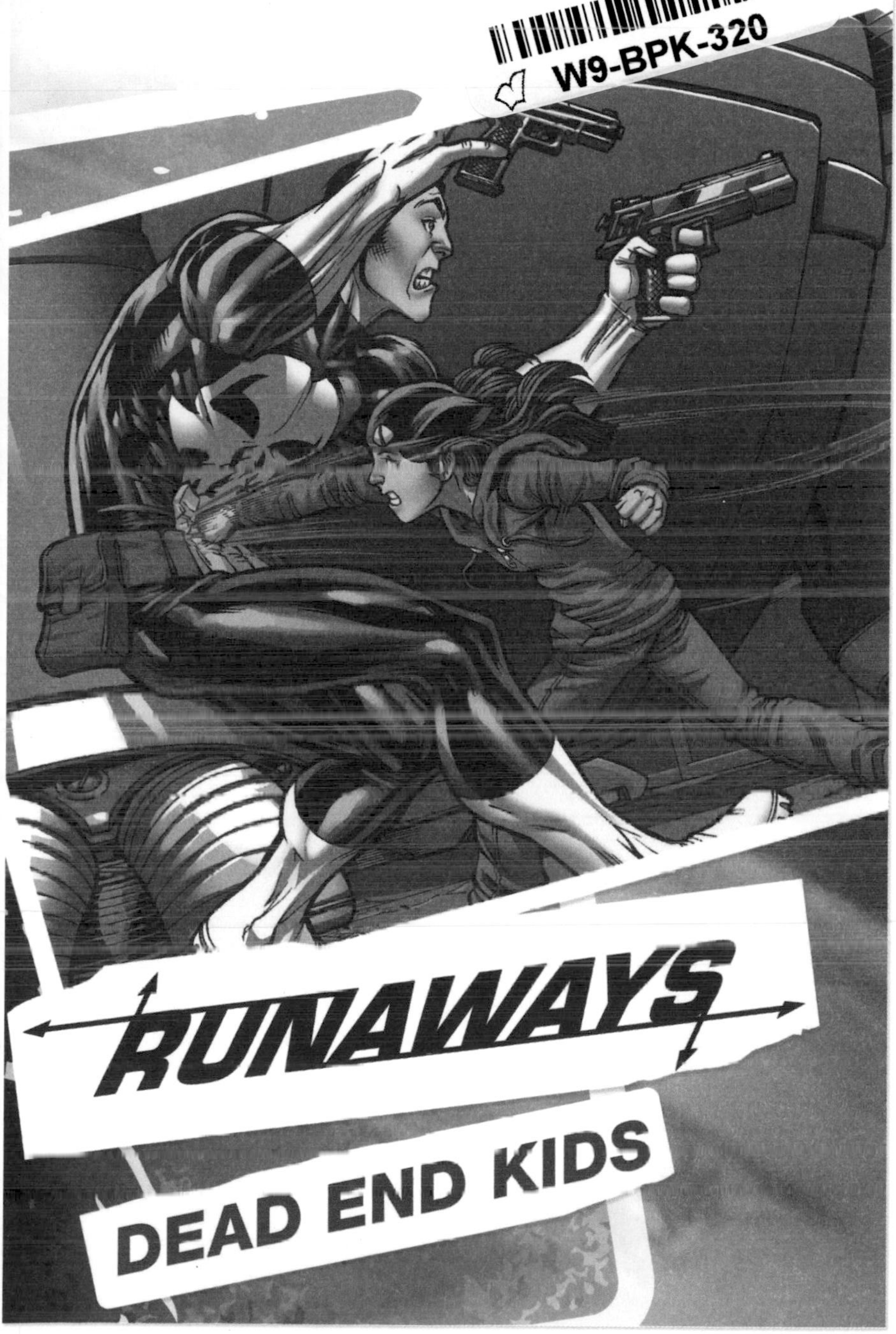
RUNAWAYS
DEAD END KIDS

RUNAWAYS

DEAD END KIDS

WRITER: **JOSS WHEDON**
PENCILER: **MICHAEL RYAN**
INKER: **RICK KETCHAM** WITH **JAY LEISTEN, ANDREW HENNESSY, VICTOR OLAZABA & ROLAND PARIS**
COLORIST: **CHRISTINA STRAIN**
LETTERER: **VC'S RANDY GENTILE, JOE CARAMAGNA & CORY PETIT**
COVER ARTIST: **JO CHEN**
ASSISTANT EDITOR: **DANIEL KETCHUM**
EDITOR: **NICK LOWE**

RUNAWAYS CREATED BY
BRIAN K. VAUGHAN & ADRIAN ALPHONA

COLLECTION EDITOR: **JENNIFER GRÜNWALD**
EDITORIAL ASSISTANT: **ALEX STARBUCK**
ASSISTANT EDITORS: **CORY LEVINE & JOHN DENNING**
EDITOR, SPECIAL PROJECTS: **MARK D. BEAZLEY**
SENIOR EDITOR, SPECIAL PROJECTS: **JEFF YOUNGQUIST**
SENIOR VICE PRESIDENT OF SALES: **DAVID GABRIEL**
BOOK DESIGNER: **RODOLFO MURAGUCHI**

EDITOR IN CHIEF: **JOE QUESADA**
PUBLISHER: **DAN BUCKLEY**
EXECUTIVE PRODUCER: **ALAN FINE**

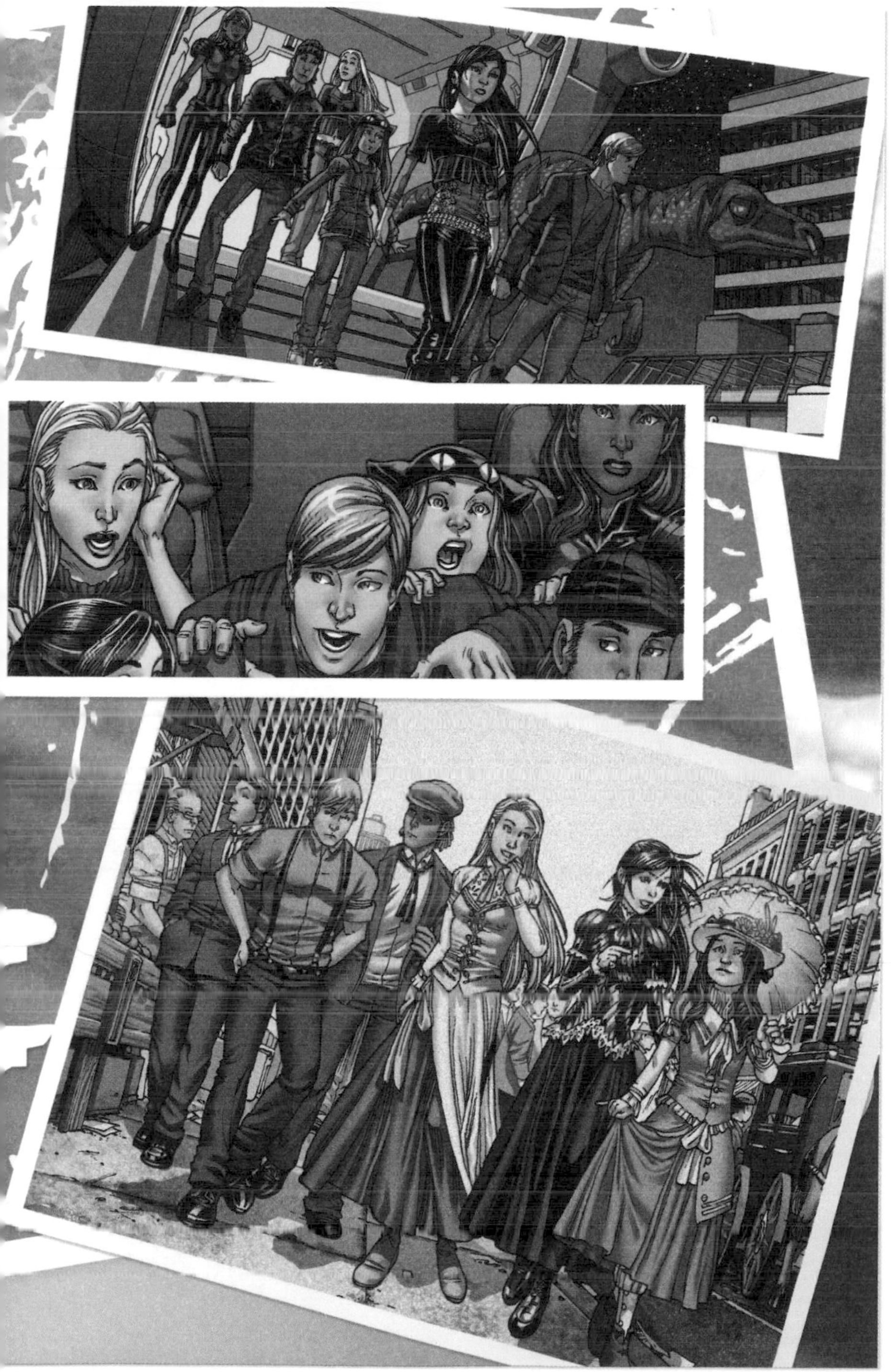

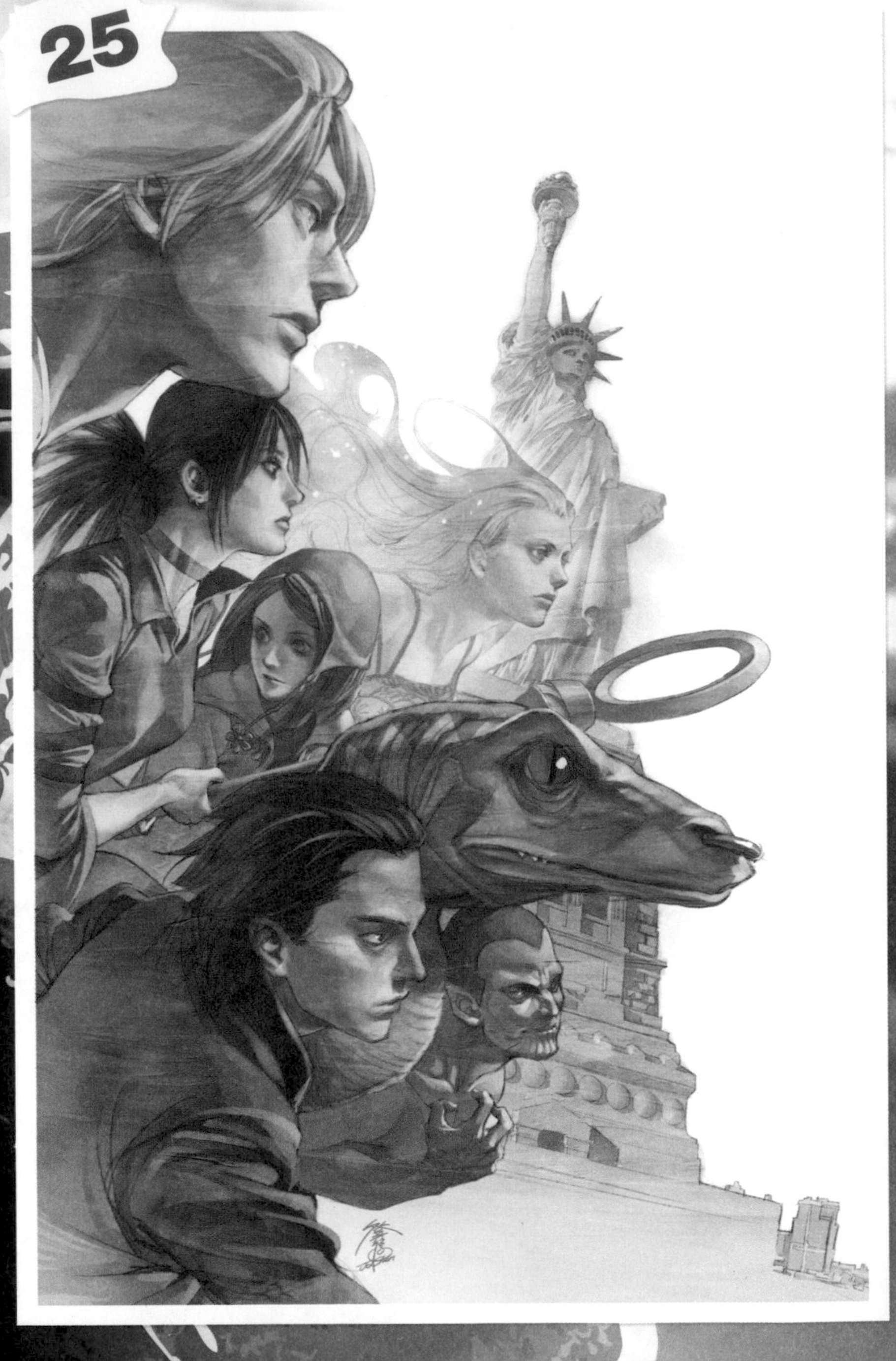
25

DEAD-END KIDS

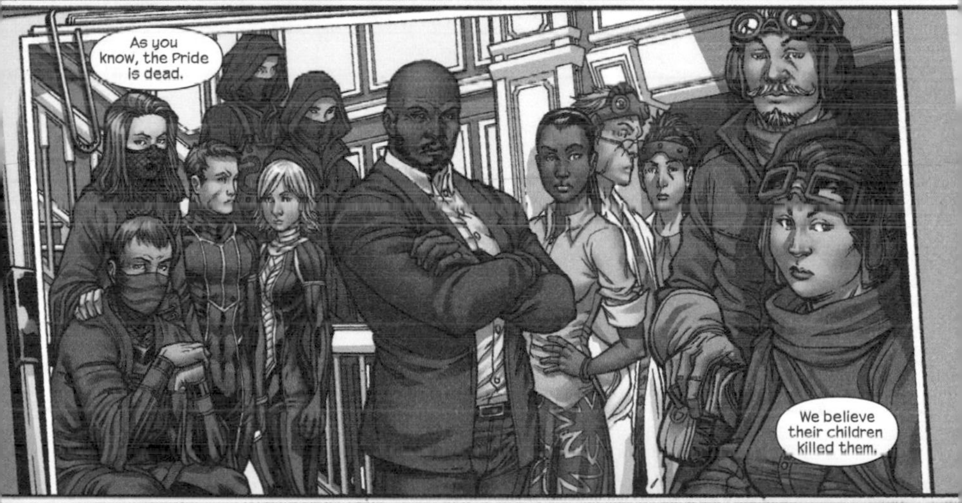
As you know, the Pride is dead.
We believe their children killed them.

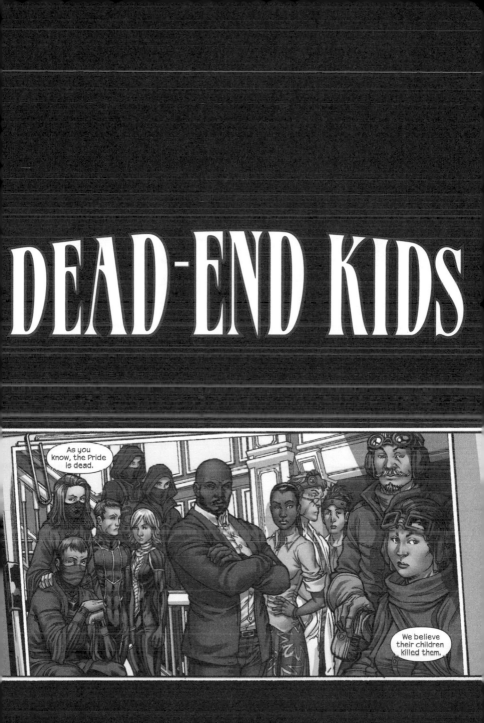

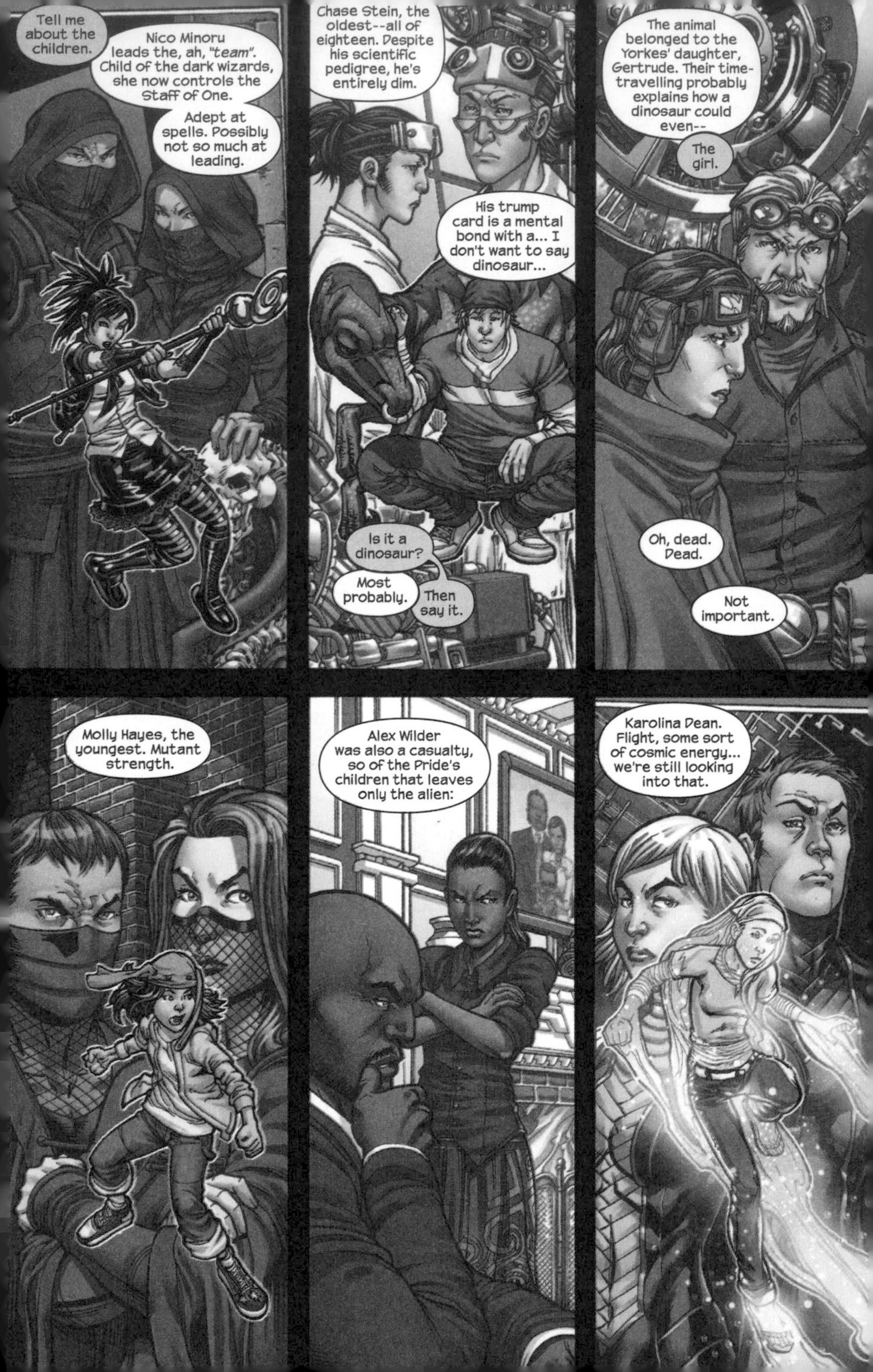

Tell me about the children.
Nico Minoru leads the, ah, "team". Child of the dark wizards, she now controls the Staff of One.
Adept at spells. Possibly not so much at leading.
Chase Stein, the oldest--all of eighteen. Despite his scientific pedigree, he's entirely dim.
His trump card is a mental bond with a... I don't want to say dinosaur...
Is it a dinosaur?
Most probably.
Then say it.
The animal belonged to the Yorkes' daughter, Gertrude. Their time-travelling probably explains how a dinosaur could even--
The girl.
Oh, dead. Dead.
Not important.
Molly Hayes, the youngest. Mutant strength.
Alex Wilder was also a casualty, so of the Pride's children that leaves only the alien:
Karolina Dean. Flight, some sort of cosmic energy... we're still looking into that.

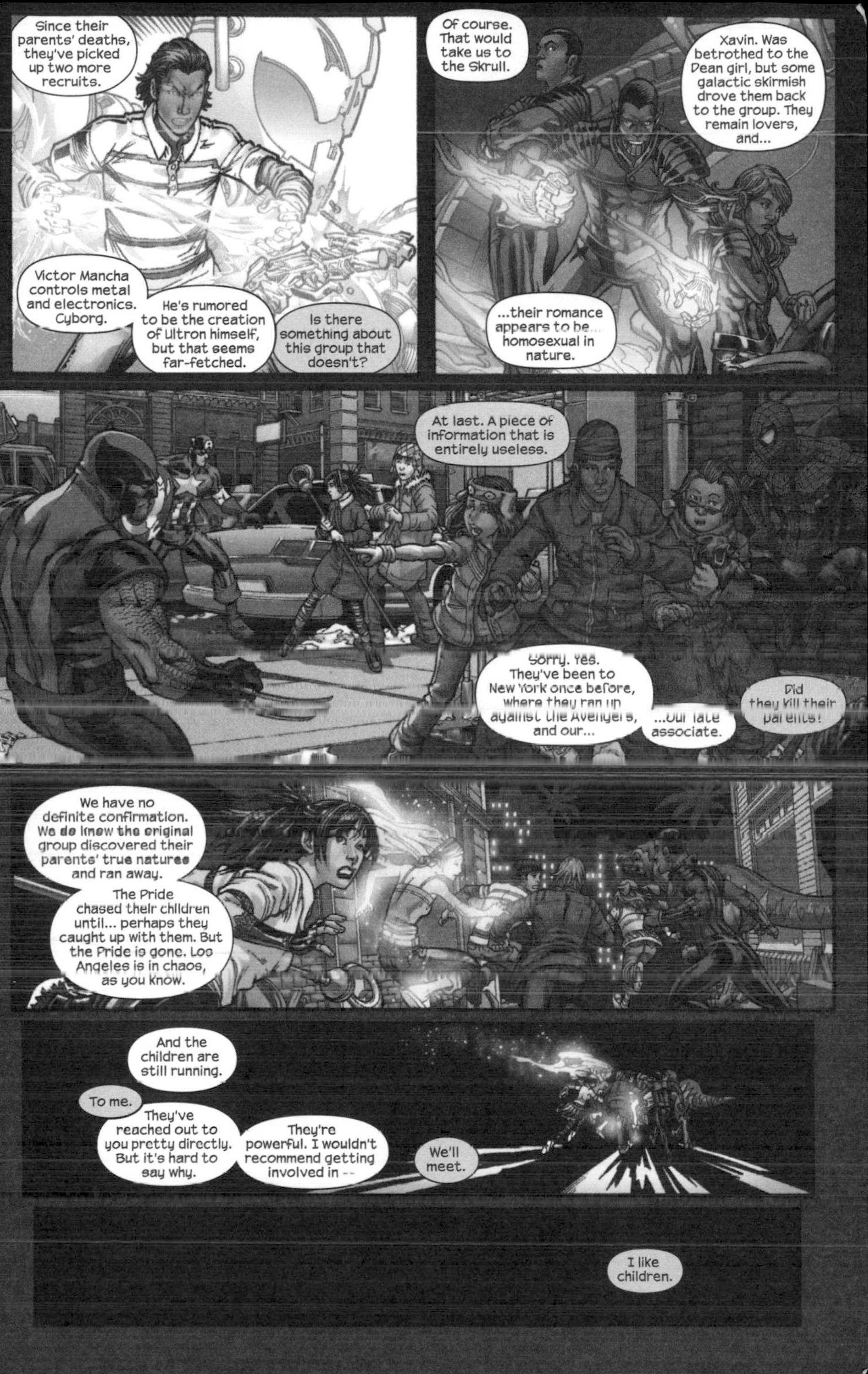
Since their parents' deaths, they've picked up two more recruits.
Victor Mancha controls metal and electronics. Cyborg.
He's rumored to be the creation of Ultron himself, but that seems far-fetched.
Is there something about this group that doesn't?
Of course. That would take us to the Skrull.
Xavin. Was betrothed to the Dean girl, but some galactic skirmish drove them back to the group. They remain lovers, and...
...their romance appears to be... homosexual in nature.
At last. A piece of information that is entirely useless.
Sorry. Yes. They've been to New York once before, where they ran up against the Avengers, and our...
...our late associate.
Did they kill their parents?
We have no definite confirmation. We do know the original group discovered their parents' true natures and ran away.
The Pride chased their children until... perhaps they caught up with them. But the Pride is gone. Los Angeles is in chaos, as you know.
And the children are still running.
To me.
They've reached out to you pretty directly. But it's hard to say why.
They're powerful. I wouldn't recommend getting involved in --
We'll meet.
I like children.

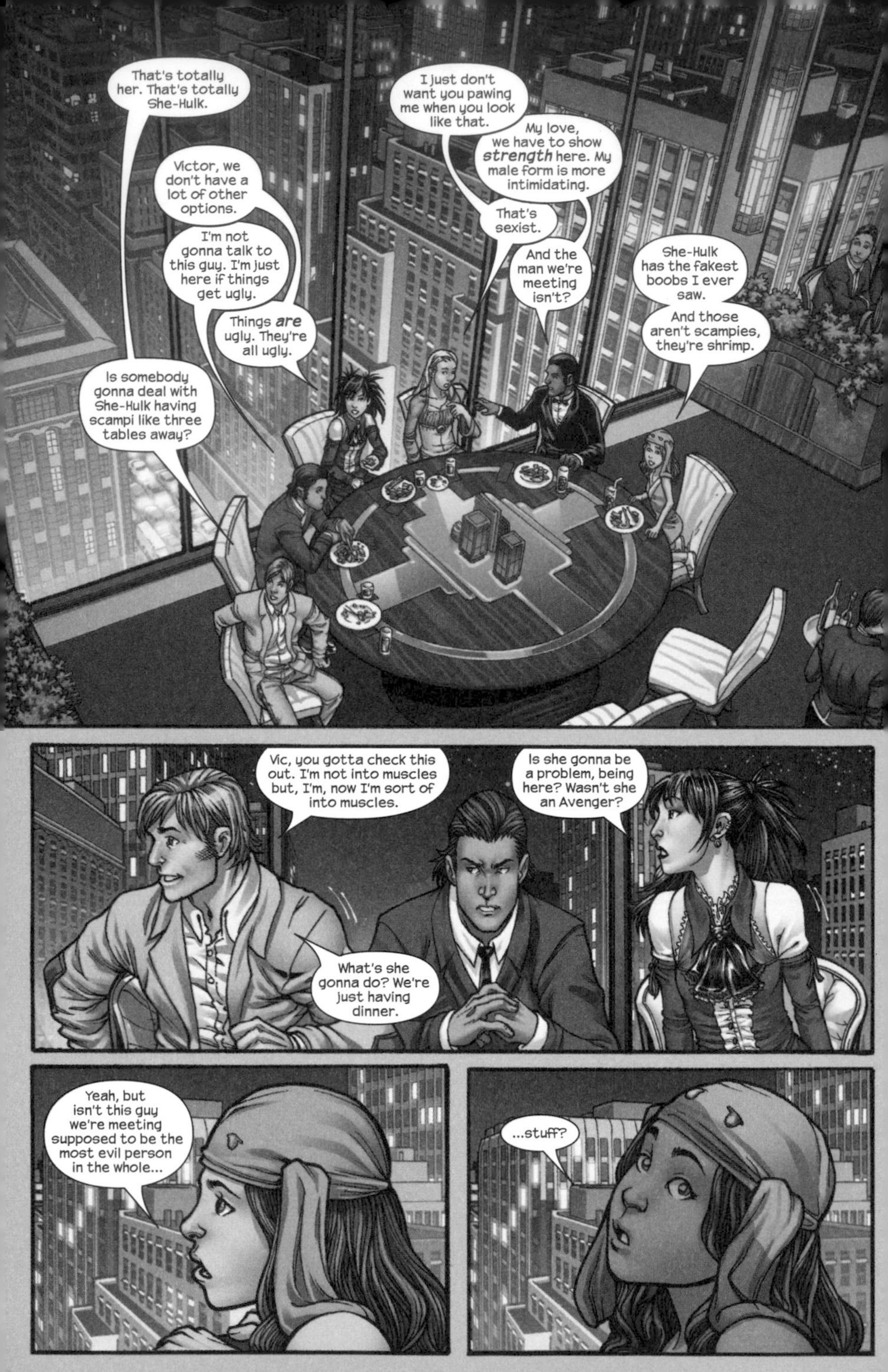
That's totally her. That's totally She-Hulk.
Victor, we don't have a lot of other options.
I'm not gonna talk to this guy. I'm just here if things get ugly.
Things *are* ugly. They're all ugly.
Is somebody gonna deal with She-Hulk having scampi like three tables away?
I just don't want you pawing me when you look like that.
My love, we have to show *strength* here. My male form is more intimidating.
That's sexist.
And the man we're meeting isn't?
She-Hulk has the fakest boobs I ever saw.
And those aren't scampies, they're shrimp.
Vic, you gotta check this out. I'm not into muscles but, I'm, now I'm sort of into muscles.
What's she gonna do? We're just having dinner.
Is she gonna be a problem, being here? Wasn't she an Avenger?
Yeah, but isn't this guy we're meeting supposed to be the most evil person in the whole...
...stuff?

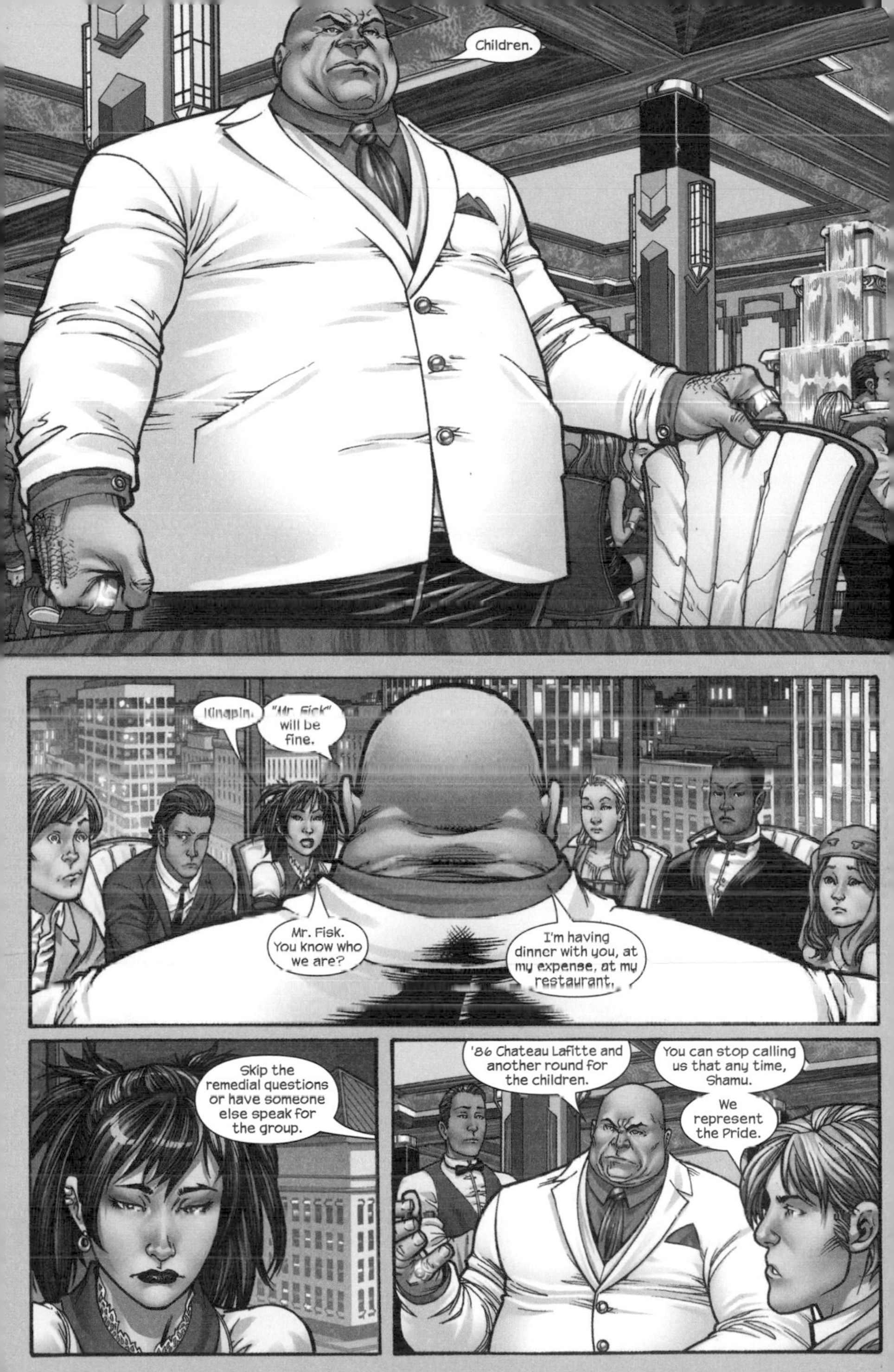
Children.
Kingpin.
"Mr. Fisk" will be fine.
Mr. Fisk. You know who we are?
I'm having dinner with you, at my expense, at my restaurant.
Skip the remedial questions or have someone else speak for the group.
'86 Chateau Lafitte and another round for the children.
You can stop calling us that any time, Shamu.
We represent the Pride.

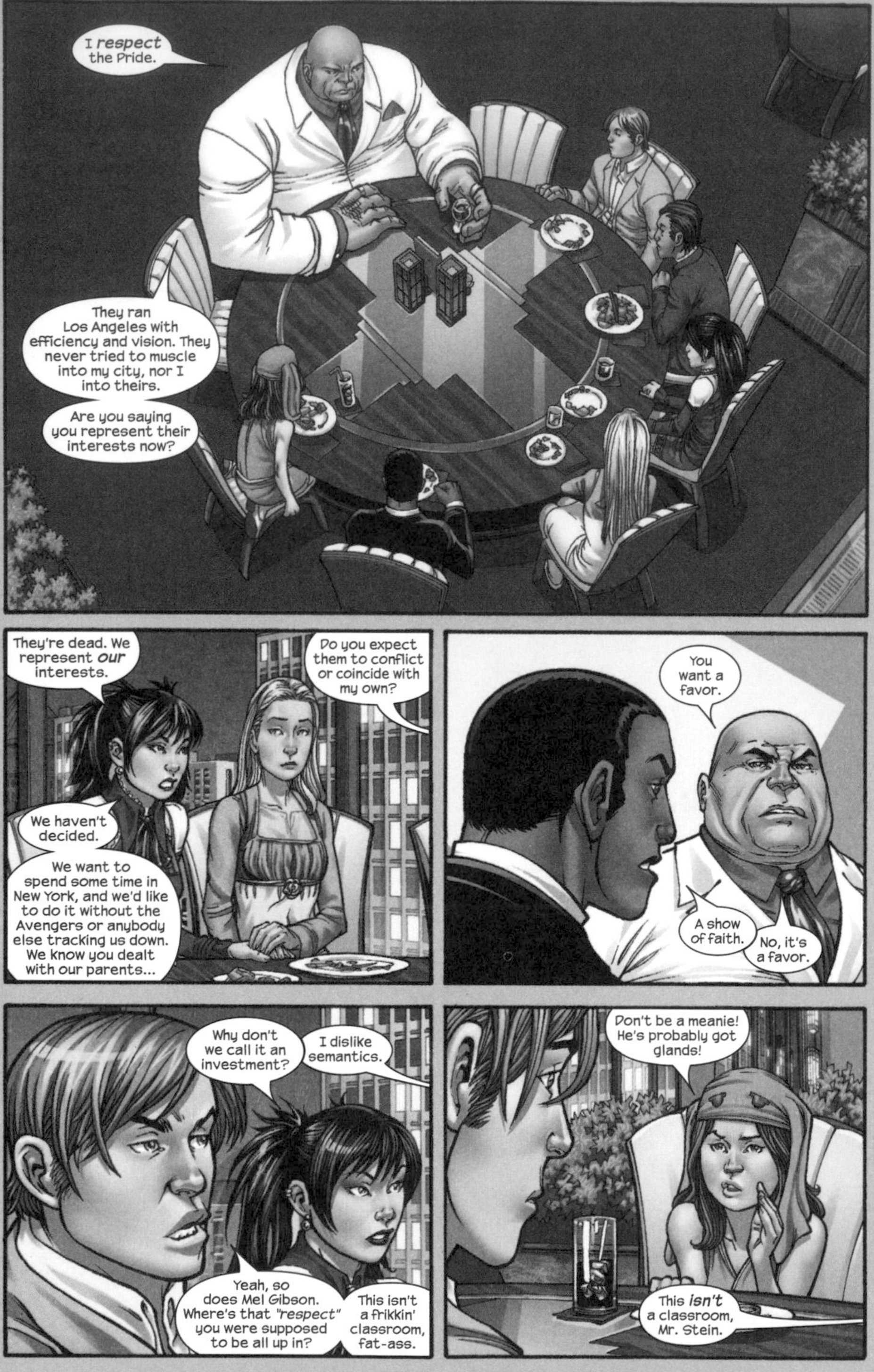
I *respect* the Pride.
They ran Los Angeles with efficiency and vision. They never tried to muscle into my city, nor I into theirs.
Are you saying you represent their interests now?
They're dead. We represent *our* interests.
Do you expect them to conflict or coincide with my own?
We haven't decided.
We want to spend some time in New York, and we'd like to do it without the Avengers or anybody else tracking us down. We know you dealt with our parents...
You want a favor.
A show of faith.
No, it's a favor.
Why don't we call it an investment?
I dislike semantics.
Yeah, so does Mel Gibson. Where's that *"respect"* you were supposed to be all up in?
This isn't a frikkin' classroom, fat-ass.
Don't be a meanie! He's probably got glands!
This *isn't* a classroom, Mr. Stein.

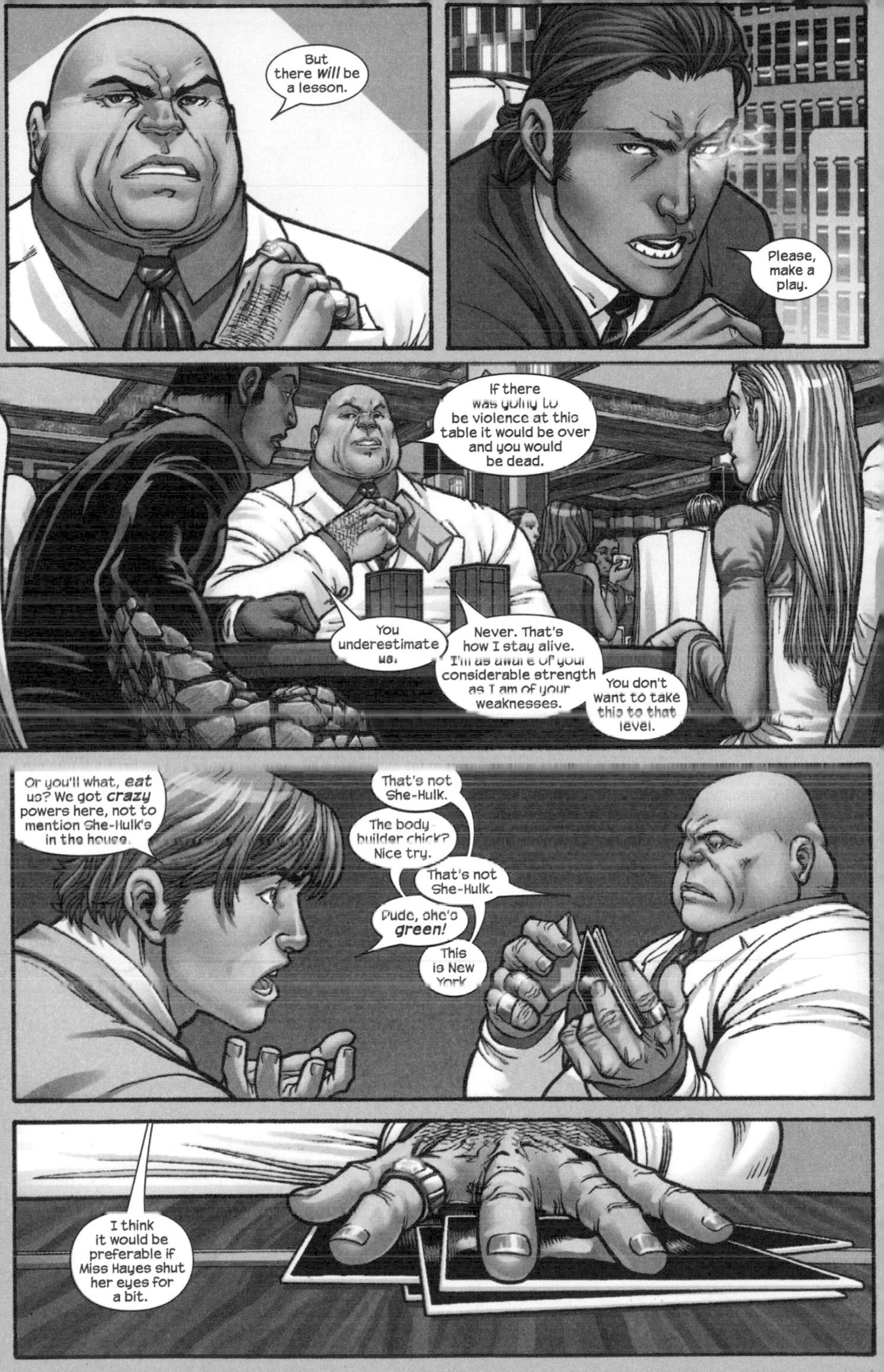

But there *will* be a lesson.
Please, make a play.
If there was going to be violence at this table it would be over and you would be dead.
You underestimate us.
Never. That's how I stay alive. I'm as aware of your considerable strength as I am of your weaknesses.
You don't want to take this to that level.
Or you'll what, *eat* us? We got *crazy* powers here, not to mention She-Hulk's in the house.
That's not She-Hulk.
The body-builder chick? Nice try.
That's not She-Hulk.
Dude, she's *green!*
This is New York.
I think it would be preferable if Miss Hayes shut her eyes for a bit.

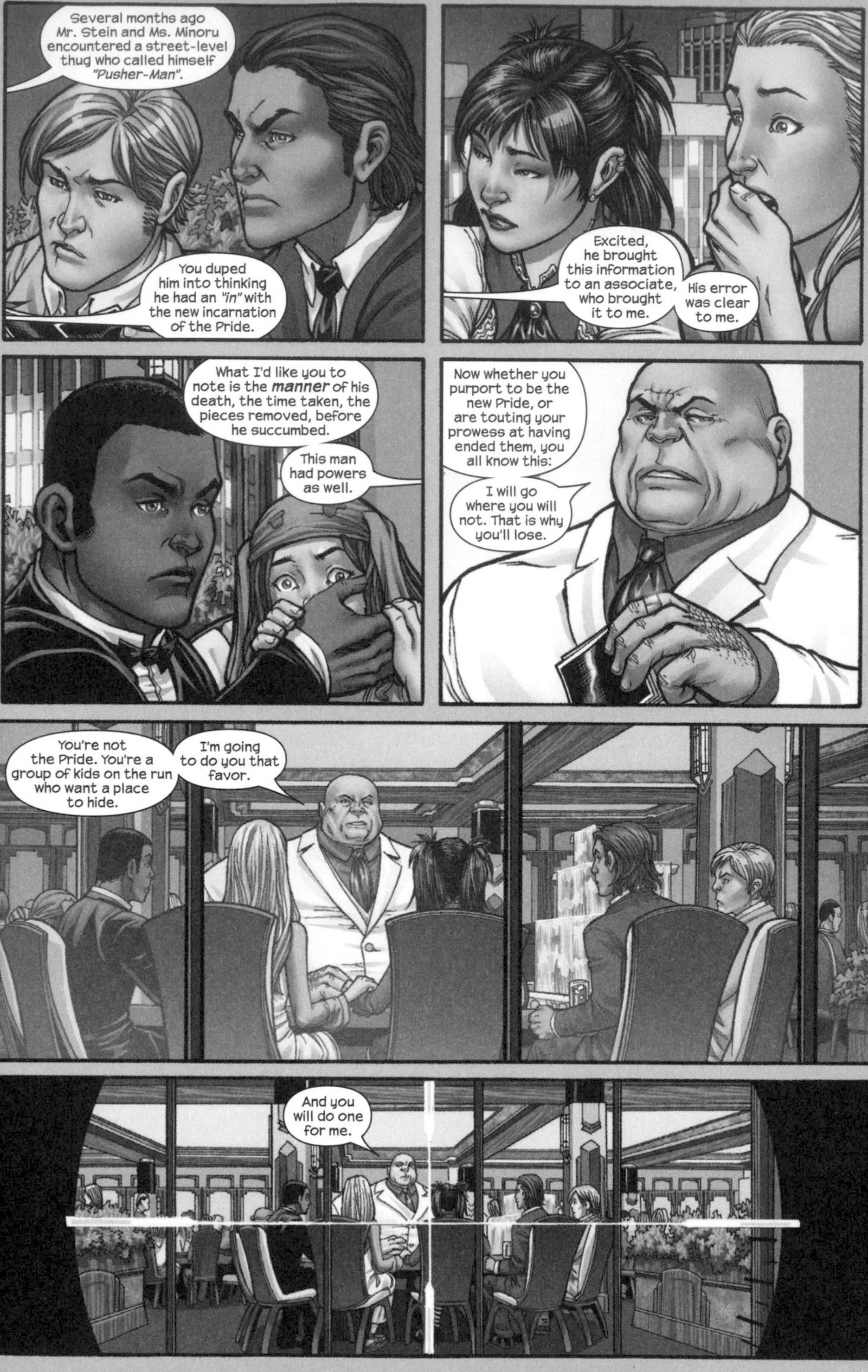
Several months ago Mr. Stein and Ms. Minoru encountered a street-level thug who called himself "Pusher-Man".
You duped him into thinking he had an "in" with the new incarnation of the Pride.
Excited, he brought this information to an associate, who brought it to me.
His error was clear to me.
What I'd like you to note is the manner of his death, the time taken, the pieces removed, before he succumbed.
This man had powers as well.
Now whether you purport to be the new Pride, or are touting your prowess at having ended them, you all know this:
I will go where you will not. That is why you'll lose.
You're not the Pride. You're a group of kids on the run who want a place to hide.
I'm going to do you that favor.
And you will do one for me.

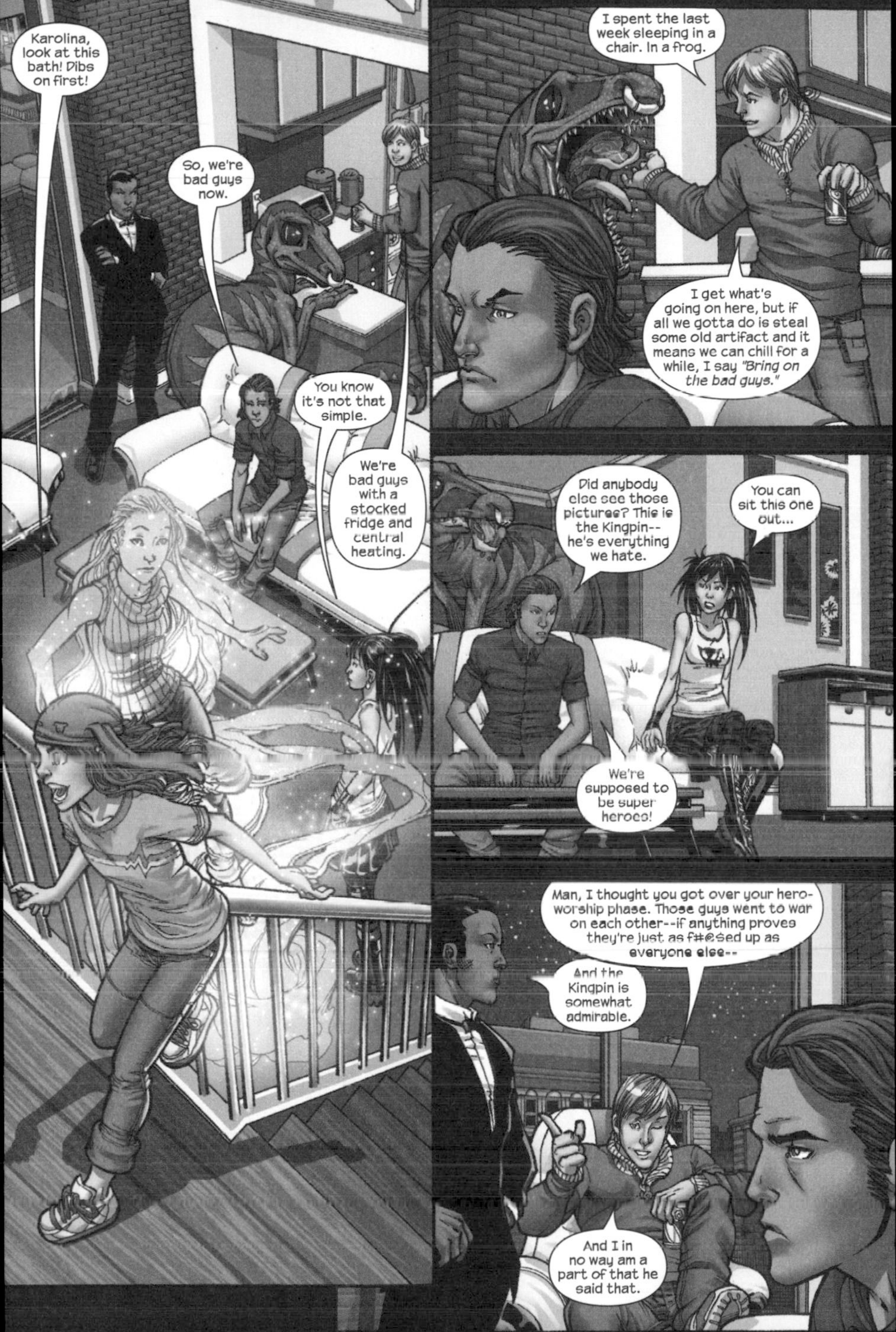
Karolina, look at this bath! Dibs on first!
So, we're bad guys now.
You know it's not that simple.
We're bad guys with a stocked fridge and central heating.
I spent the last week sleeping in a chair. In a frog.
I get what's going on here, but if all we gotta do is steal some old artifact and it means we can chill for a while, I say *"Bring on the bad guys."*
Did anybody else see those pictures? This is the Kingpin-- he's everything we hate.
You can sit this one out...
We're supposed to be super heroes!
Man, I thought you got over your hero-worship phase. Those guys went to war on each other--if anything proves they're just as f#@$ed up as everyone else--
And the Kingpin is somewhat admirable.
And I in no way am a part of that he said that.

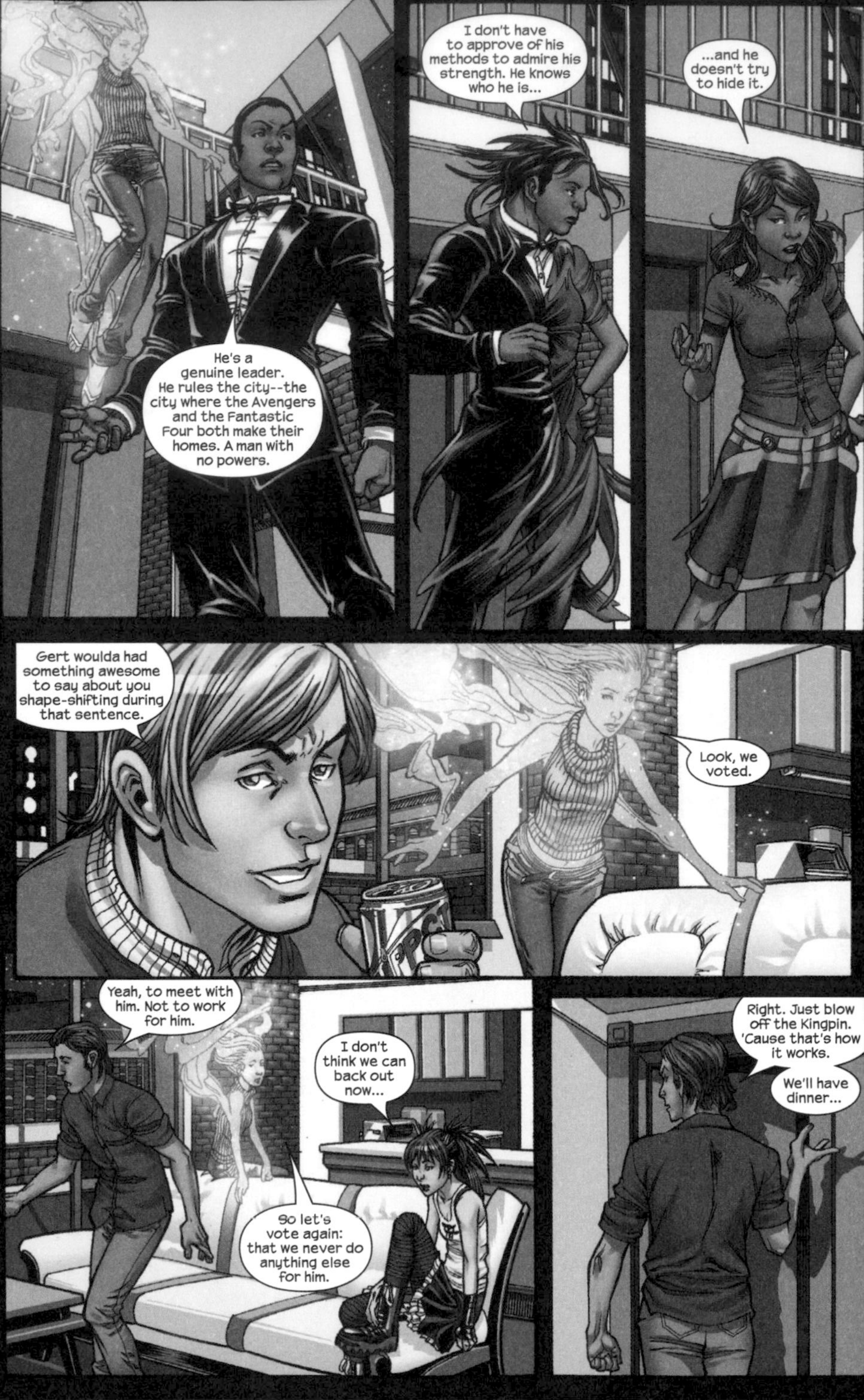
He's a genuine leader. He rules the city--the city where the Avengers and the Fantastic Four both make their homes. A man with no powers.
I don't have to approve of his methods to admire his strength. He knows who he is...
...and he doesn't try to hide it.
Gert woulda had something awesome to say about you shape-shifting during that sentence.
Look, we voted.
Yeah, to meet with him. Not to work for him.
I don't think we can back out now...
So let's vote again: that we never do anything else for him.
Right. Just blow off the Kingpin. 'Cause that's how it works.
We'll have dinner...

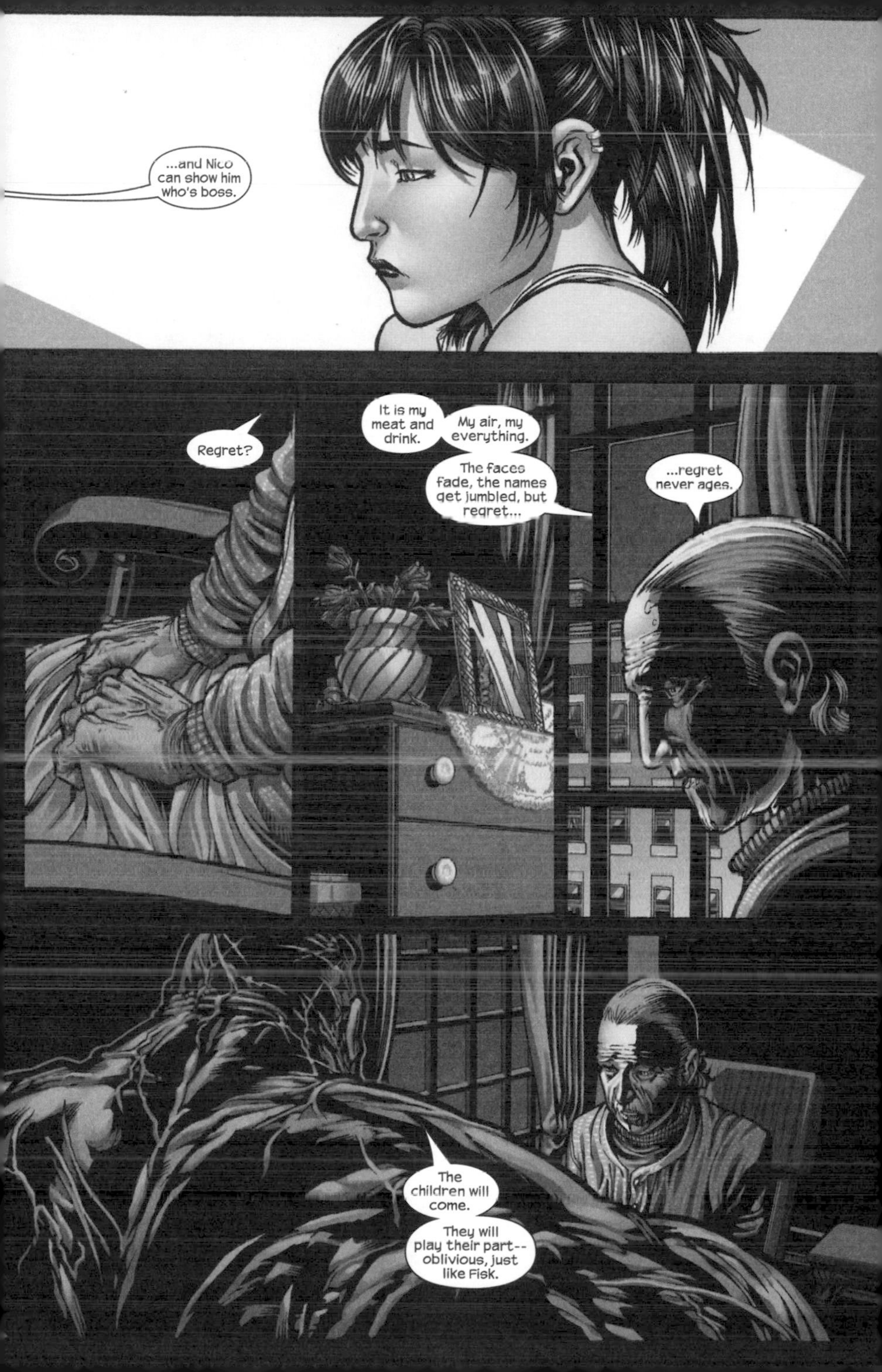
...and Nico can show him who's boss.
Regret?
It is my meat and drink.
My air, my everything.
The faces fade, the names get jumbled, but regret...
...regret never ages.
The children will come.
They will play their part-- oblivious, just like Fisk.

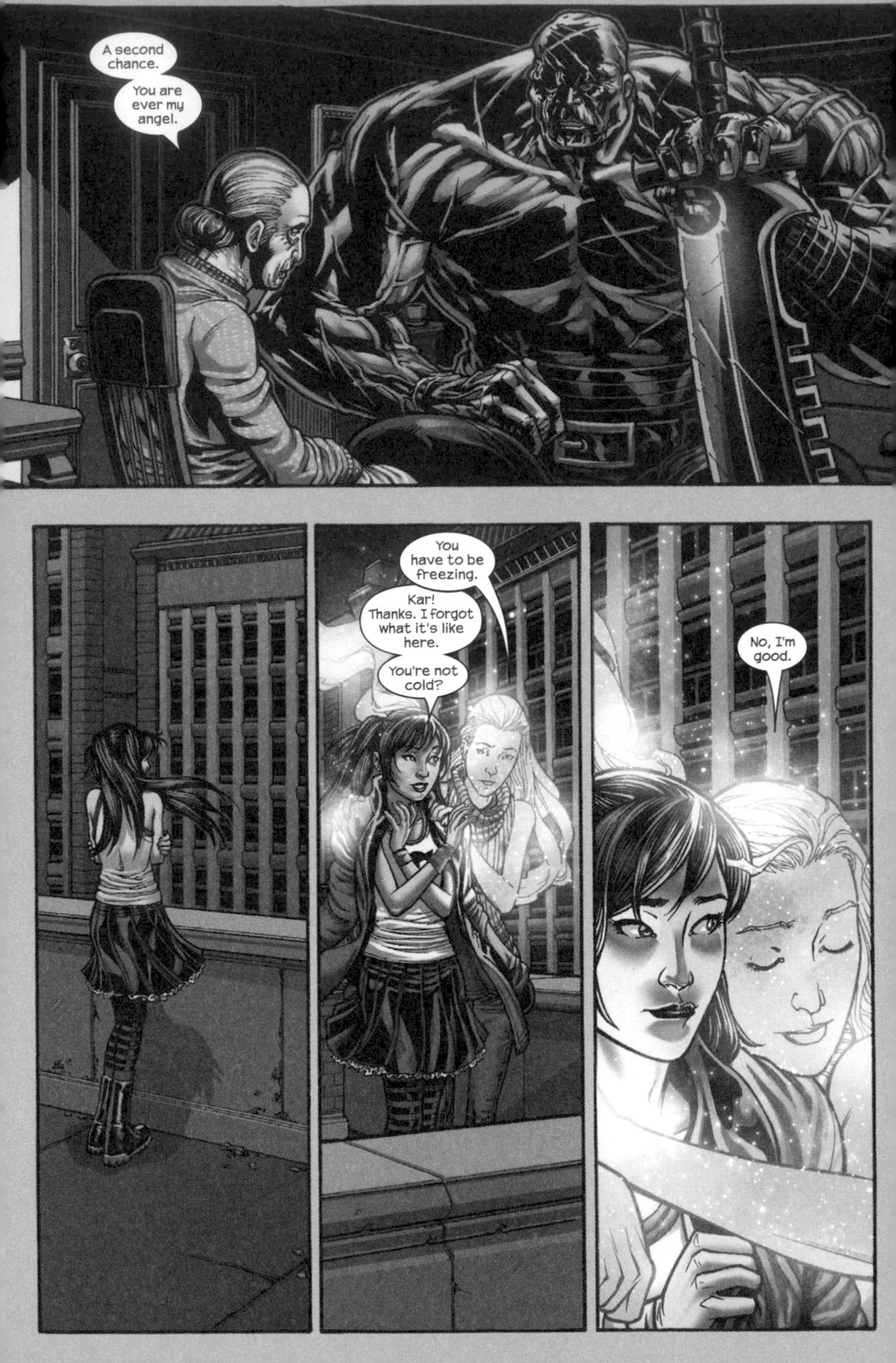
A second chance.
You are ever my angel.
You have to be freezing.
Kar! Thanks. I forgot what it's like here.
You're not cold?
No, I'm good.

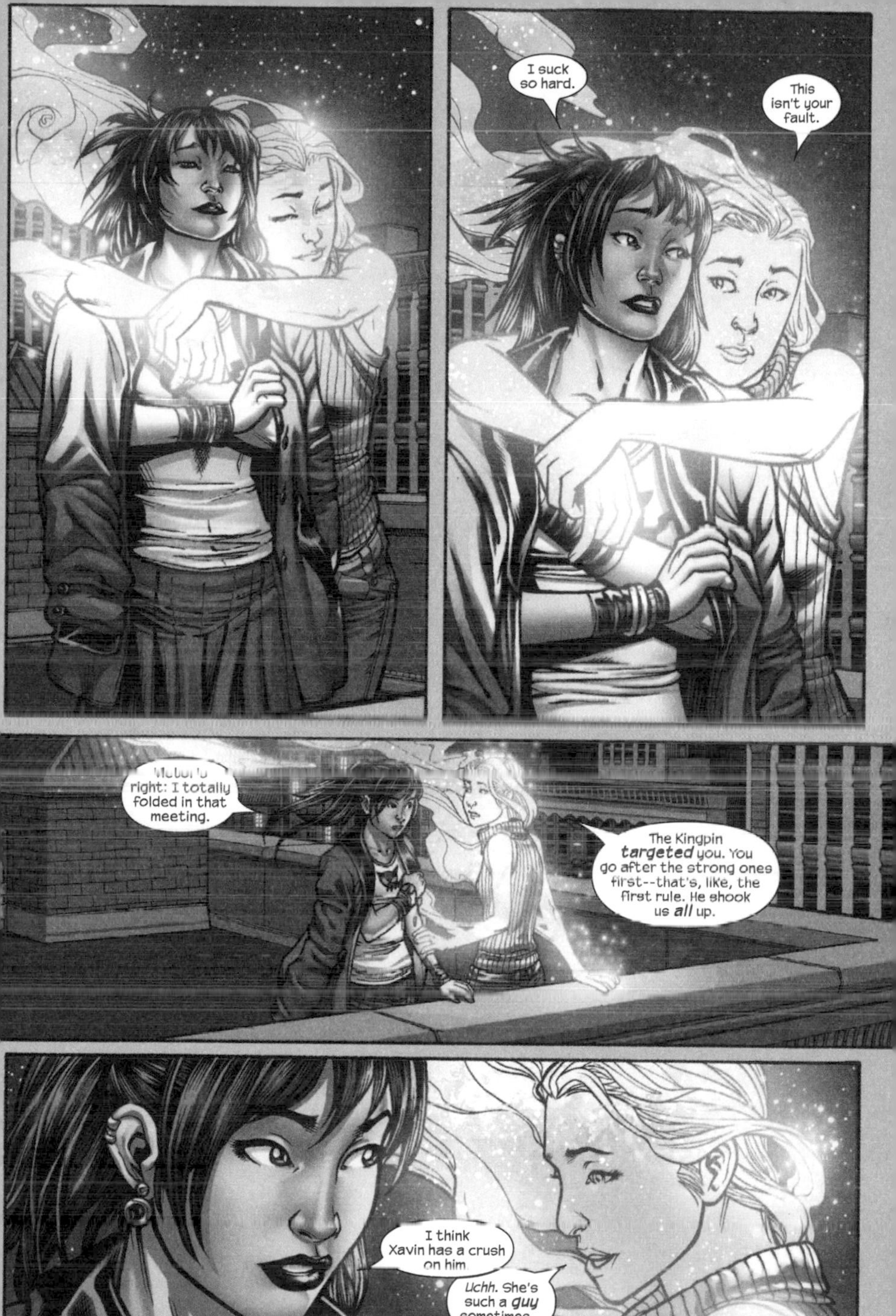

I suck so hard.
This isn't your fault.
right: I totally folded in that meeting.
The Kingpin ***targeted*** you. You go after the strong ones first--that's, like, the first rule. He shook us ***all*** up.
I think Xavin has a crush on him.
Uchh. She's such a ***guy*** sometimes...

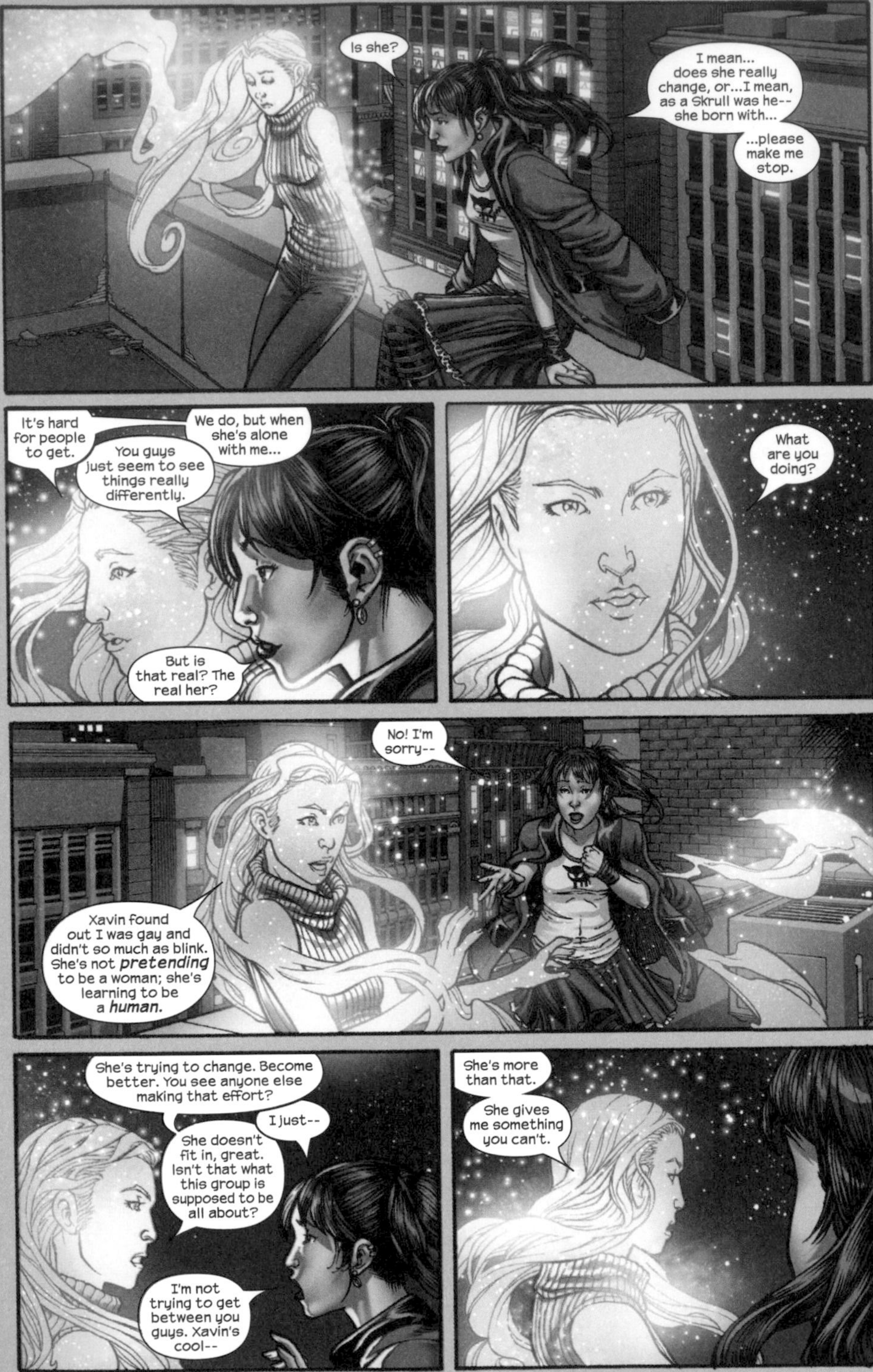
Is she?
I mean... does she really change, or...I mean, as a Skrull was he-- she born with...
...please make me stop.
It's hard for people to get.
We do, but when she's alone with me...
You guys just seem to see things really differently.
But is that real? The real her?
What are you doing?
No! I'm sorry--
Xavin found out I was gay and didn't so much as blink. She's not *pretending* to be a woman; she's learning to be a *human.*
She's trying to change. Become better. You see anyone else making that effort?
I just--
She doesn't fit in, great. Isn't that what this group is supposed to be all about?
I'm not trying to get between you guys. Xavin's cool--
She's more than that.
She gives me something you can't.

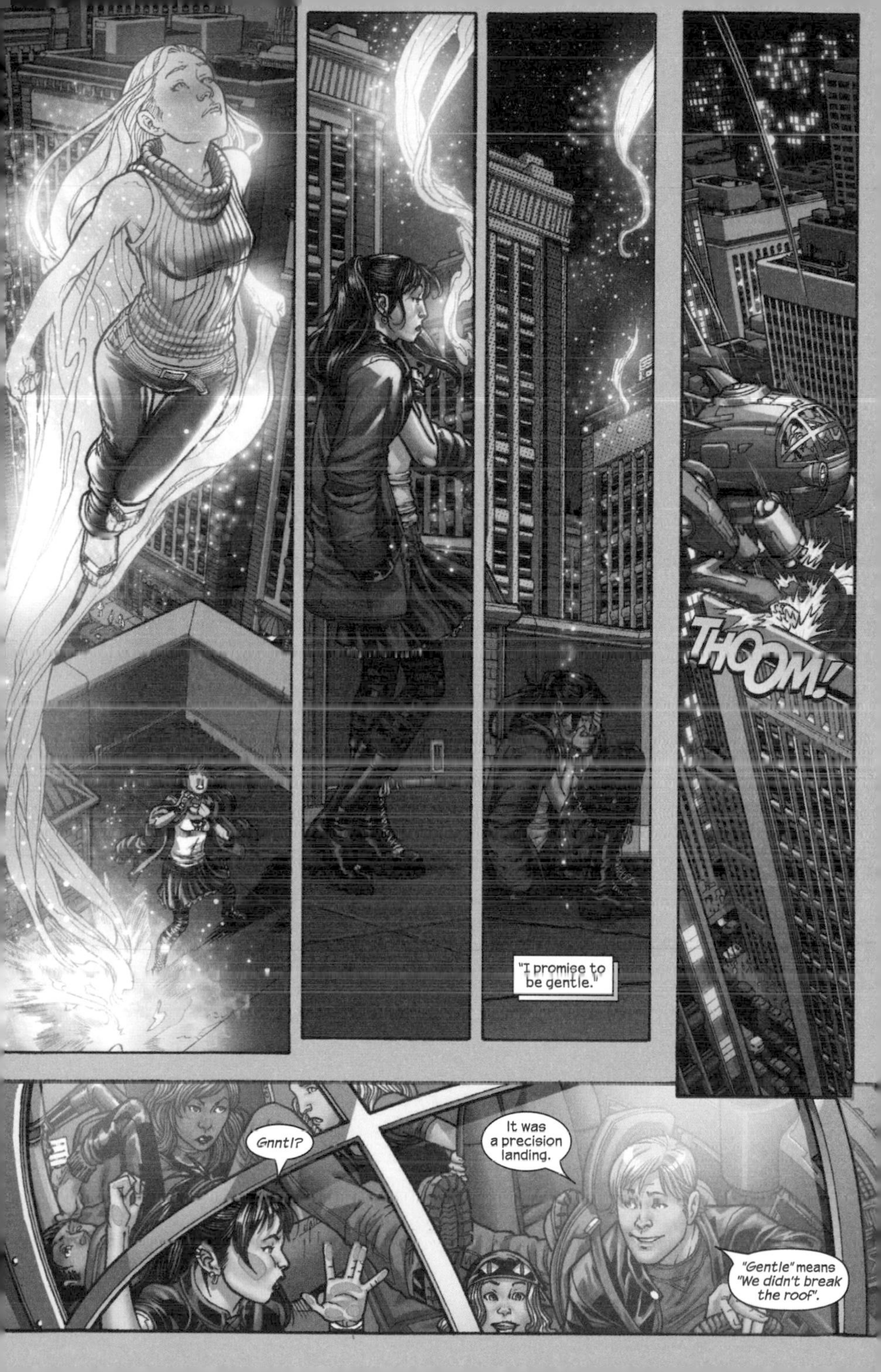

"I promise to be gentle."
THOOM!
Gnnt!?
It was a precision landing.
"Gentle" means "We didn't break the roof".

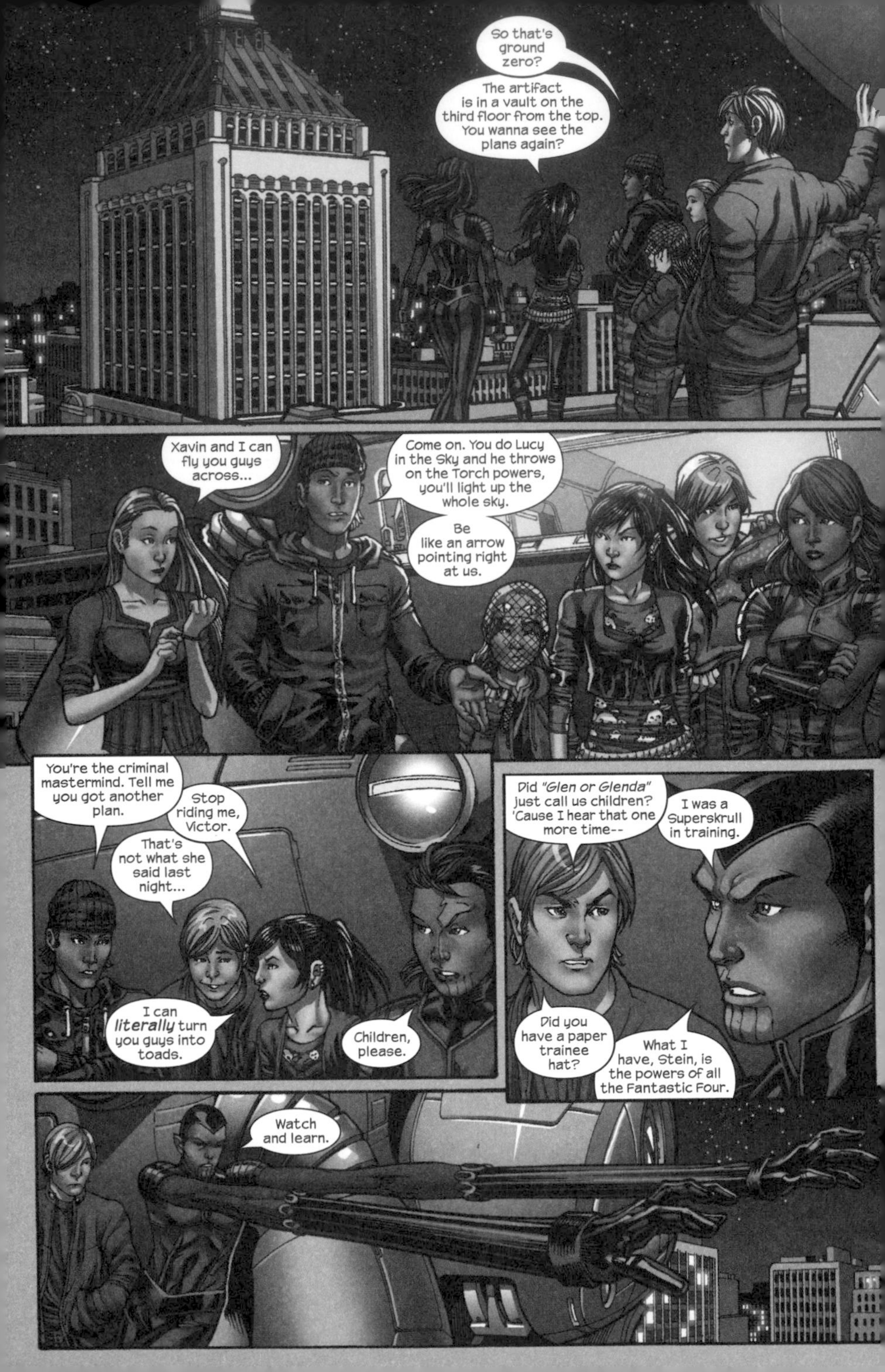

So that's ground zero?
The artifact is in a vault on the third floor from the top. You wanna see the plans again?
Xavin and I can fly you guys across...
Come on. You do Lucy in the Sky and he throws on the Torch powers, you'll light up the whole sky.
Be like an arrow pointing right at us.
You're the criminal mastermind. Tell me you got another plan.
Stop riding me, Victor.
That's not what she said last night...
I can *literally* turn you guys into toads.
Children, please.
Did *"Glen or Glenda"* just call us children? 'Cause I hear that one more time--
I was a Superskrull in training.
Did you have a paper trainee hat?
What I have, Stein, is the powers of all the Fantastic Four.
Watch and learn.

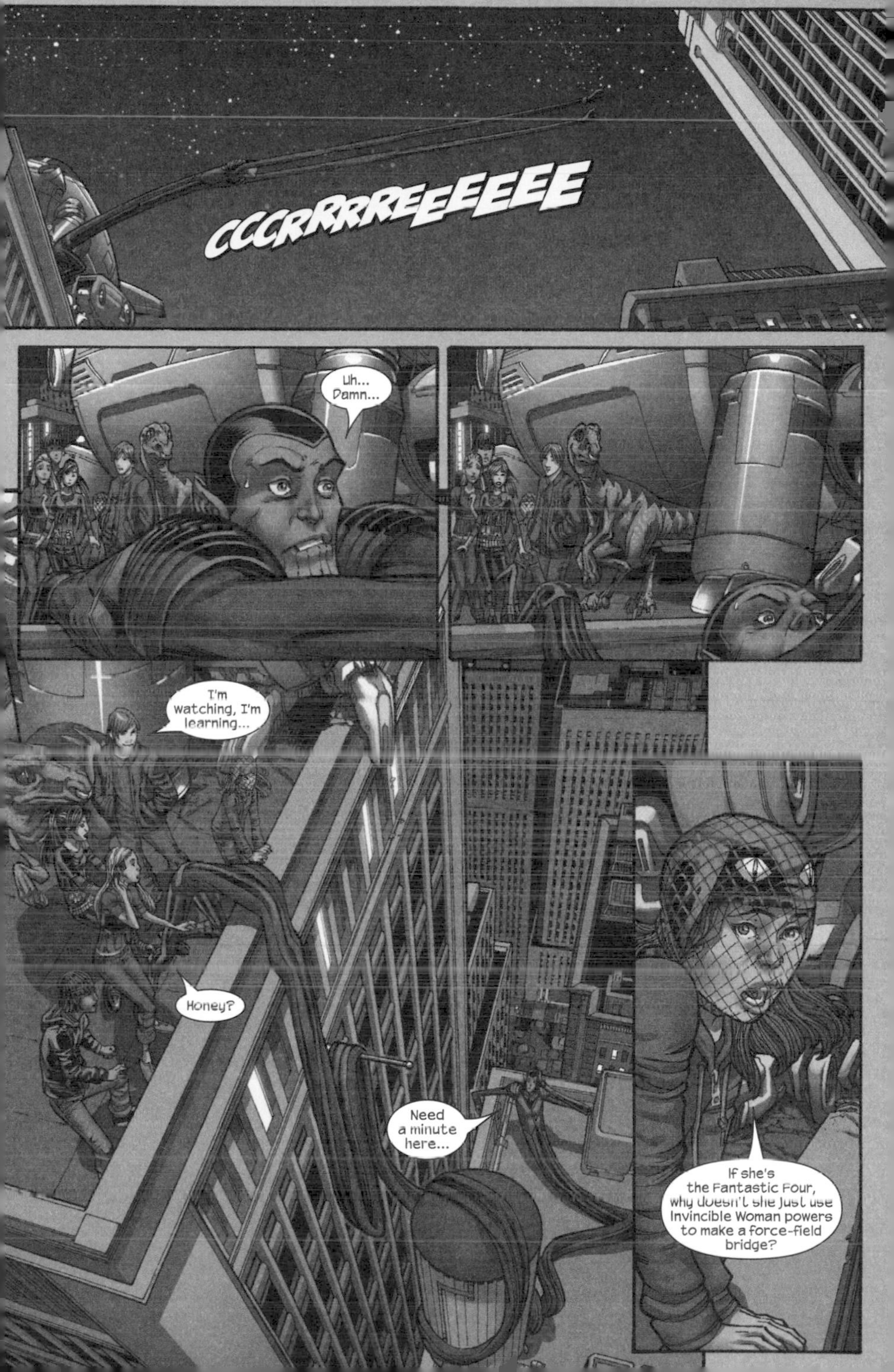
CCCRRRRREEEEEE
Uh... Damn...
I'm watching, I'm learning...
Honey?
Need a minute here...
If she's the Fantastic Four, why doesn't she just use Invincible Woman powers to make a force-field bridge?

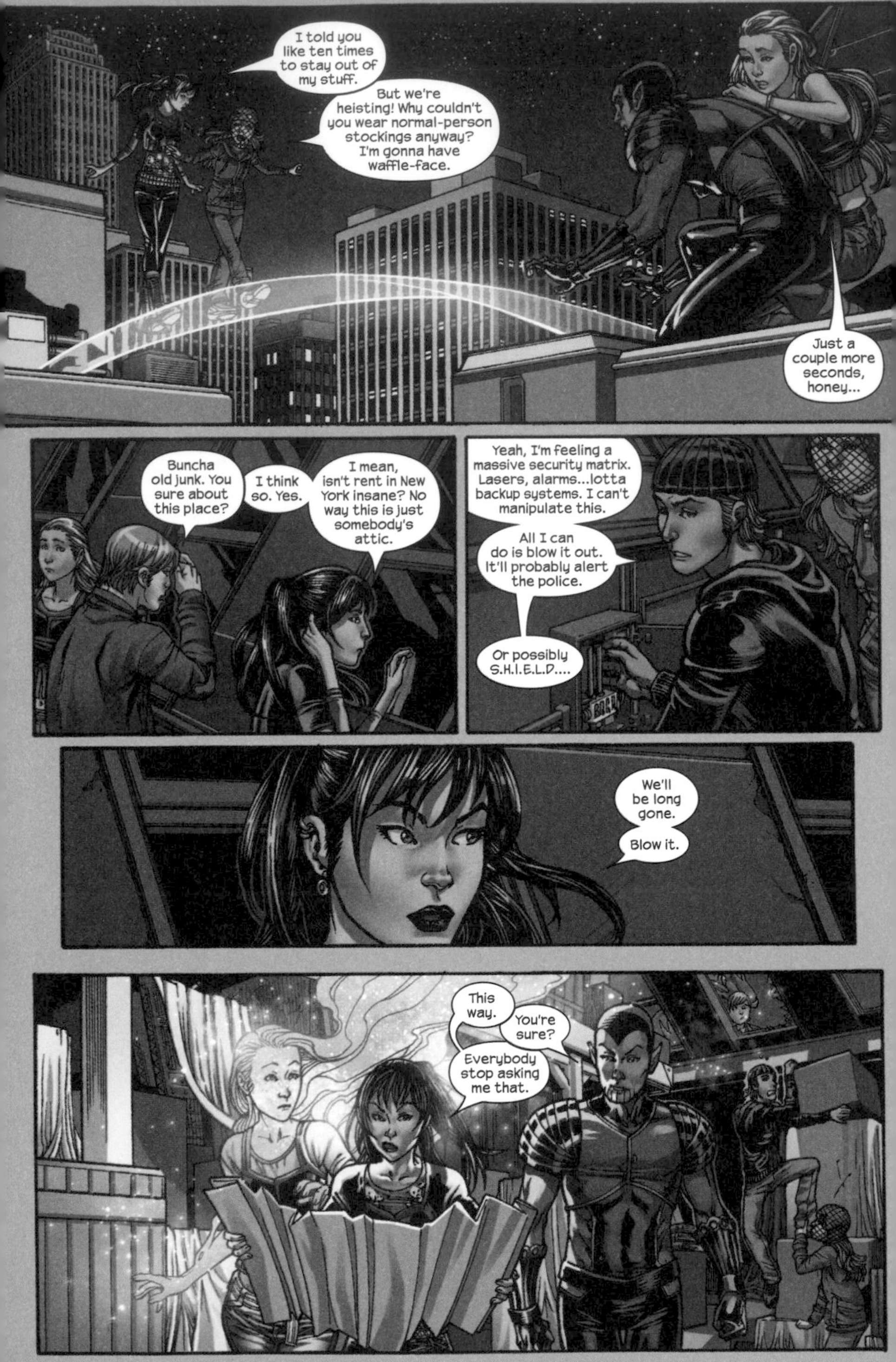
I told you like ten times to stay out of my stuff.
But we're heisting! Why couldn't you wear normal-person stockings anyway? I'm gonna have waffle-face.
Just a couple more seconds, honey...
Buncha old junk. You sure about this place?
I think so. Yes.
I mean, isn't rent in New York insane? No way this is just somebody's attic.
Yeah, I'm feeling a massive security matrix. Lasers, alarms...lotta backup systems. I can't manipulate this.
All I can do is blow it out. It'll probably alert the police.
Or possibly S.H.I.E.L.D....
We'll be long gone.
Blow it.
This way.
You're sure?
Everybody stop asking me that.

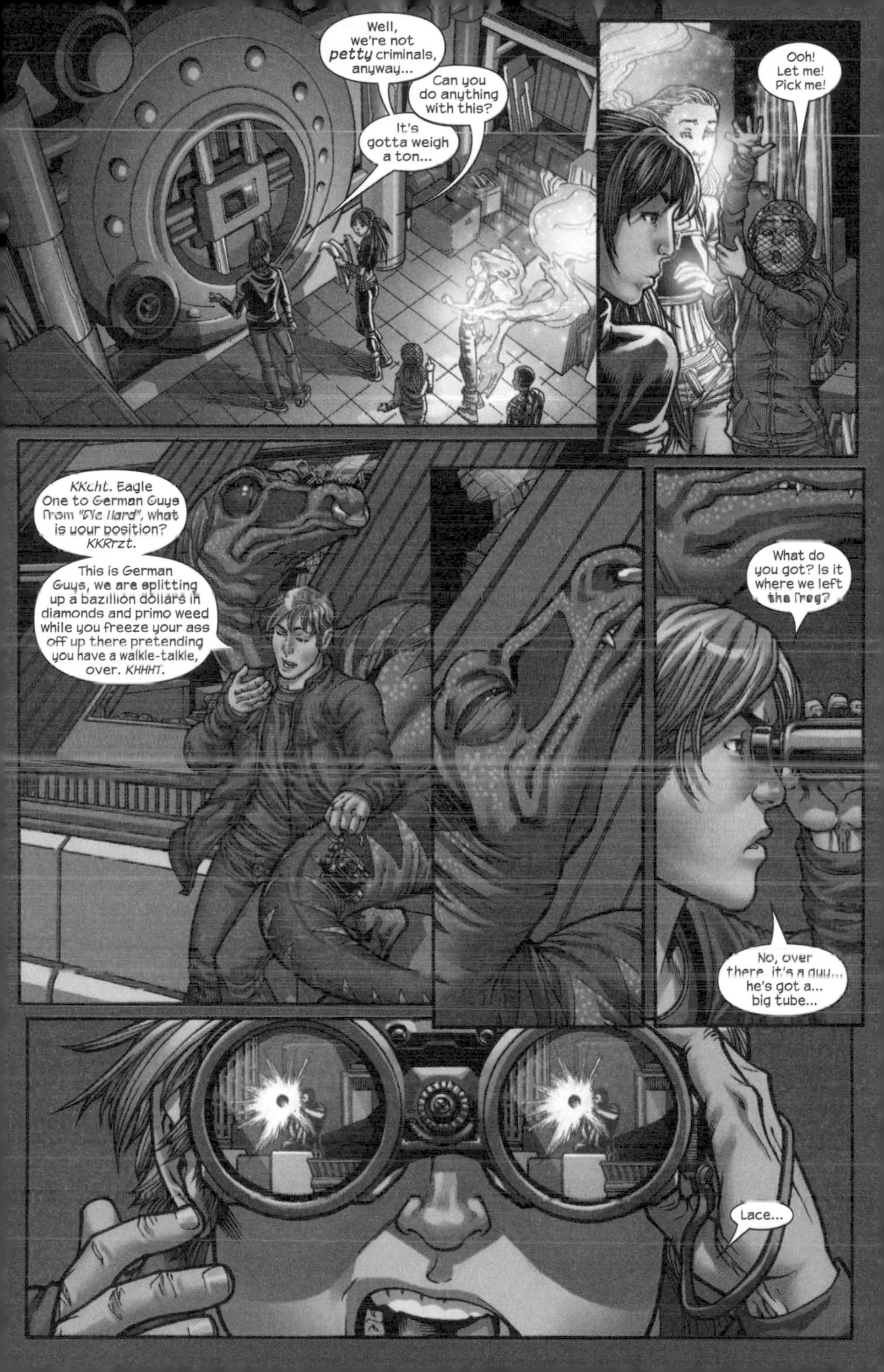
Well, we're not *petty* criminals, anyway...
Can you do anything with this?
It's gotta weigh a ton...
Ooh! Let me! Pick me!
KKcht. Eagle One to German Guys from "*Die Hard*", what is your position? *KKRrzt.*
This is German Guys, we are splitting up a bazillion dollars in diamonds and primo weed while you freeze your ass off up there pretending you have a walkie-talkie, over. *KHHHT.*
What do you got? Is it where we left the frog?
No, over there, it's a guy... he's got a... big tube...
Lace...

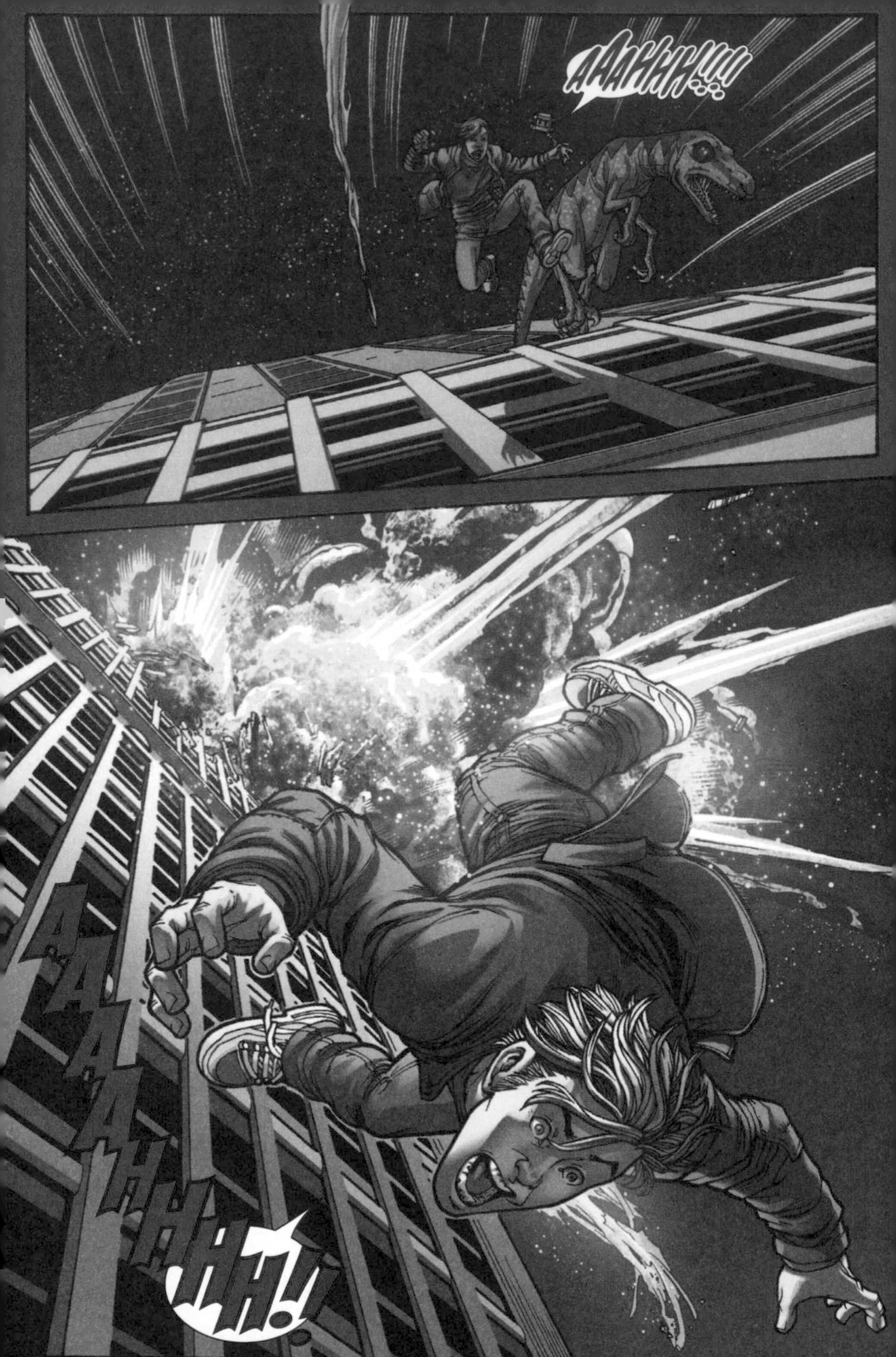
AAAHHH!!!...
AAAAHHHHH!

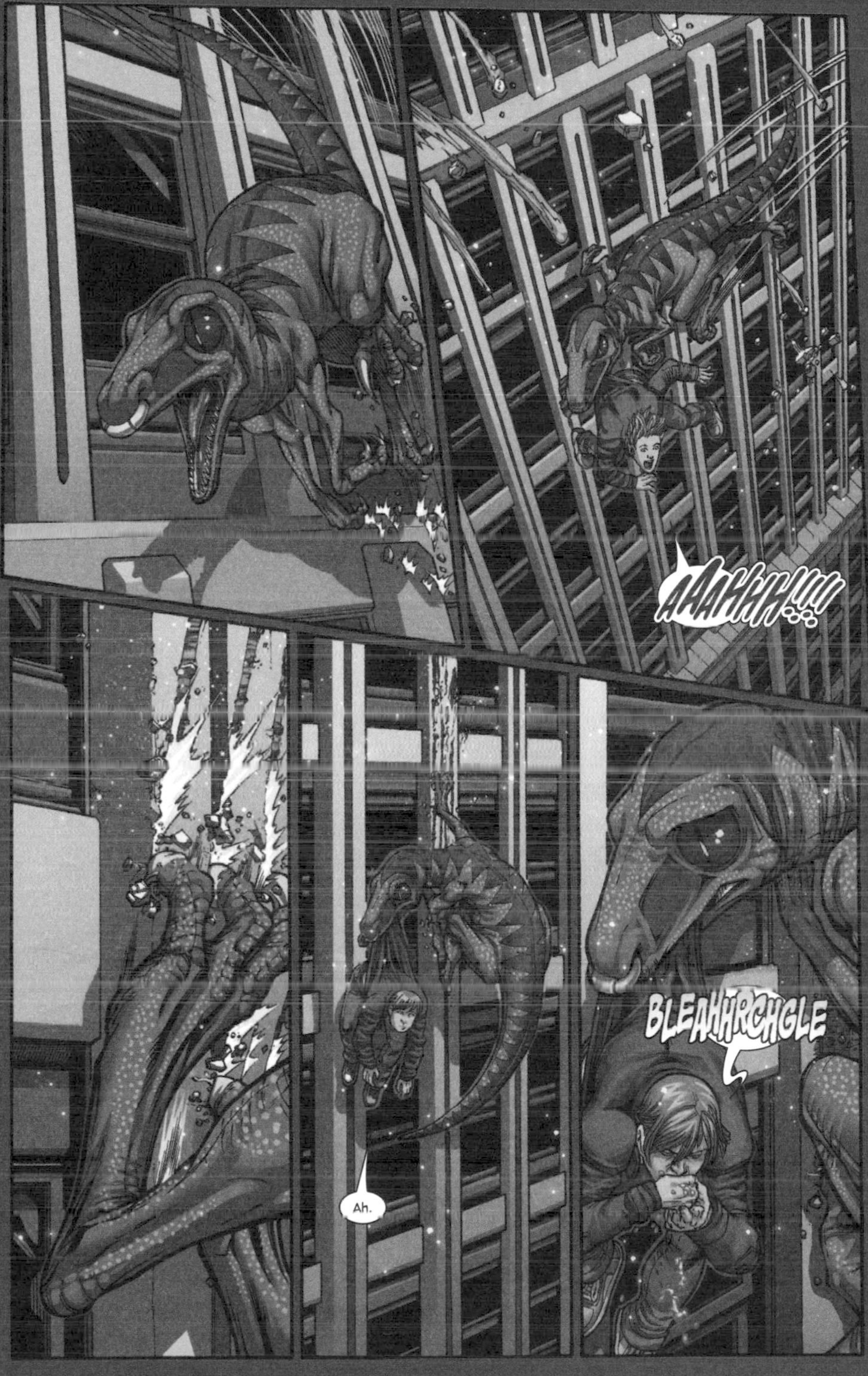
AAAHHH!!!
Ah.
BLEAHHRCHGLE

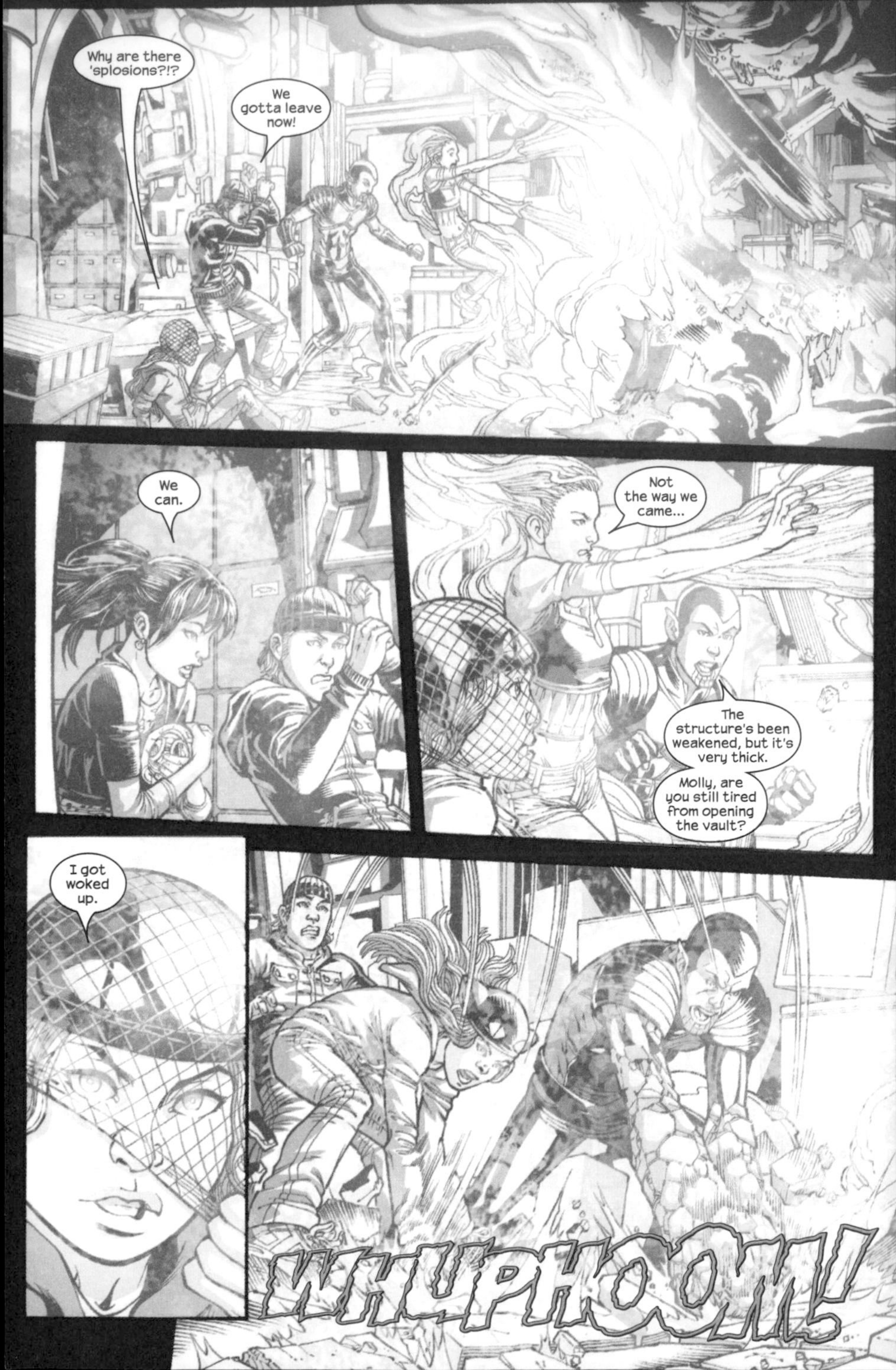
Why are there 'splosions?!?
We gotta leave now!
We can.
Not the way we came...
The structure's been weakened, but it's very thick.
Molly, are you still tired from opening the vault?
I got woked up.
WHUPHOOM!

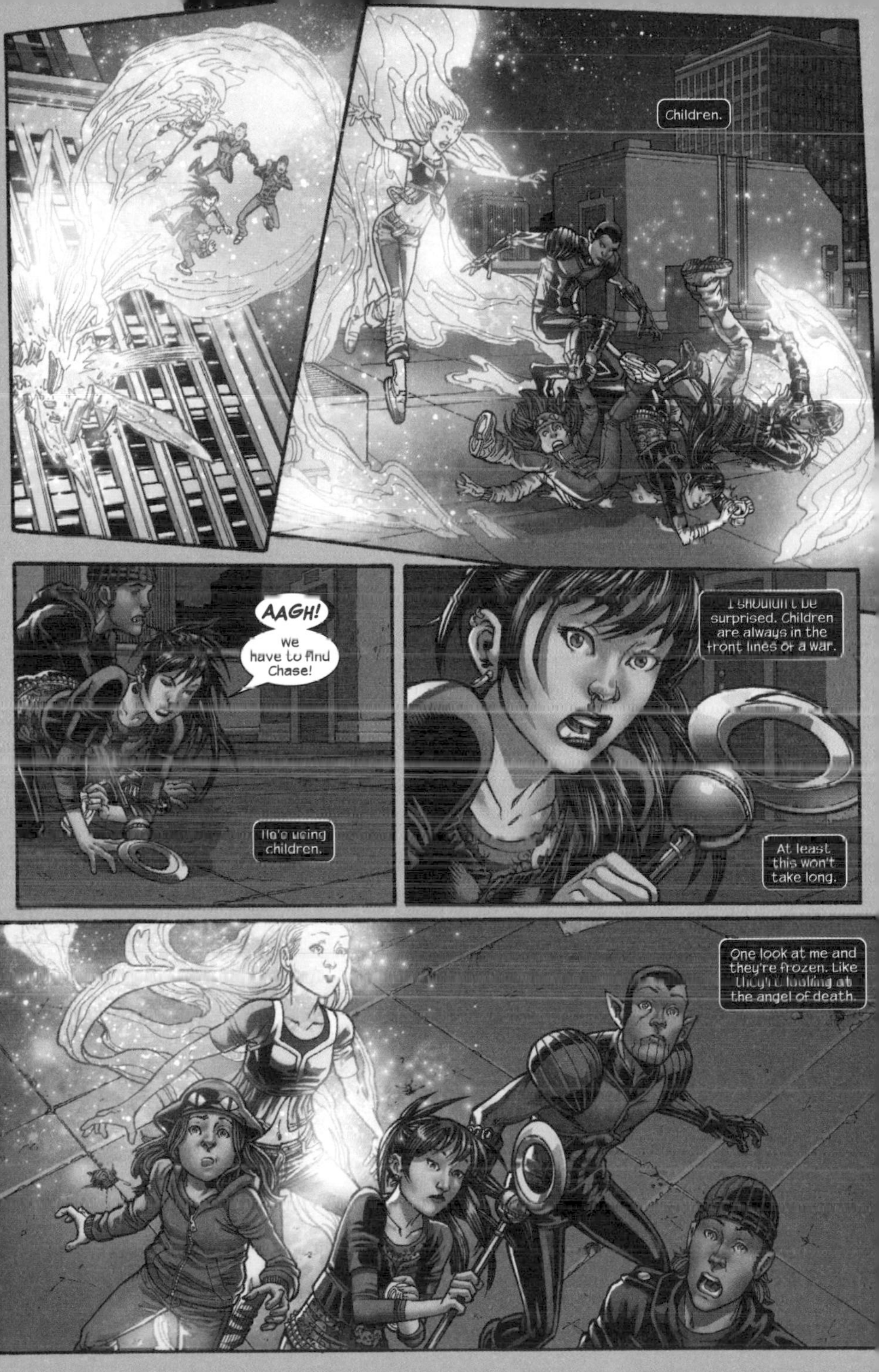
Children.
AAGH!
We have to find Chase!
He's using children.
I shouldn't be surprised. Children are always in the front lines of a war.
At least this won't take long.
One look at me and they're frozen. Like they're looking at the angel of death.

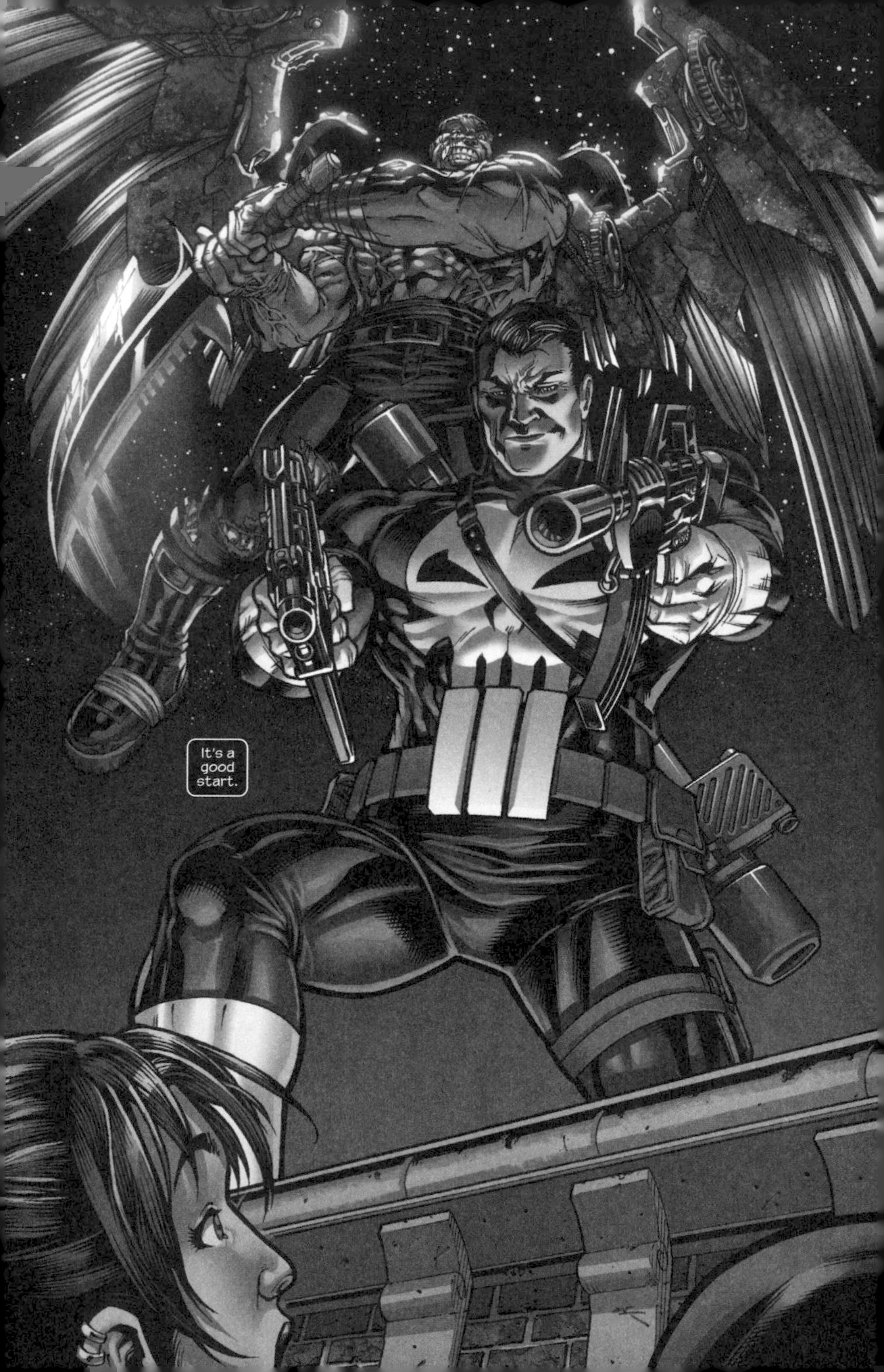
It's a good start.

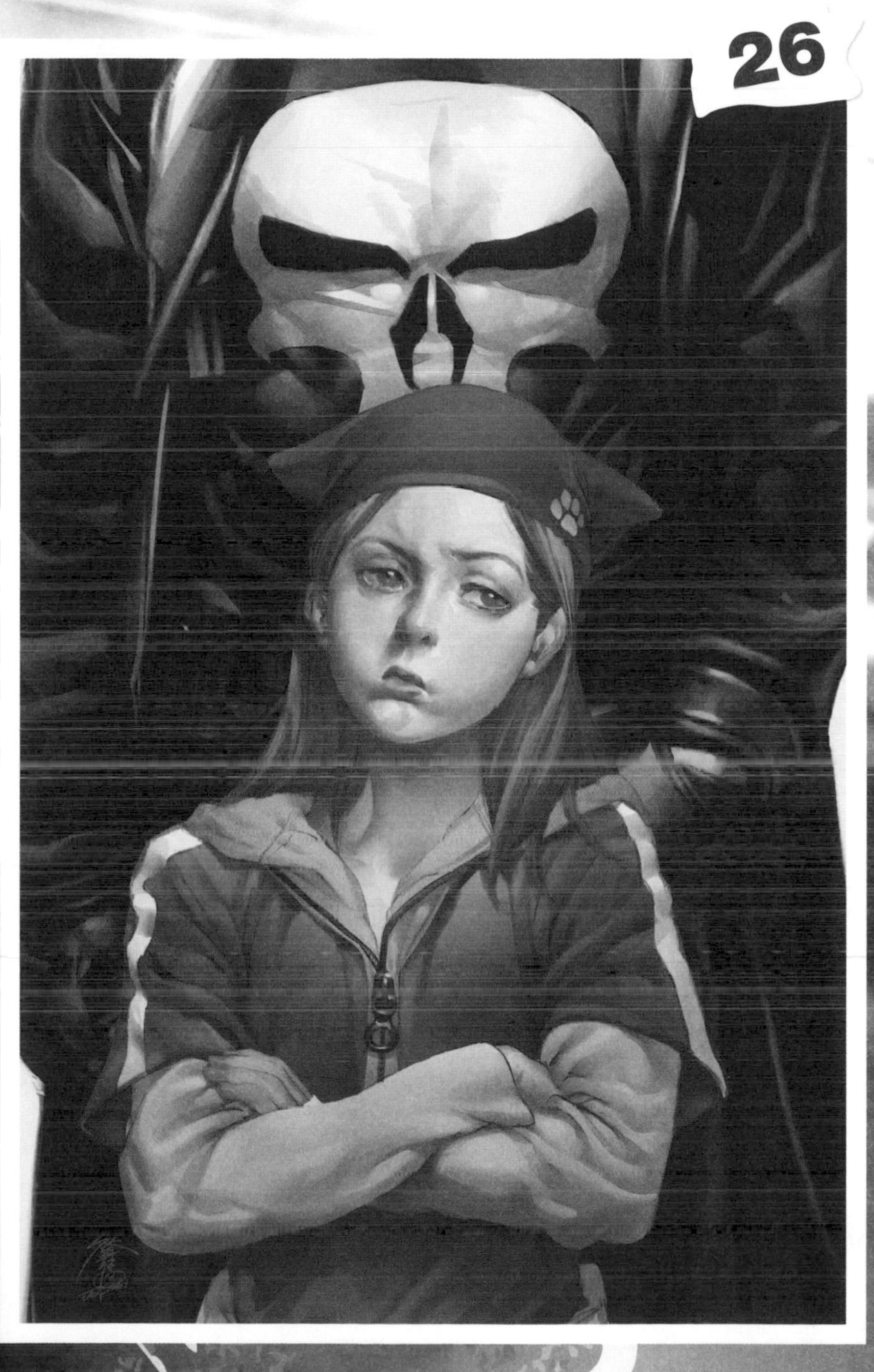
26

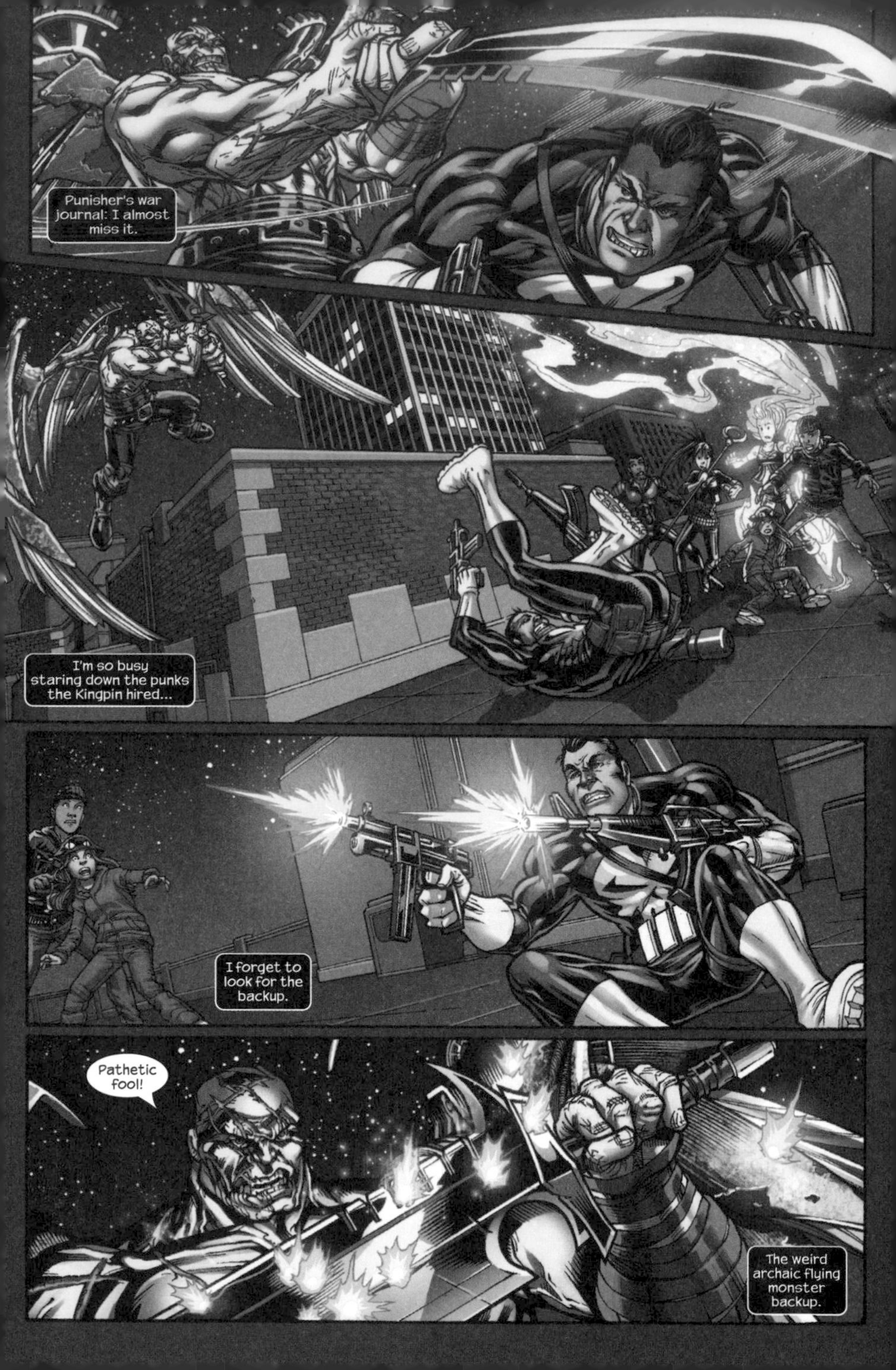
Punisher's war journal: I almost miss it.
I'm so busy staring down the punks the Kingpin hired...
I forget to look for the backup.
Pathetic fool!
The weird archaic flying monster backup.

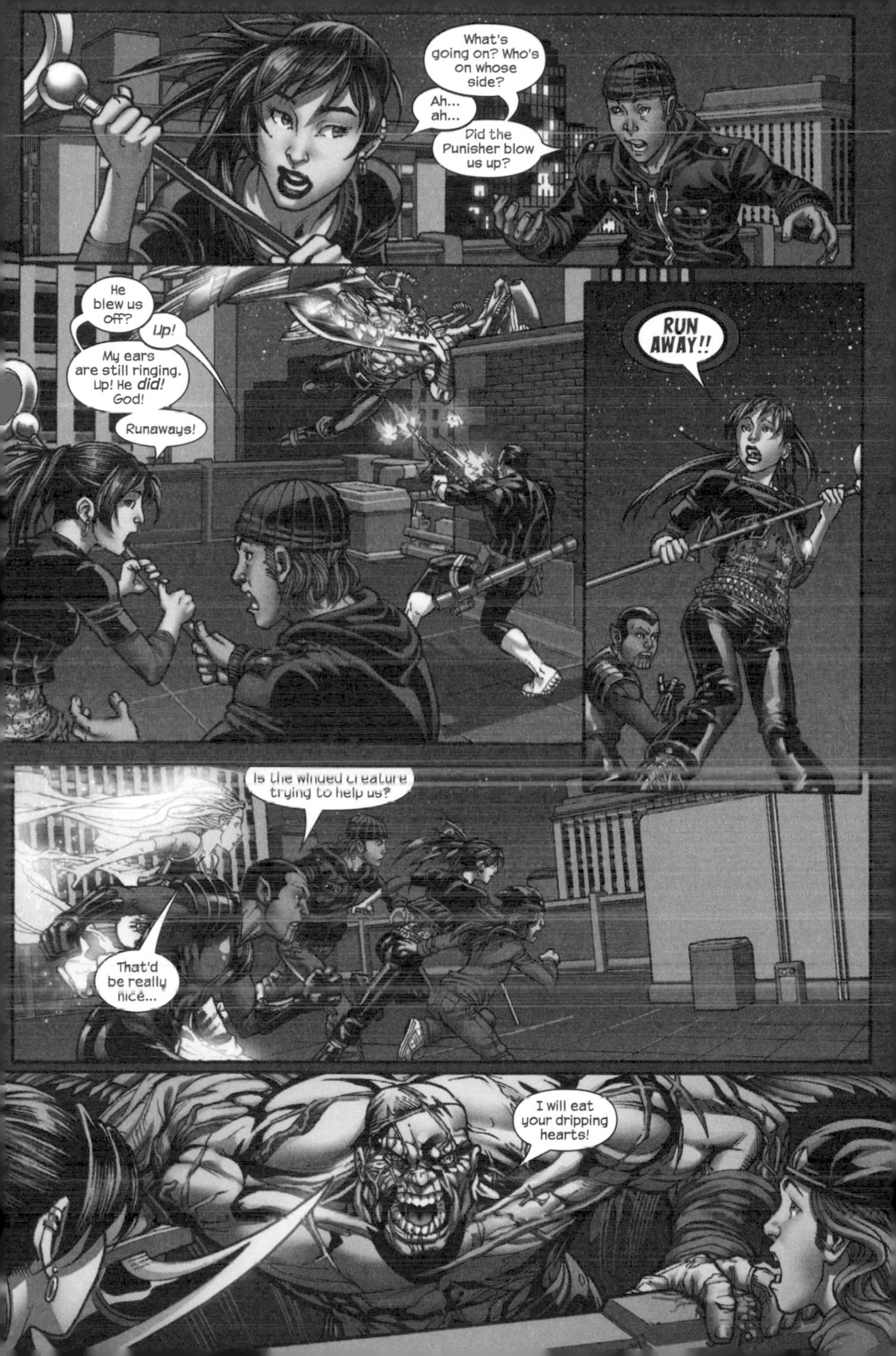
What's going on? Who's on whose side?
Ah... ah...
Did the Punisher blow us up?
He blew us off?
Up!
My ears are still ringing. Up! He did! God!
Runaways!
RUN AWAY!!
Is the winged creature trying to help us?
That'd be really nice...
I will eat your dripping hearts!

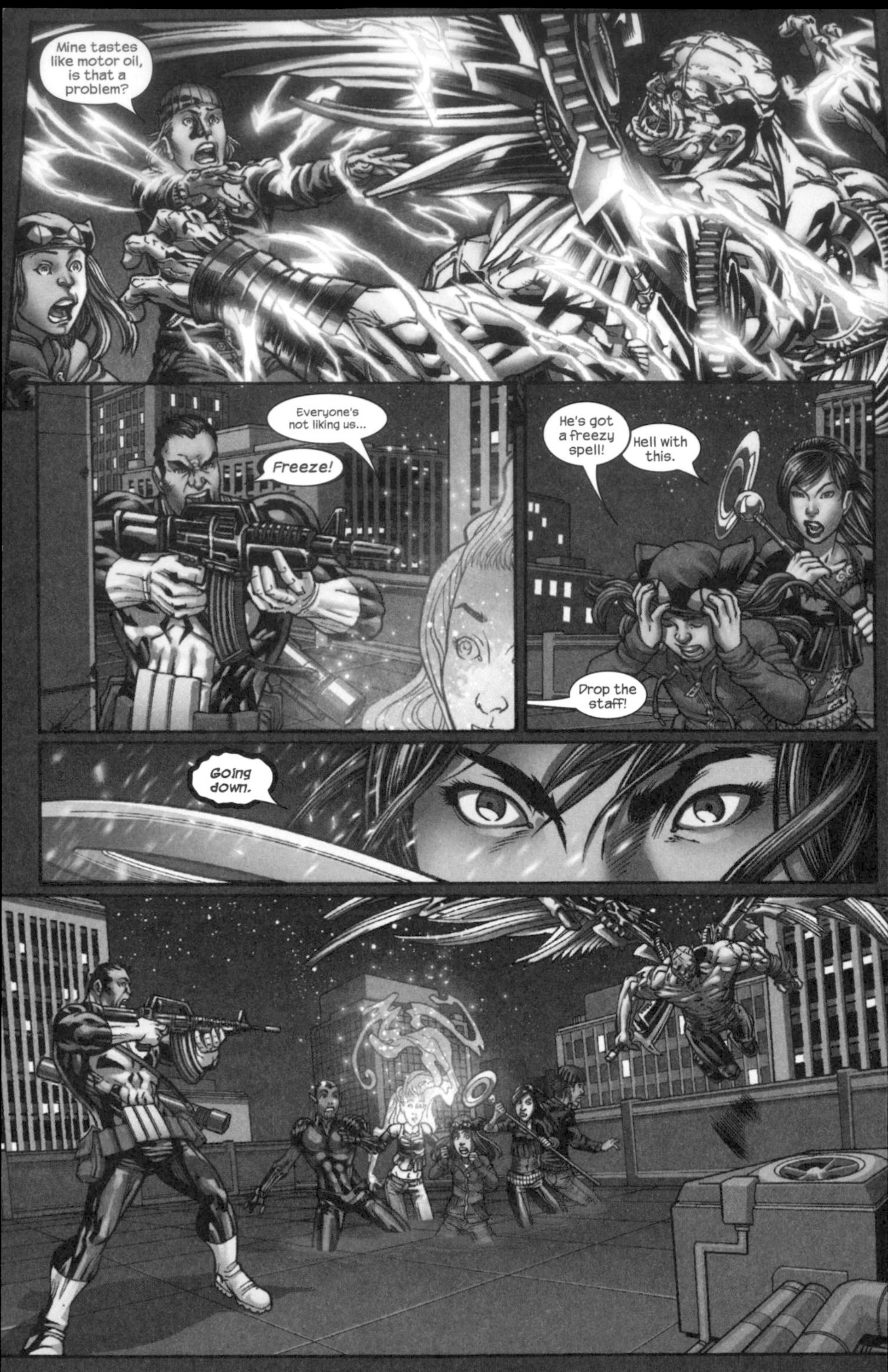
Mine tastes like motor oil, is that a problem?
Everyone's not liking us...
Freeze!
He's got a freezy spell!
Hell with this.
Drop the staff!
Going down.

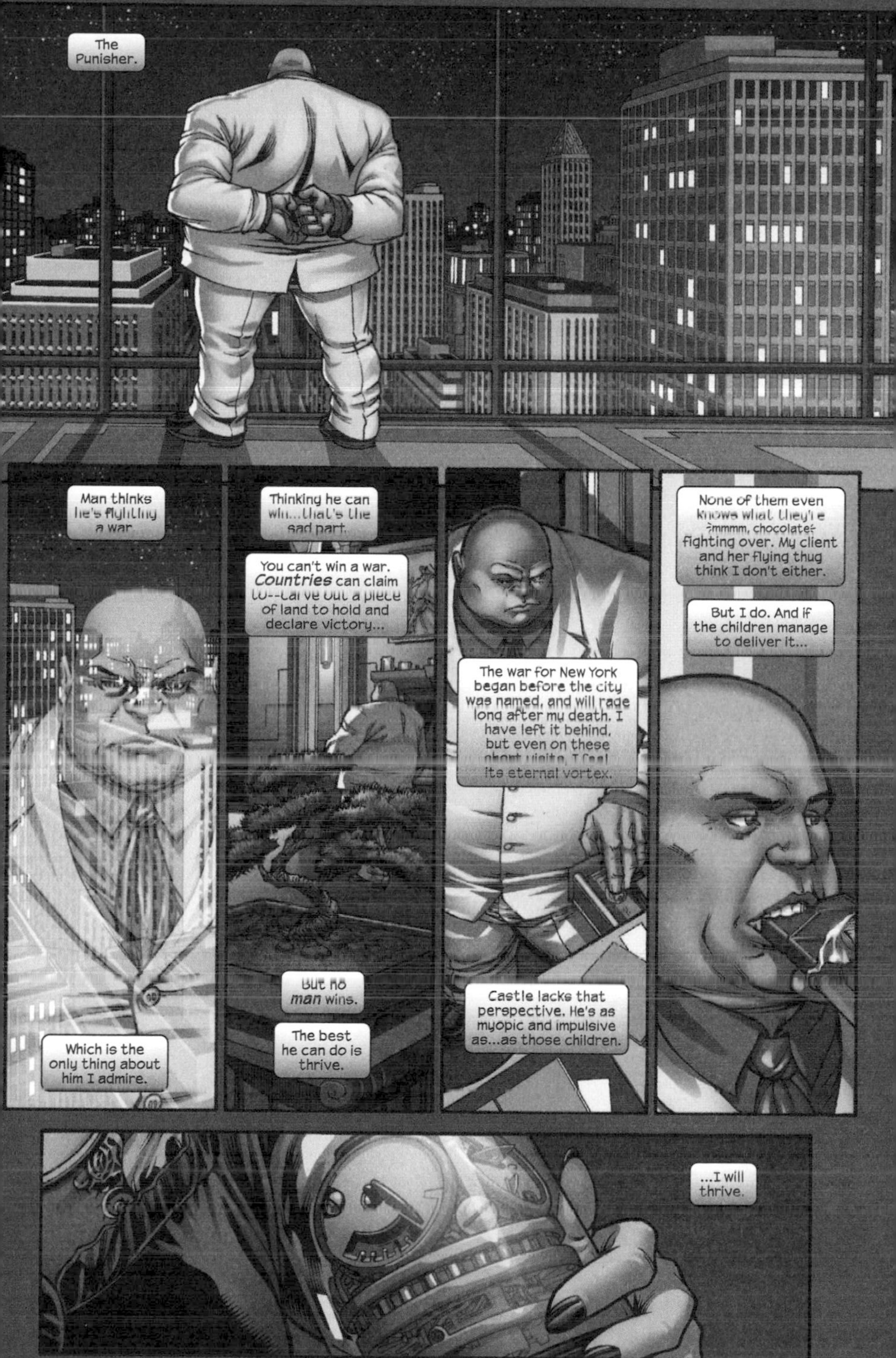

The Punisher.
Man thinks he's fighting a war.
Which is the only thing about him I admire.
Thinking he can win...that's the sad part.
You can't win a war. *Countries* can claim to--carve out a piece of land to hold and declare victory...
But no *man* wins.
The best he can do is thrive.
The war for New York began before the city was named, and will rage long after my death. I have left it behind, but even on these short visits, I feel its eternal vortex.
Castle lacks that perspective. He's as myopic and impulsive as...as those children.
None of them even knows what they're -mmmm, chocolate- fighting over. My client and her flying thug think I don't either.
But I do. And if the children manage to deliver it...
...I will thrive.

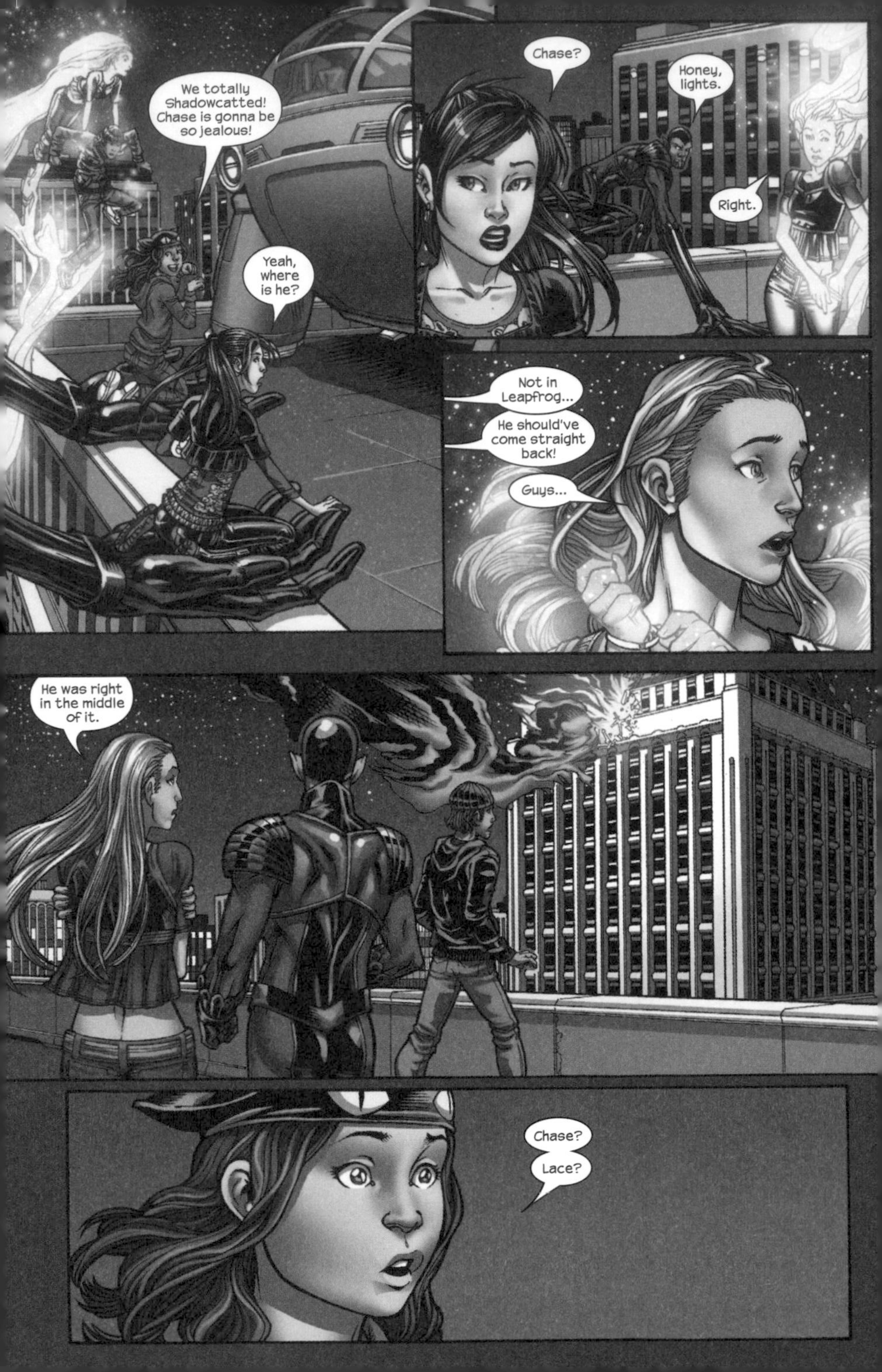
We totally Shadowcatted! Chase is gonna be so jealous!
Yeah, where is he?
Chase?
Honey, lights.
Right.
Not in Leapfrog...
He should've come straight back!
Guys...
He was right in the middle of it.
Chase?
Lace?

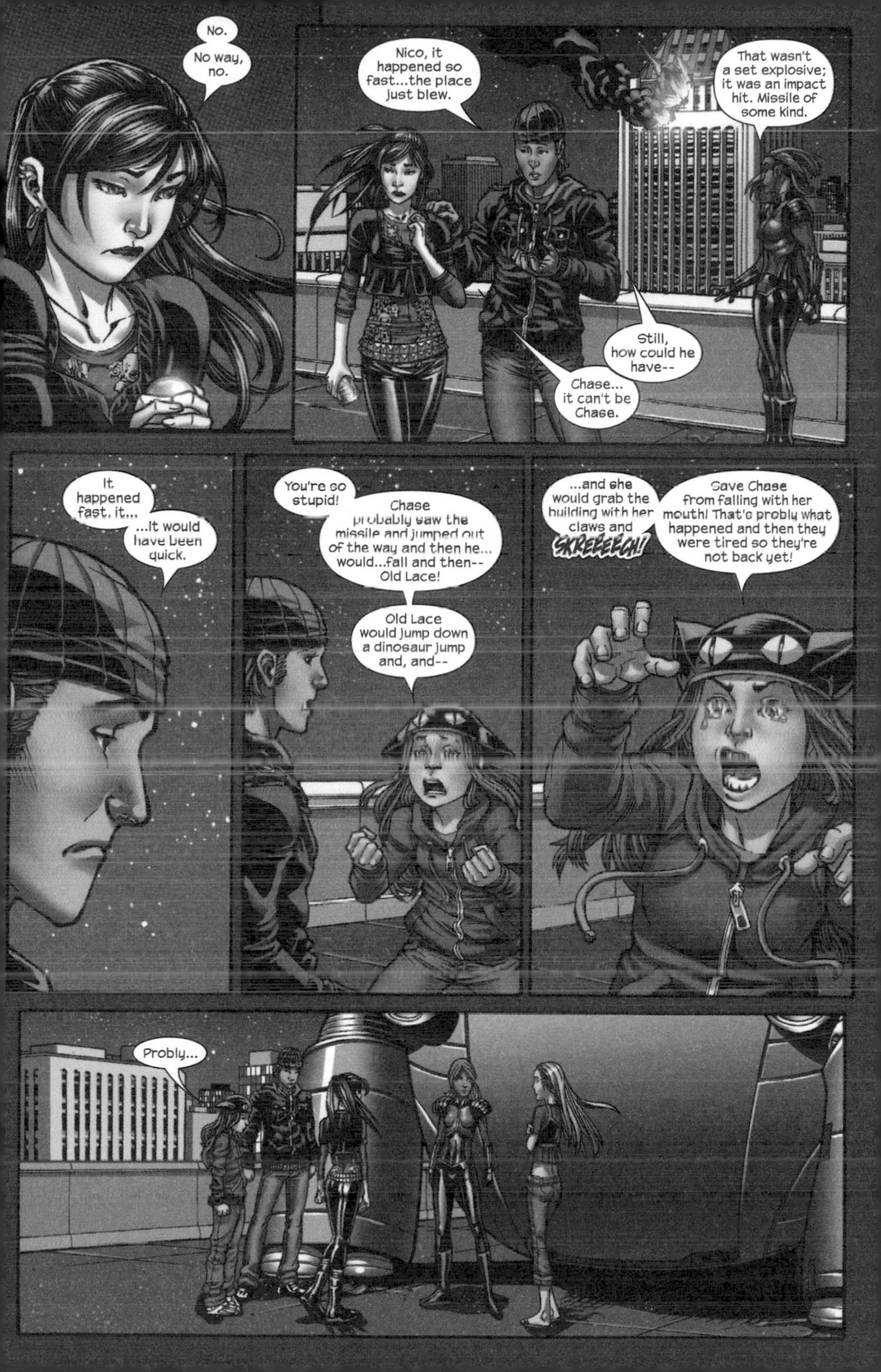
No.
No way, no.
Nico, it happened so fast...the place just blew.
That wasn't a set explosive; it was an impact hit. Missile of some kind.
Still, how could he have--
Chase... it can't be Chase.
It happened fast, it...
...it would have been quick.
You're so stupid!
Chase probably saw the missile and jumped out of the way and then he... would...fall and then-- Old Lace!
Old Lace would jump down a dinosaur jump and, and--
...and she would grab the building with her claws and
SKREEEECH!
Save Chase from falling with her mouth! That's probly what happened and then they were tired so they're not back yet!
Probly...

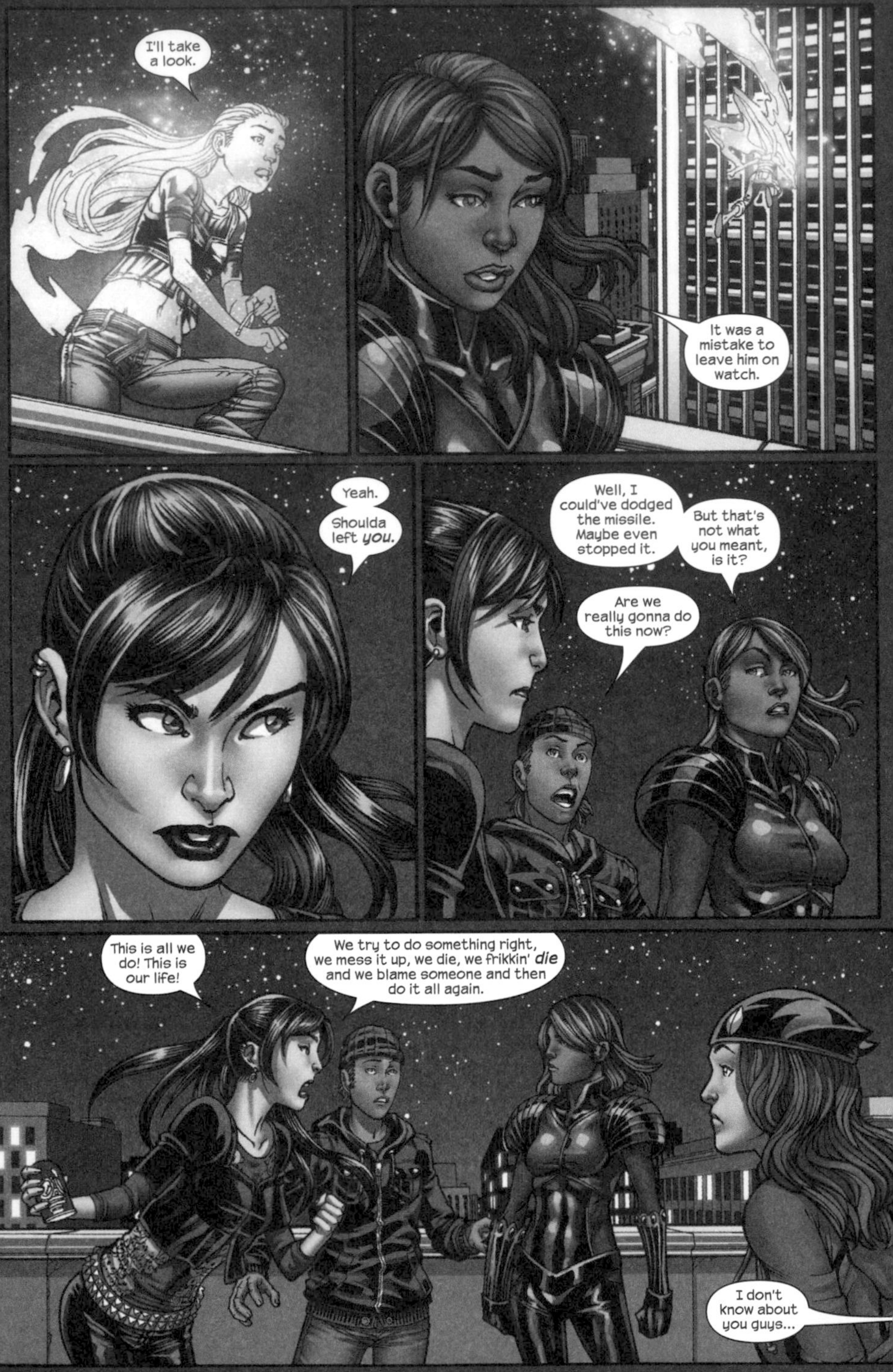
I'll take a look.
It was a mistake to leave him on watch.
Yeah.
Shoulda left *you.*
Well, I could've dodged the missile. Maybe even stopped it.
But that's not what you meant, is it?
Are we really gonna do this now?
This is all we do! This is our life!
We try to do something right, we mess it up, we die, we frikkin' *die* and we blame someone and then do it all again.
I don't know about you guys...

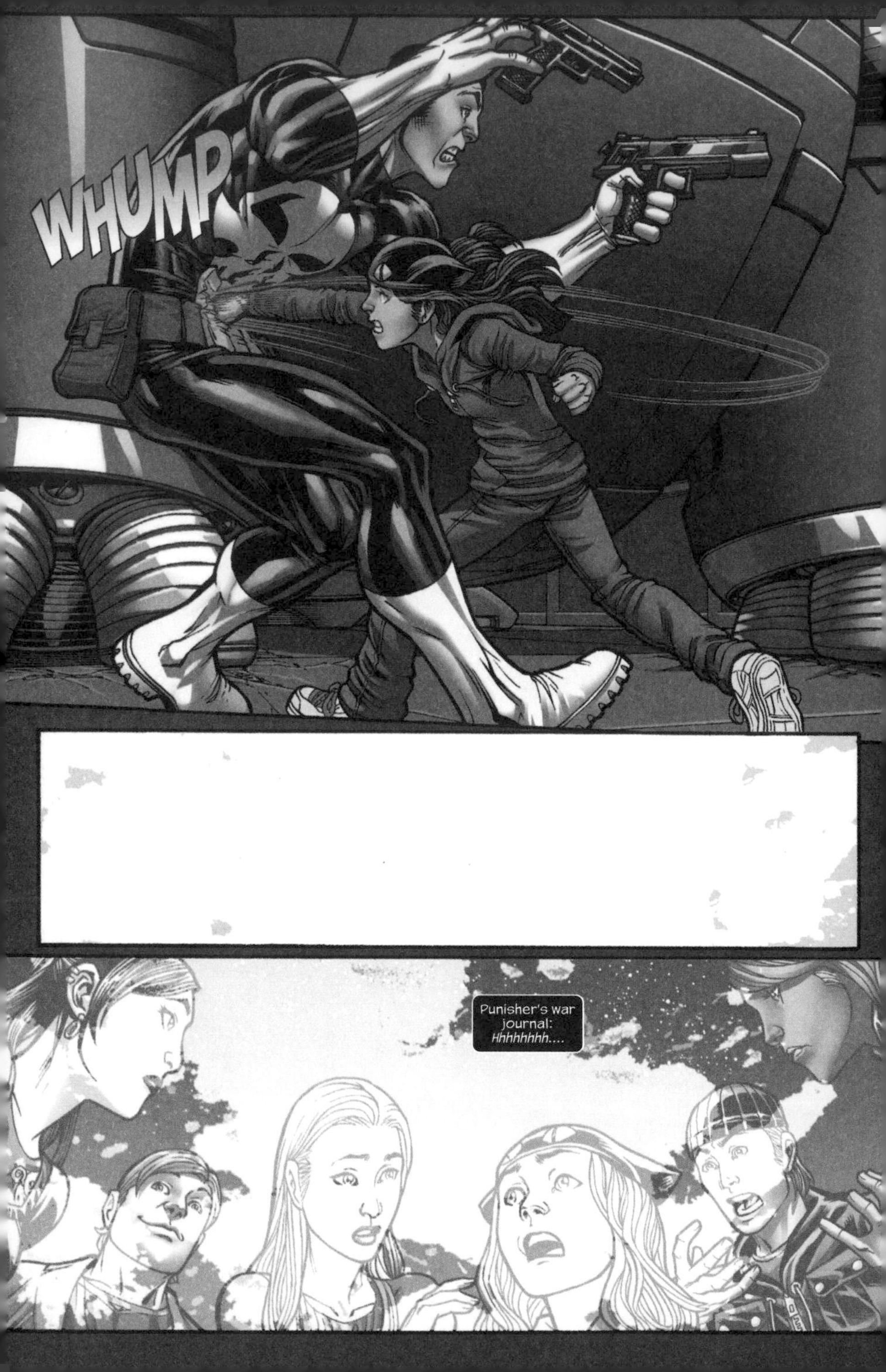
WHUMP
Punisher's war journal: *Hhhhhhhh....*

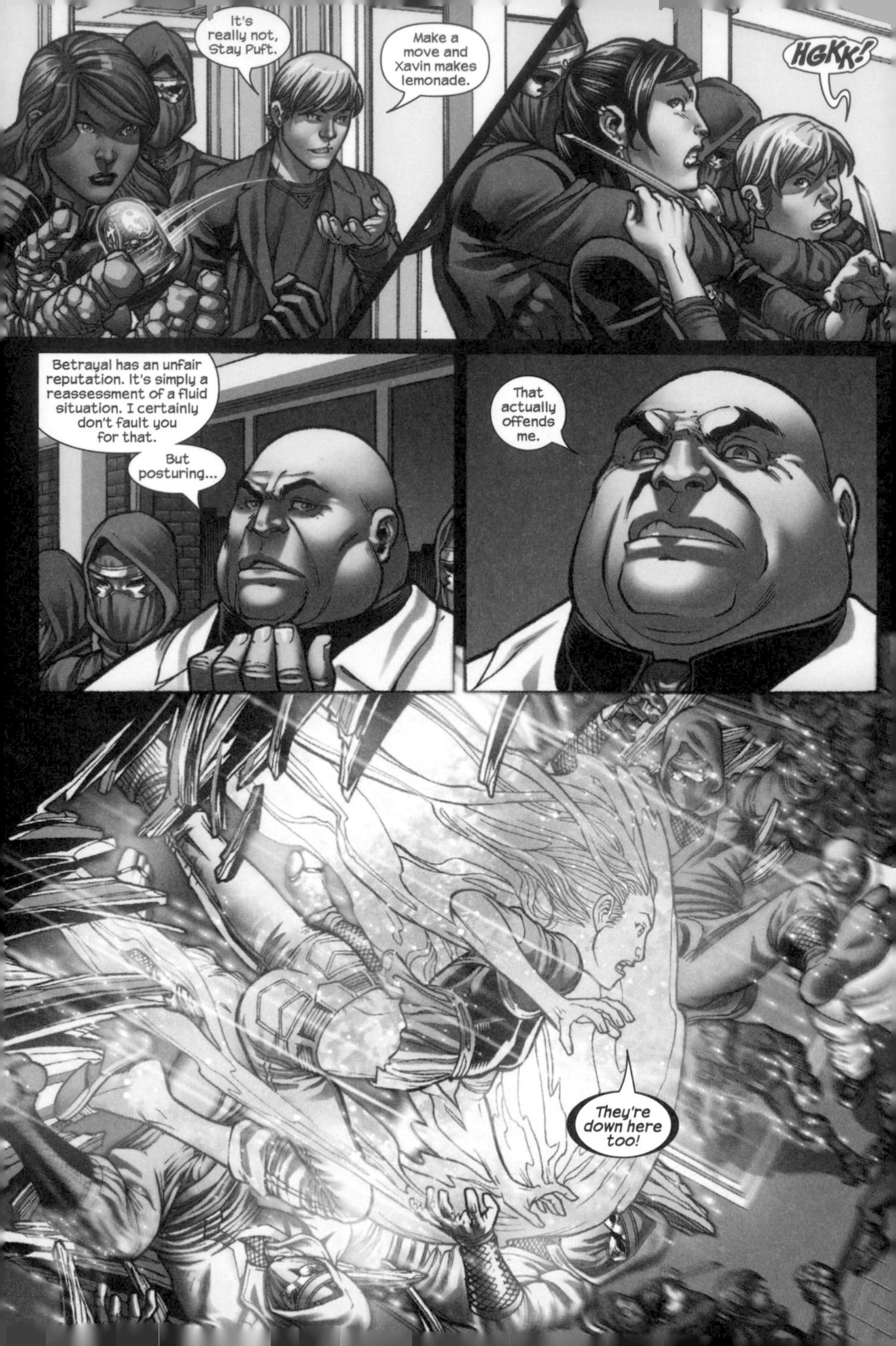
It's really not, Stay Puft.
Make a move and Xavin makes lemonade.
HGKK!
Betrayal has an unfair reputation. It's simply a reassessment of a fluid situation. I certainly don't fault you for that.
But posturing...
That actually offends me.
They're down here too!

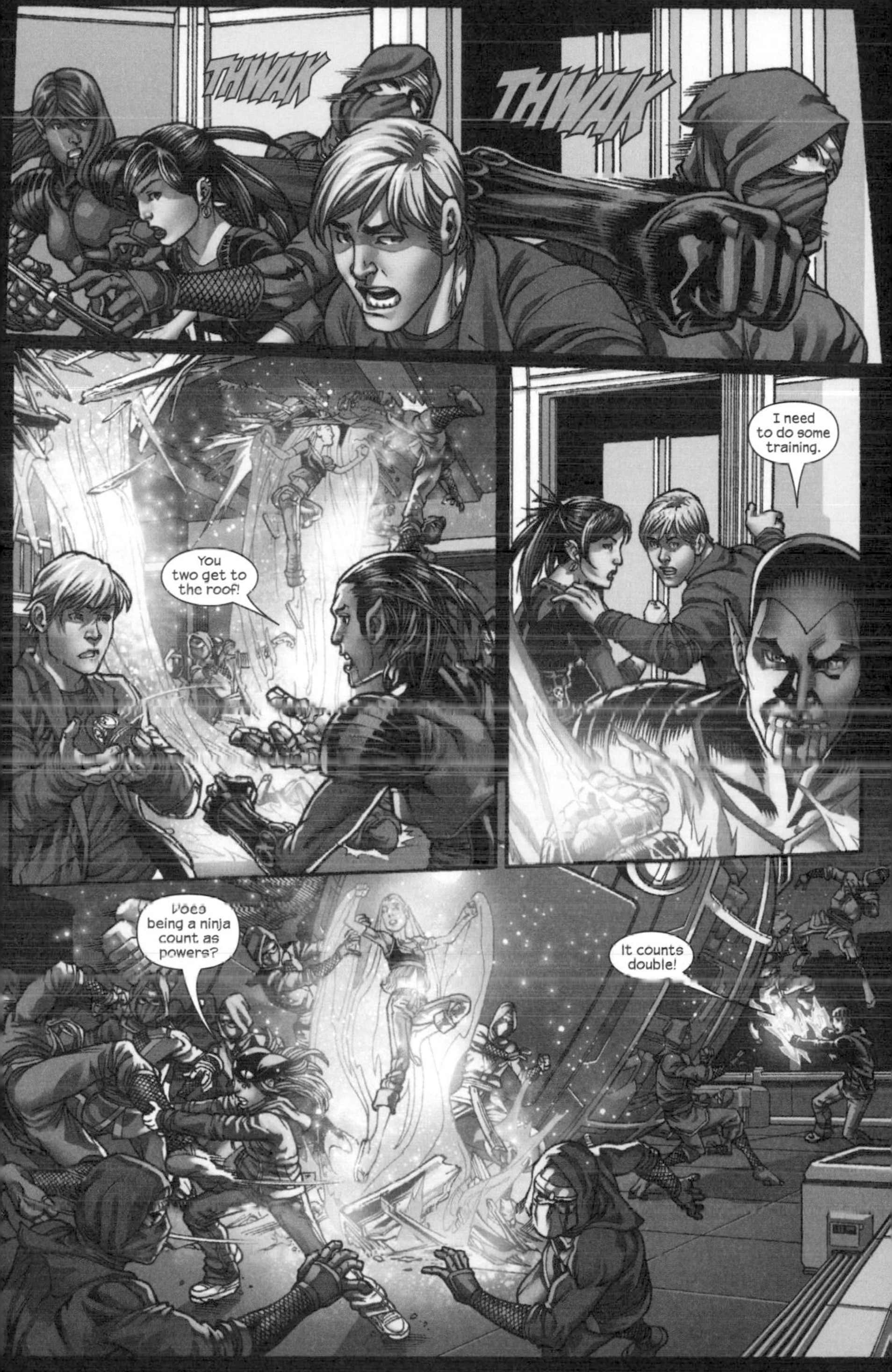
THWAK
THWAK
You two get to the roof!
I need to do some training.
Does being a ninja count as powers?
It counts double!

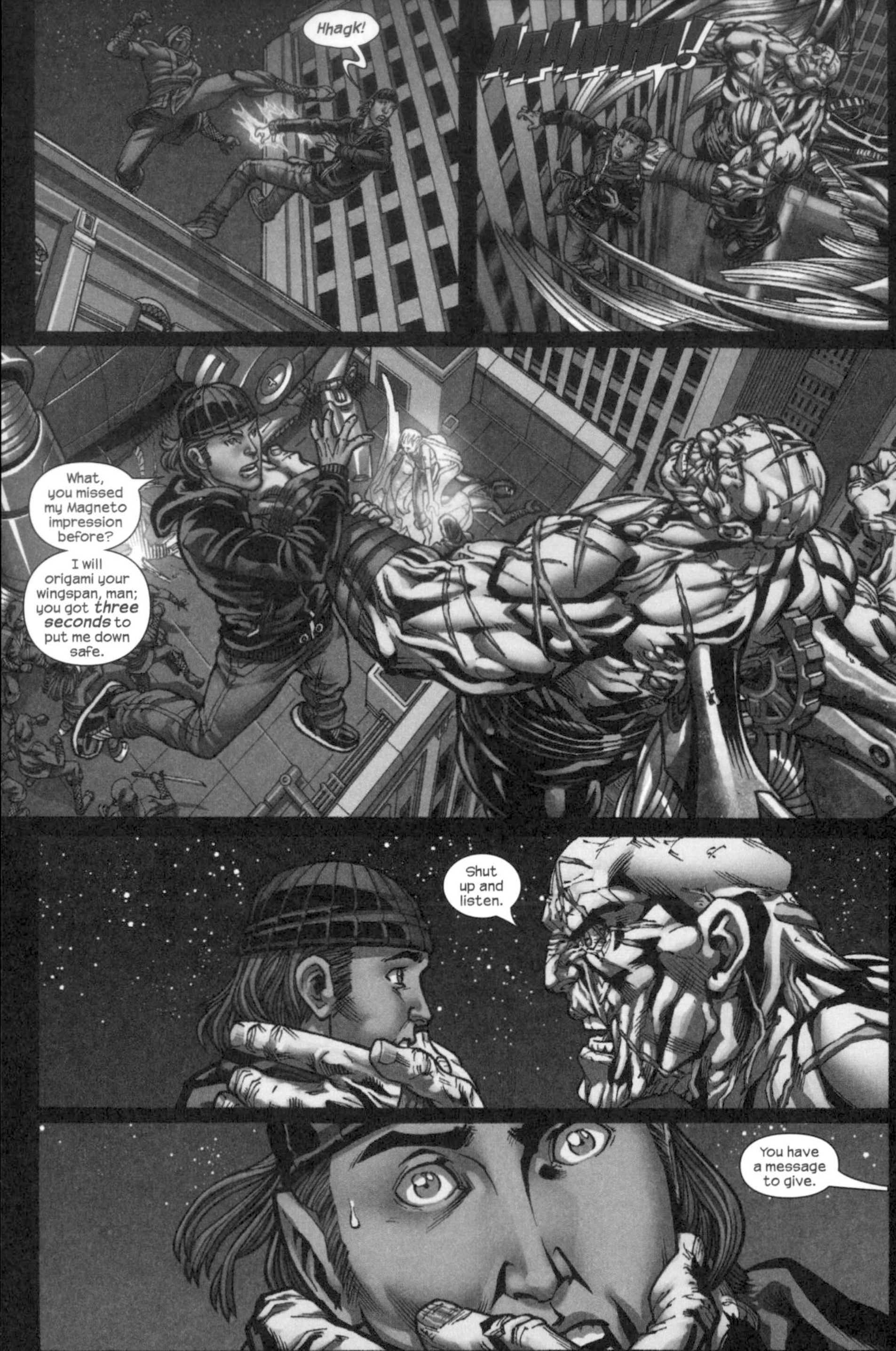
Hhagk!
What, you missed my Magneto impression before?
I will origami your wingspan, man; you got *three seconds* to put me down safe.
Shut up and listen.
You have a message to give.

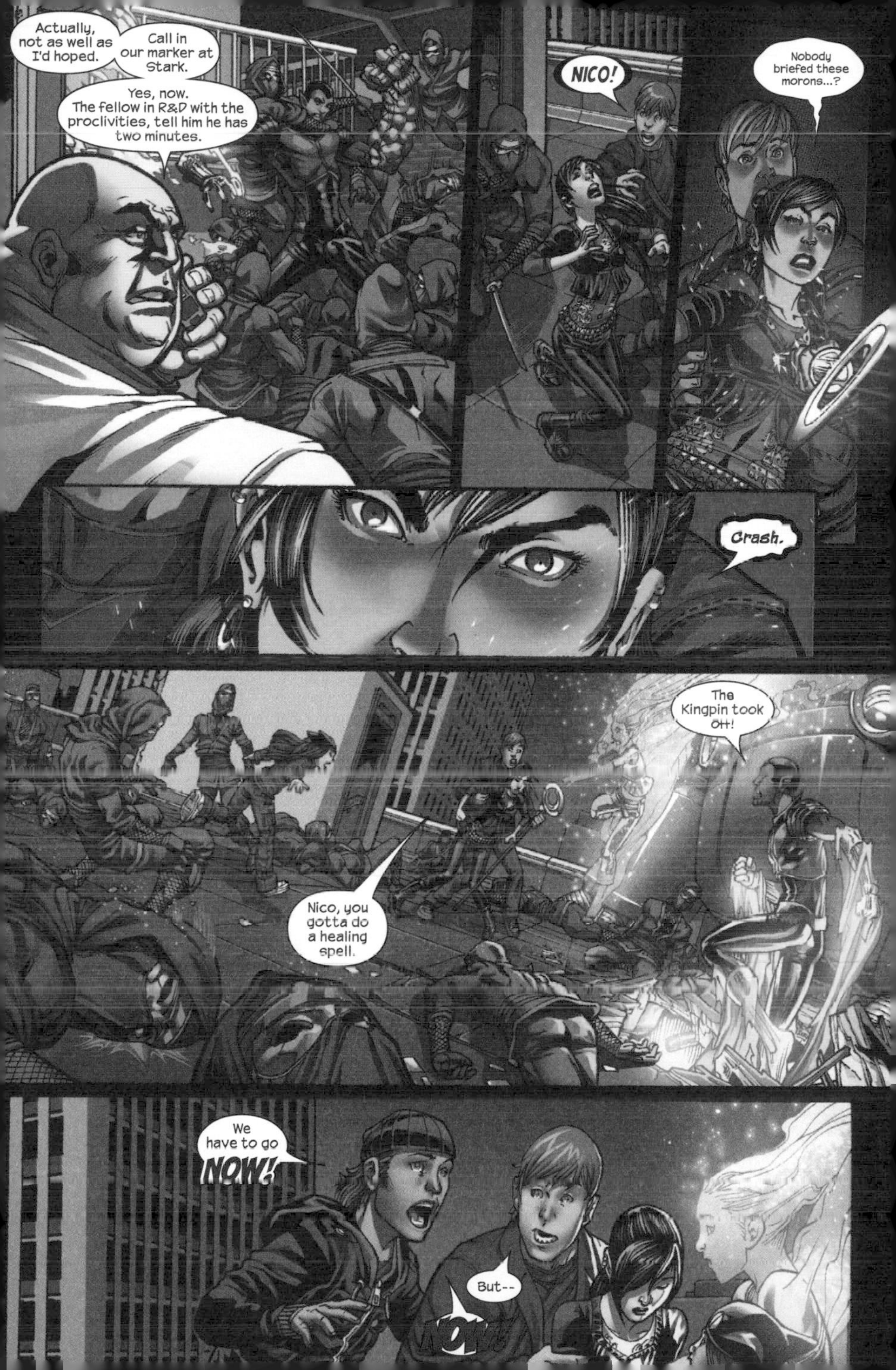
Actually, not as well as I'd hoped.
Call in our marker at Stark.
Yes, now. The fellow in R&D with the proclivities, tell him he has two minutes.
NICO!
Nobody briefed these morons...?
Crash.
The Kingpin took off!
Nico, you gotta do a healing spell.
We have to go NOW!
But--
NOW!

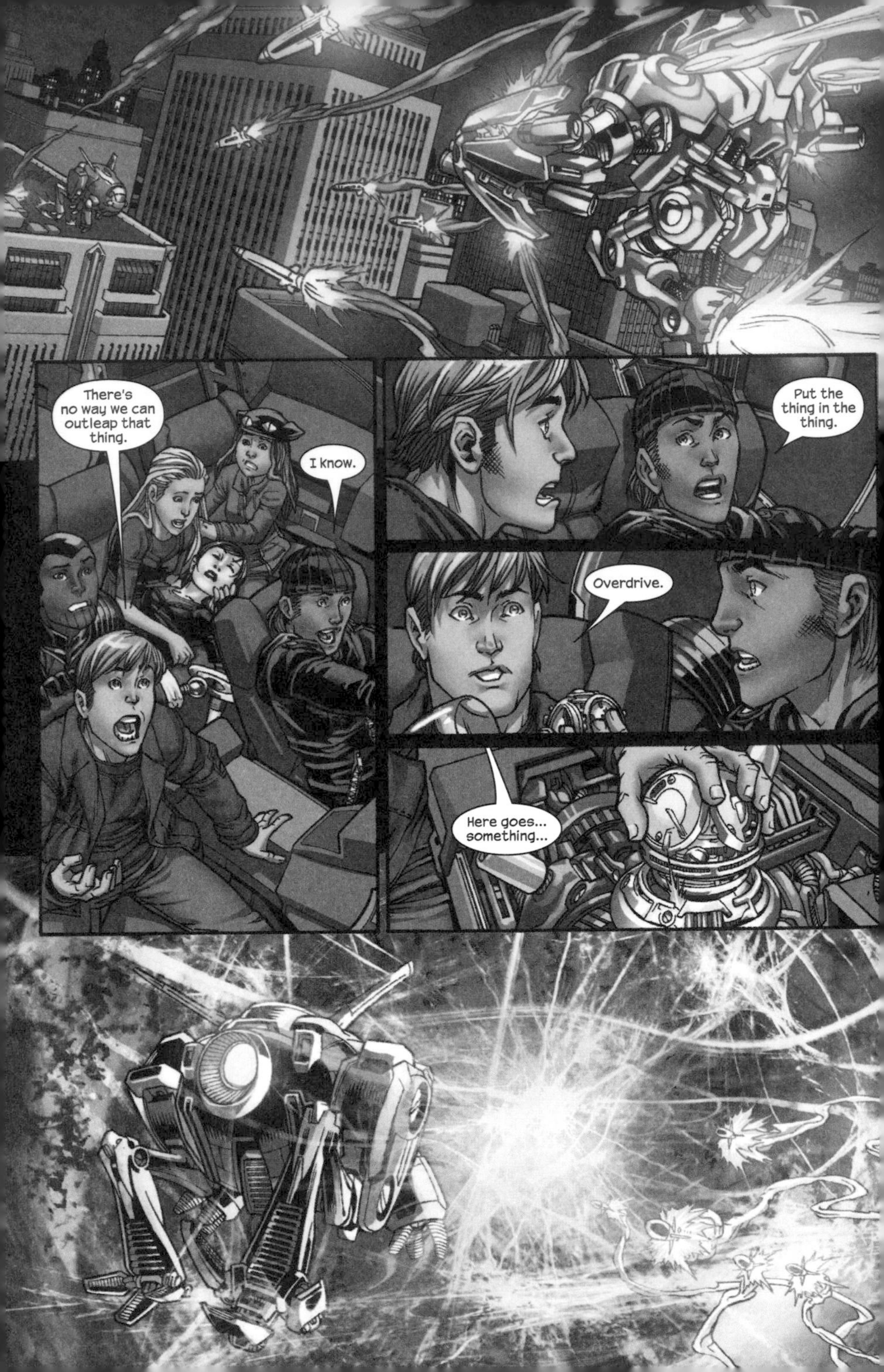
There's no way we can outleap that thing.
I know.
Put the thing in the thing.
Overdrive.
Here goes... something...

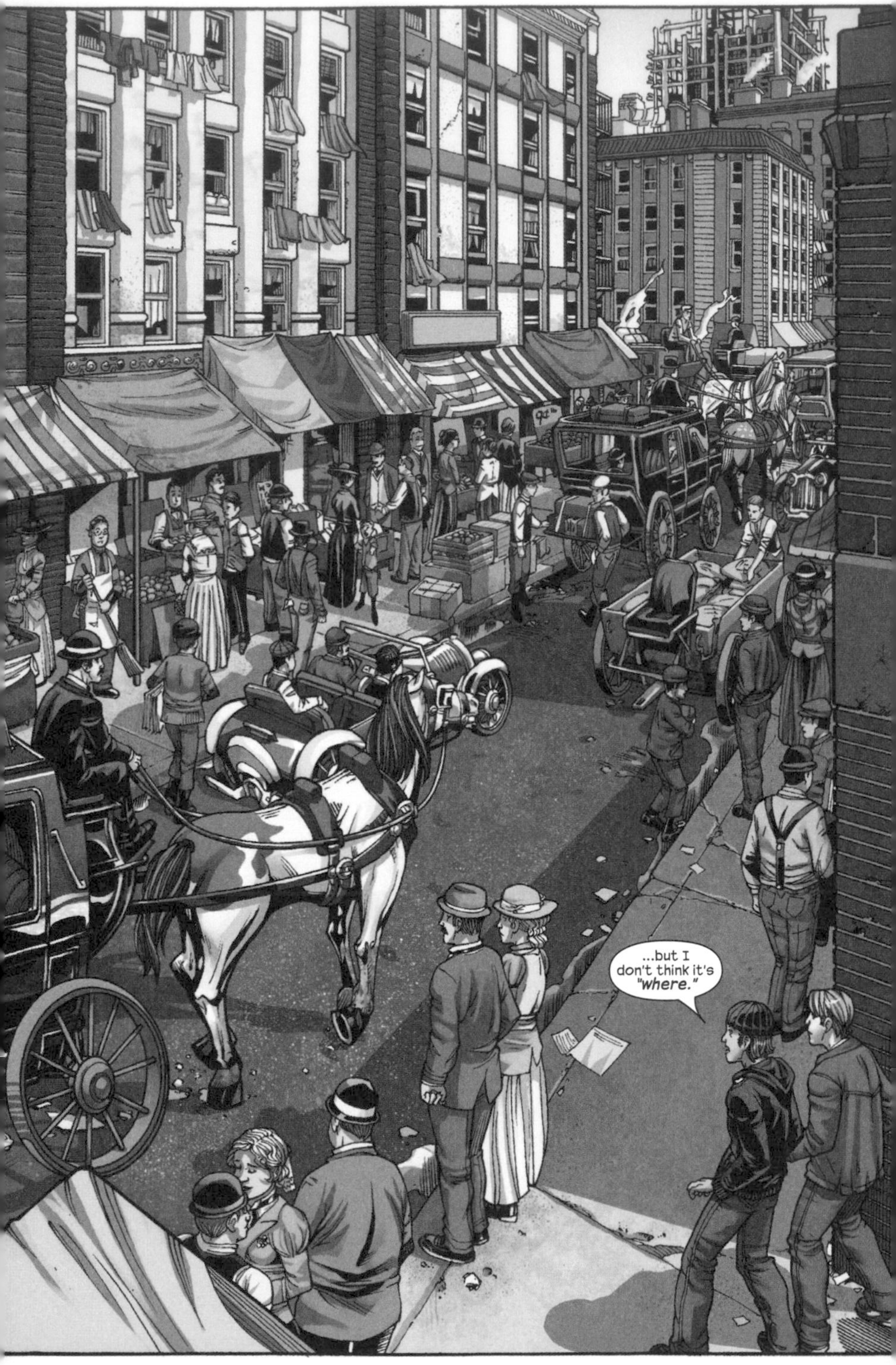
...but I don't think it's "where."

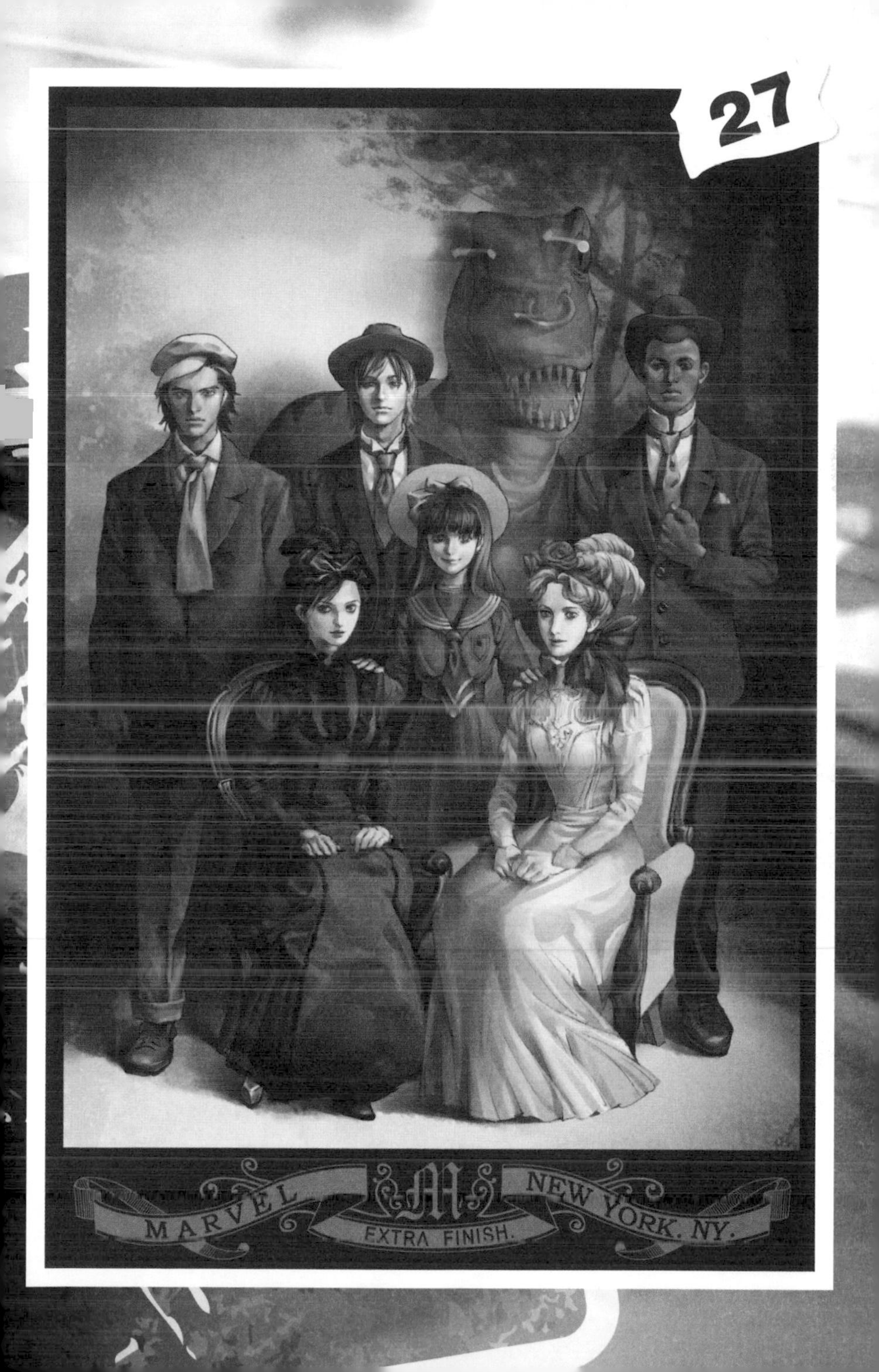
27
MARVEL
M
EXTRA FINISH.
NEW YORK. NY.

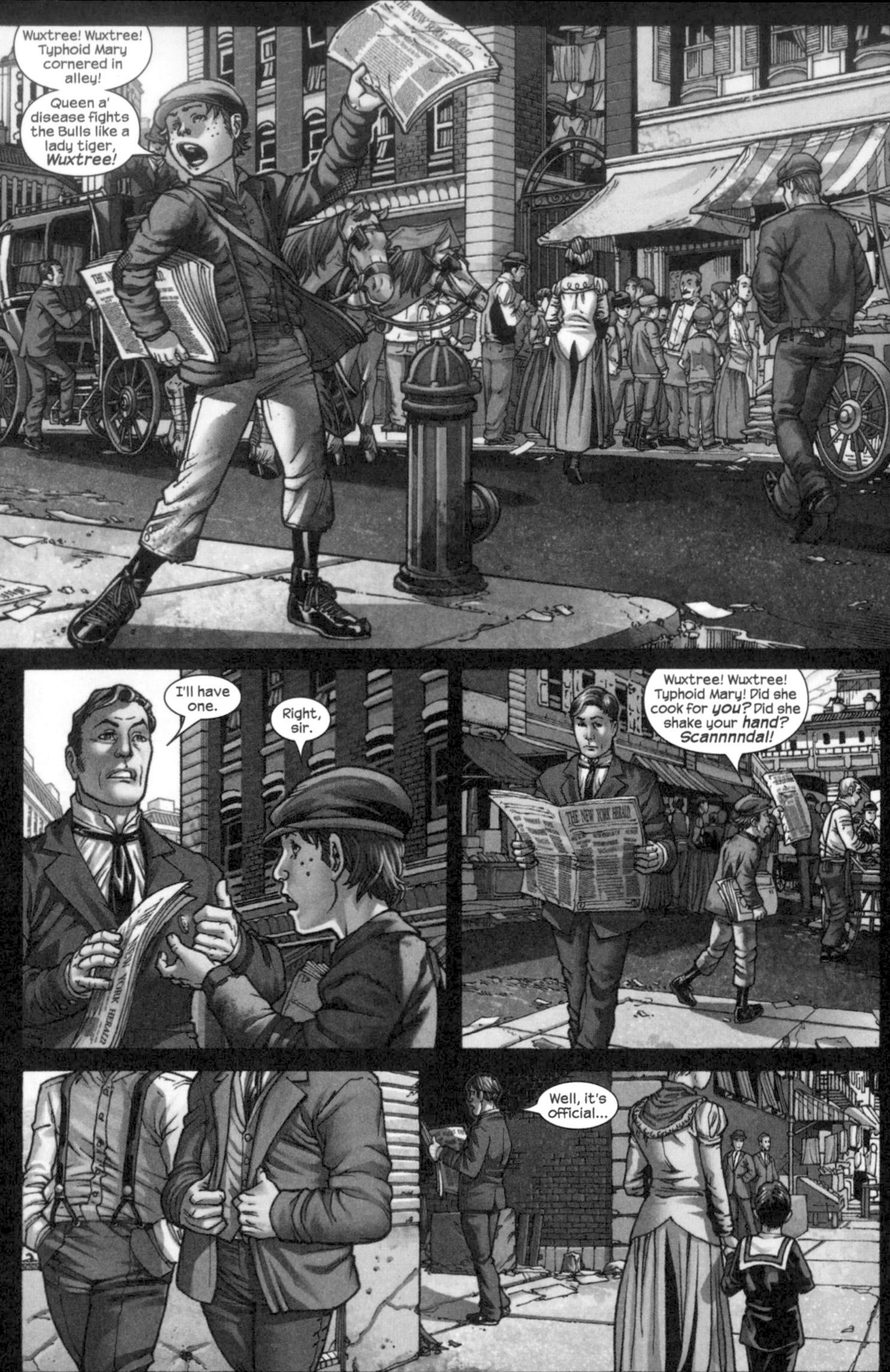

Wuxtree! Wuxtree! Typhoid Mary cornered in alley!
Queen a' disease fights the Bulls like a lady tiger, Wuxtree!
I'll have one.
Right, sir.
Wuxtree! Wuxtree! Typhoid Mary! Did she cook for you? Did she shake your hand? Scannnndal!
Well, it's official...

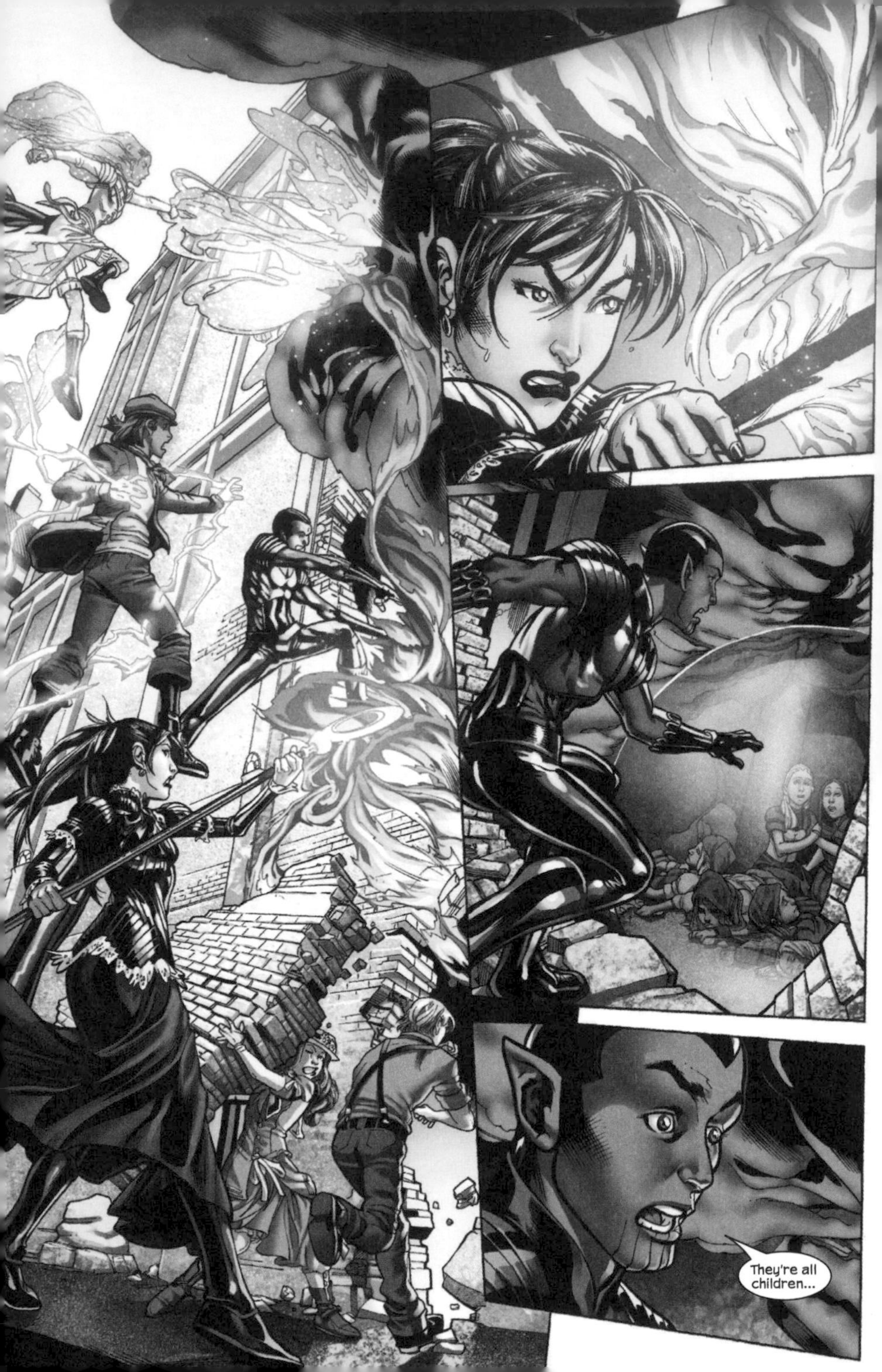
They're all children...

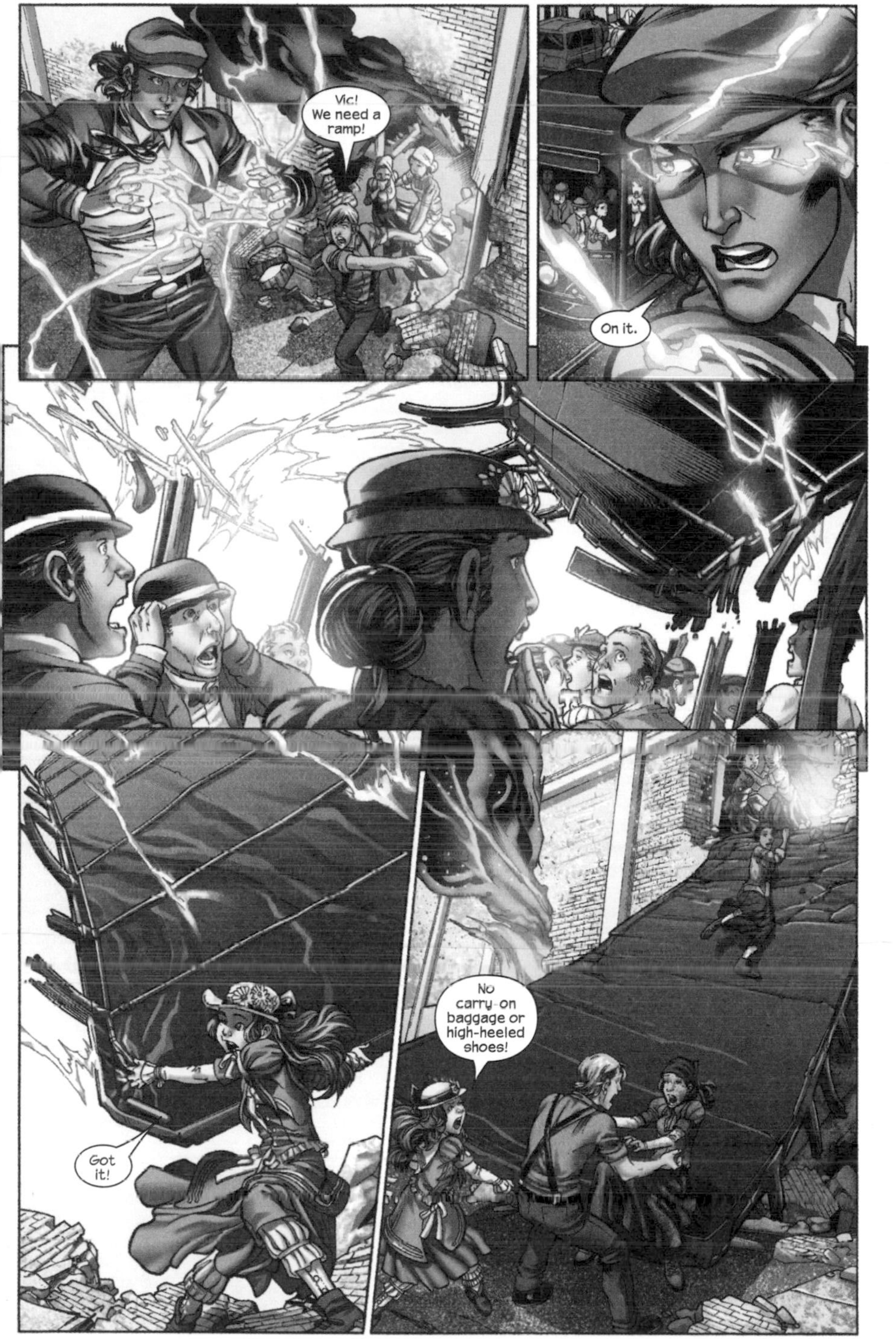
Vic! We need a ramp!
On it.
Got it!
No carry-on baggage or high-heeled shoes!

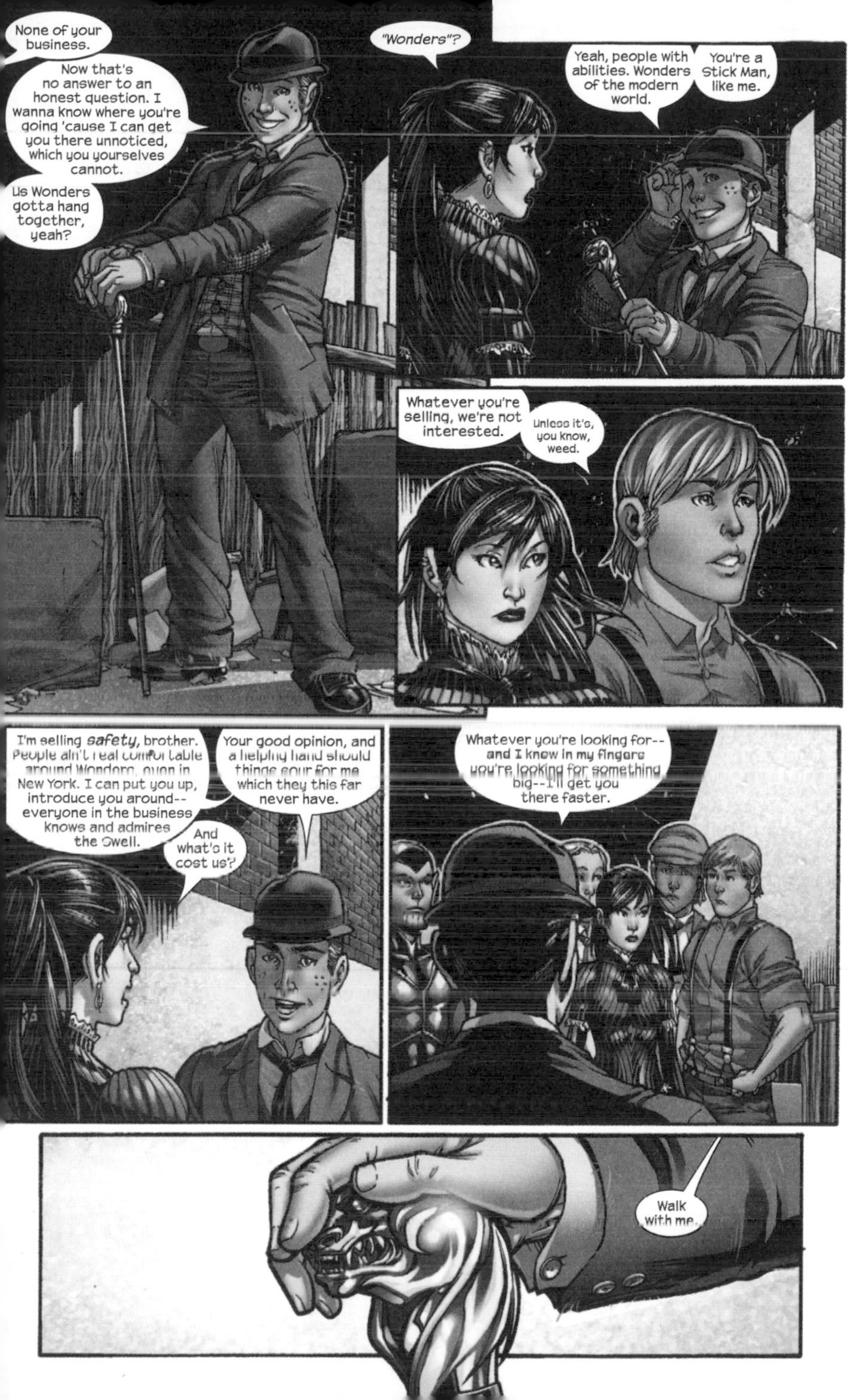

None of your business.
Now that's no answer to an honest question. I wanna know where you're going 'cause I can get you there unnoticed, which you yourselves cannot.
Us Wonders gotta hang together, yeah?
"Wonders"?
Yeah, people with abilities. Wonders of the modern world.
You're a Stick Man, like me.
Whatever you're selling, we're not interested.
Unless it's, you know, weed.
I'm selling *safety,* brother. People ain't real comfortable around Wonders, even in New York. I can put you up, introduce you around-- everyone in the business knows and admires the Swell.
Your good opinion, and a helping hand should things sour for me which they this far never have.
And what's it cost us?
Whatever you're looking for-- and I know in my fingers you're looking for something big--I'll get you there faster.
Walk with me.

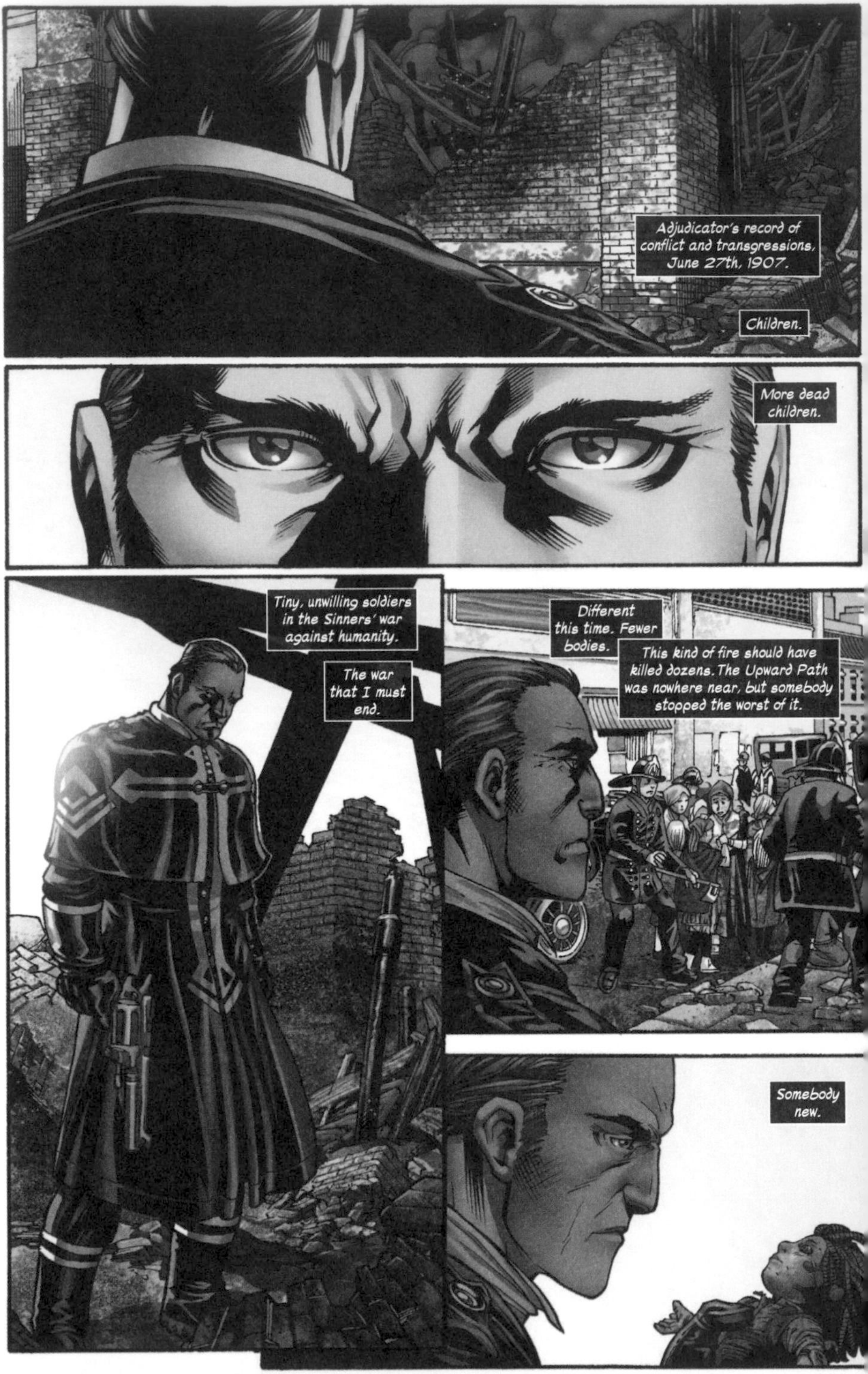
Adjudicator's record of conflict and transgressions, June 27th, 1907.
Children.
More dead children.
Tiny, unwilling soldiers in the Sinners' war against humanity.
The war that I must end.
Different this time. Fewer bodies.
This kind of fire should have killed dozens. The Upward Path was nowhere near, but somebody stopped the worst of it.
Somebody new.

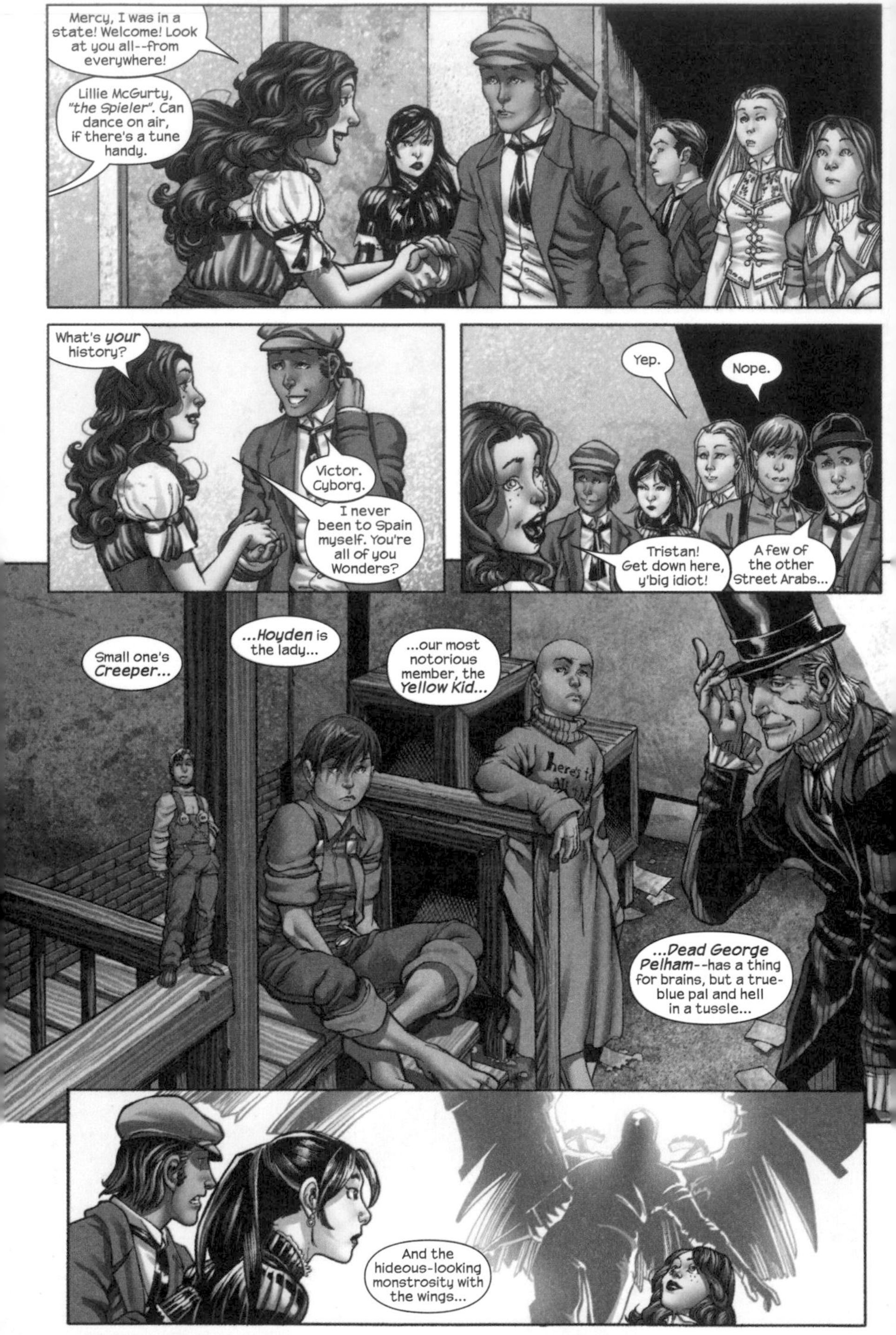

Mercy, I was in a state! Welcome! Look at you all--from everywhere!
Lillie McGurty, *"the Spieler"*. Can dance on air, if there's a tune handy.
What's ***your*** history?
Victor. Cyborg.
I never been to Spain myself. You're all of you Wonders?
Yep.
Nope.
Tristan! Get down here, y'big idiot!
A few of the other Street Arabs...
Small one's ***Creeper...***
...Hoyden is the lady...
...our most notorious member, the ***Yellow Kid...***
...Dead George Pelham--has a thing for brains, but a true-blue pal and hell in a tussle...
And the hideous-looking monstrosity with the wings...

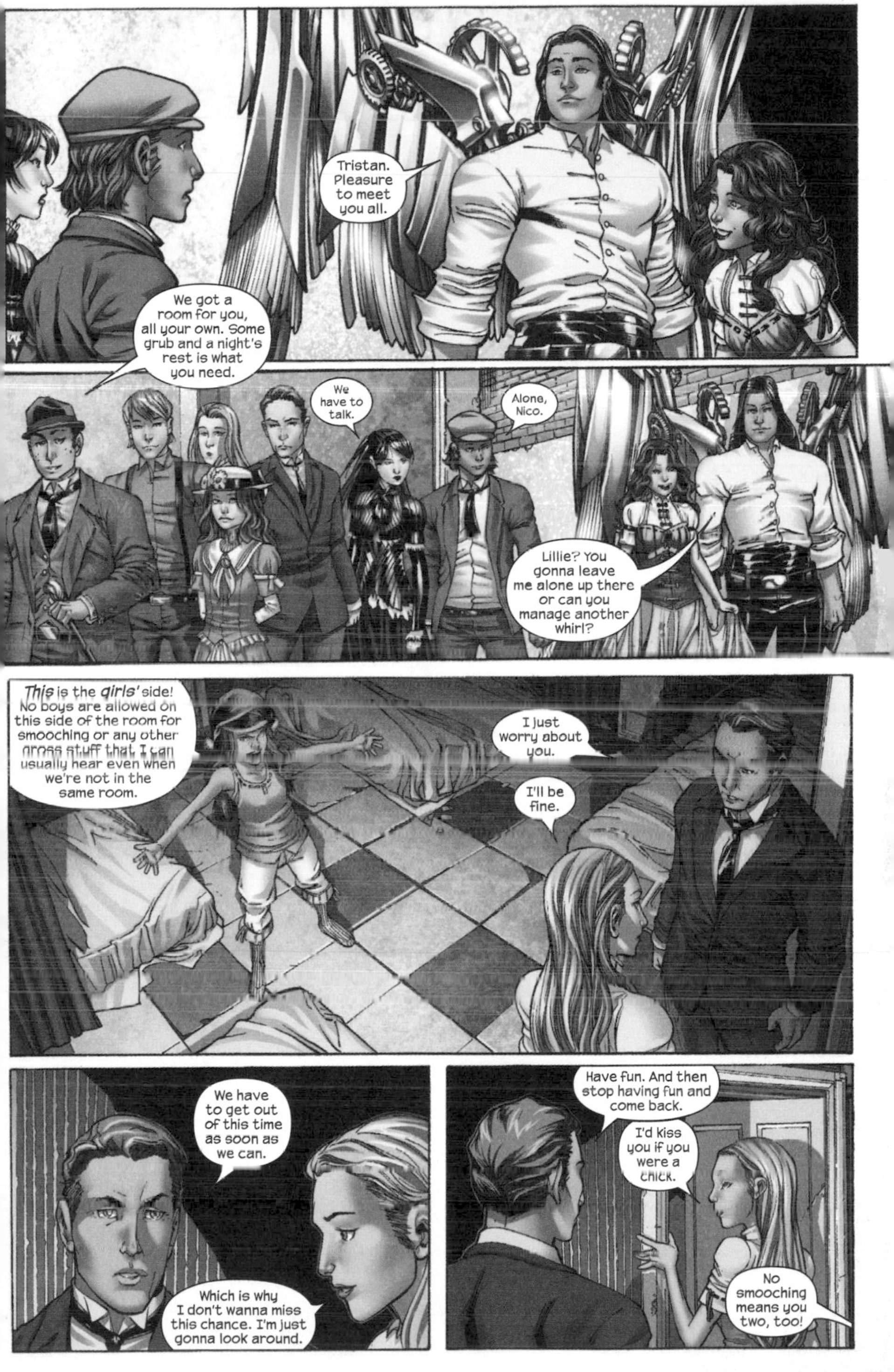
Tristan. Pleasure to meet you all.
We got a room for you, all your own. Some grub and a night's rest is what you need.
We have to talk.
Alone, Nico.
Lillie? You gonna leave me alone up there or can you manage another whirl?
This is the girls' side! No boys are allowed on this side of the room for smooching or any other gross stuff that I can usually hear even when we're not in the same room.
I just worry about you.
I'll be fine.
We have to get out of this time as soon as we can.
Which is why I don't wanna miss this chance. I'm just gonna look around.
Have fun. And then stop having fun and come back.
I'd kiss you if you were a chick.
No smooching means you two, too!

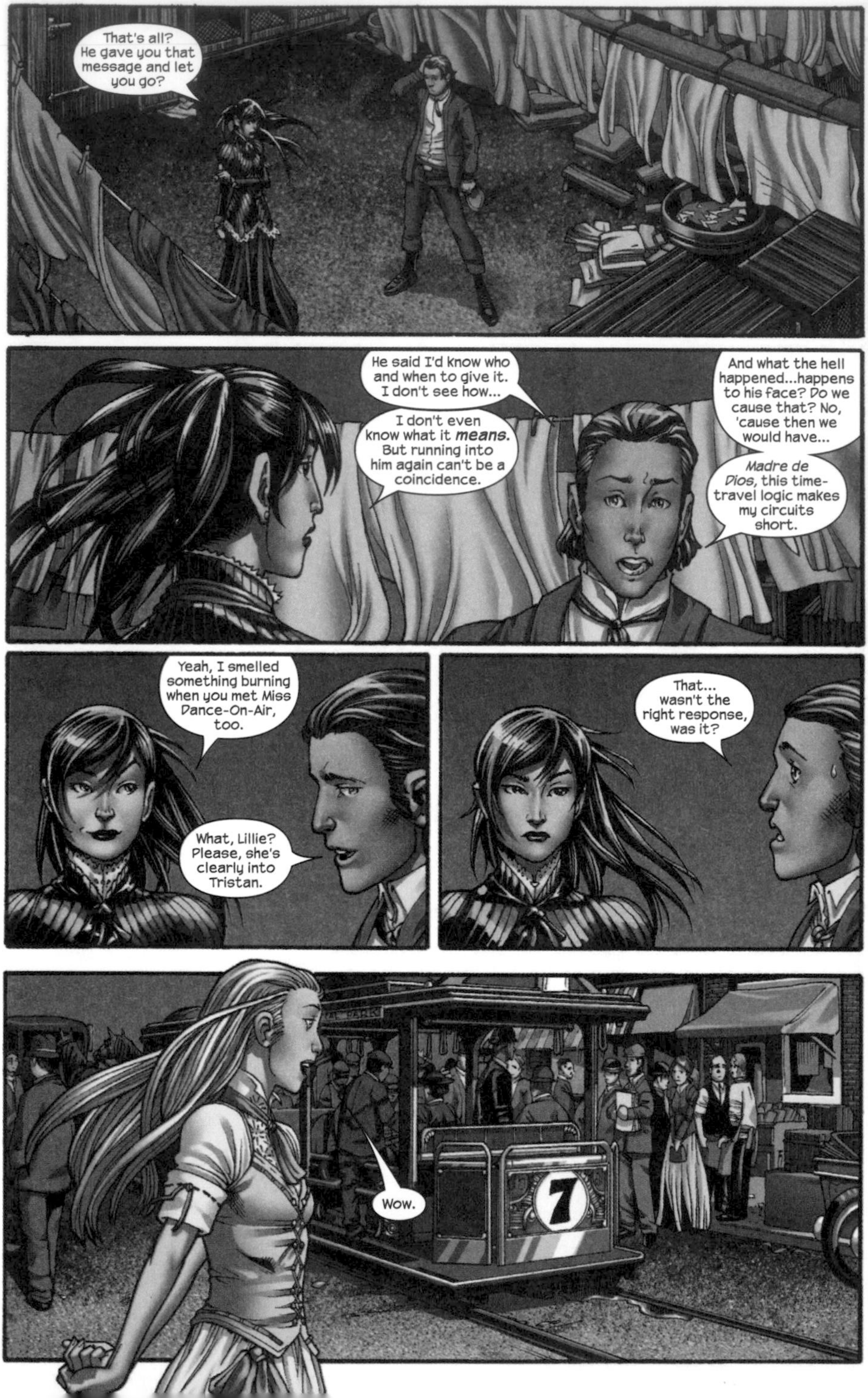
That's all? He gave you that message and let you go?
He said I'd know who and when to give it. I don't see how...
I don't even know what it *means*. But running into him again can't be a coincidence.
And what the hell happened...happens to his face? Do we cause that? No, 'cause then we would have...
Madre de Dios, this time-travel logic makes my circuits short.
Yeah, I smelled something burning when you met Miss Dance-On-Air, too.
What, Lillie? Please, she's clearly into Tristan.
That... wasn't the right response, was it?
Wow.

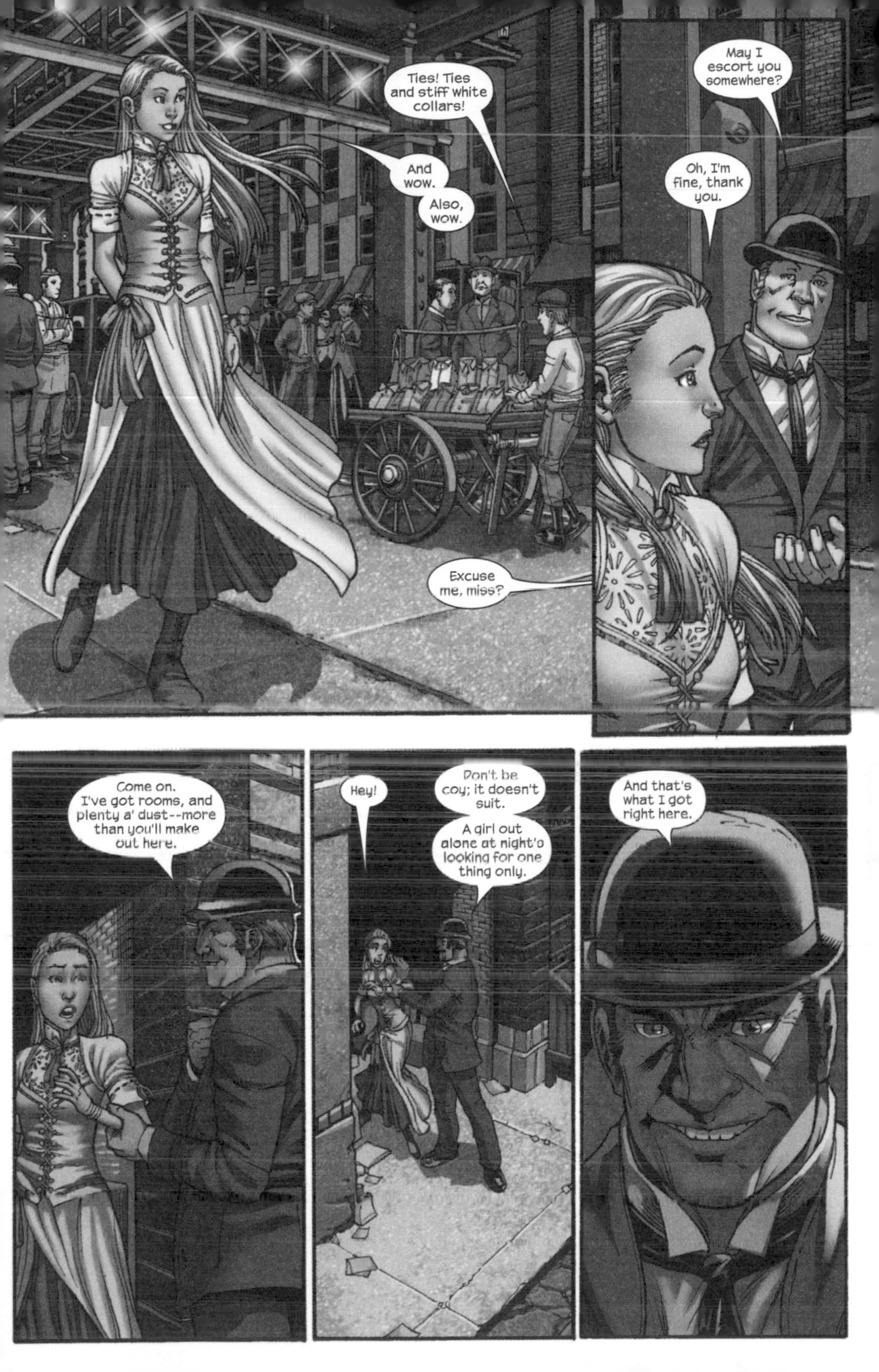
Ties! Ties and stiff white collars!
And wow.
Also, wow.
Excuse me, miss?
May I escort you somewhere?
Oh, I'm fine, thank you.
Come on. I've got rooms, and plenty a' dust--more than you'll make out here.
Hey!
Don't be coy; it doesn't suit.
A girl out alone at night's looking for one thing only.
And that's what I got right here.

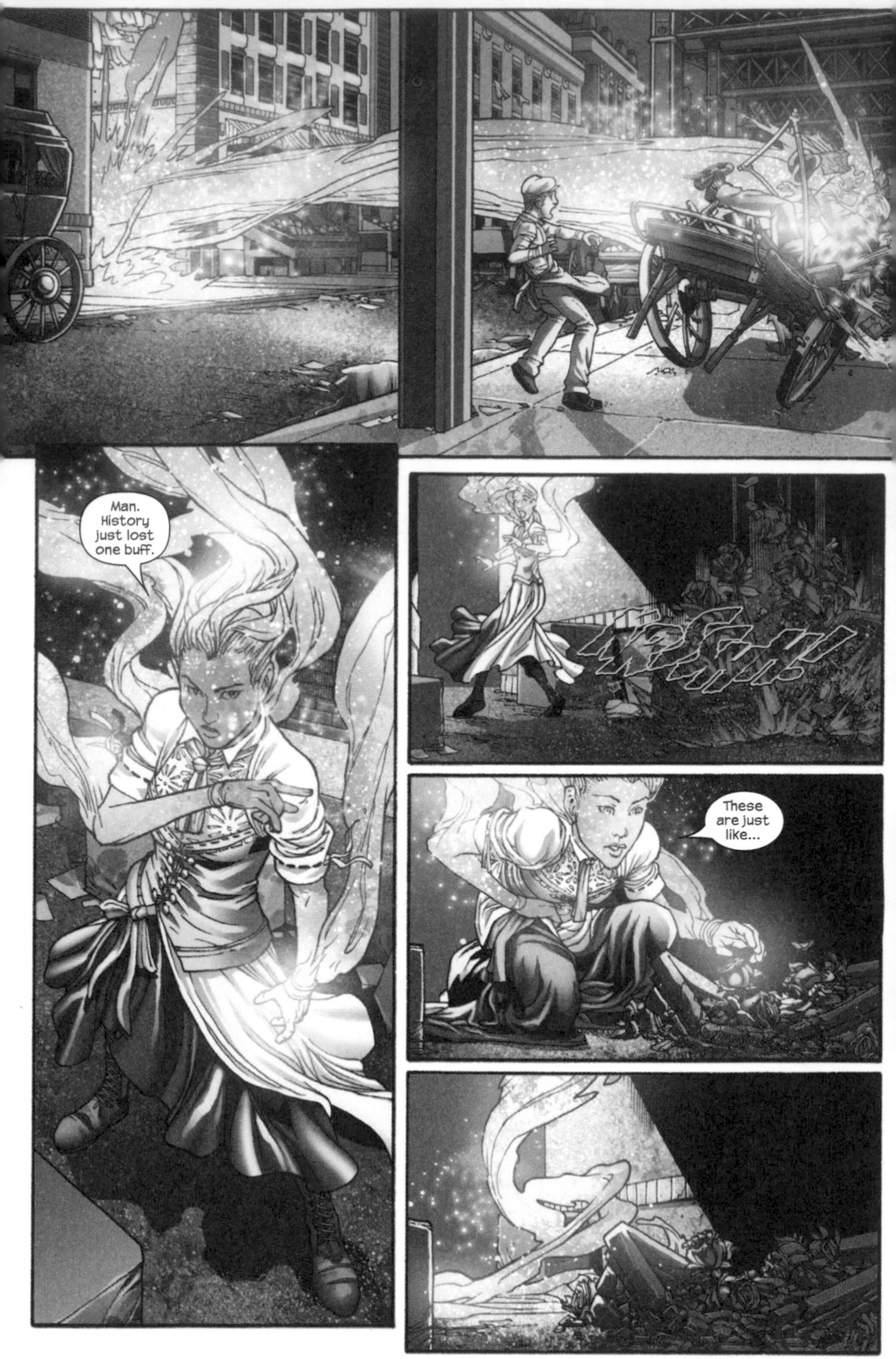
Man. History just lost one buff.
These are just like...

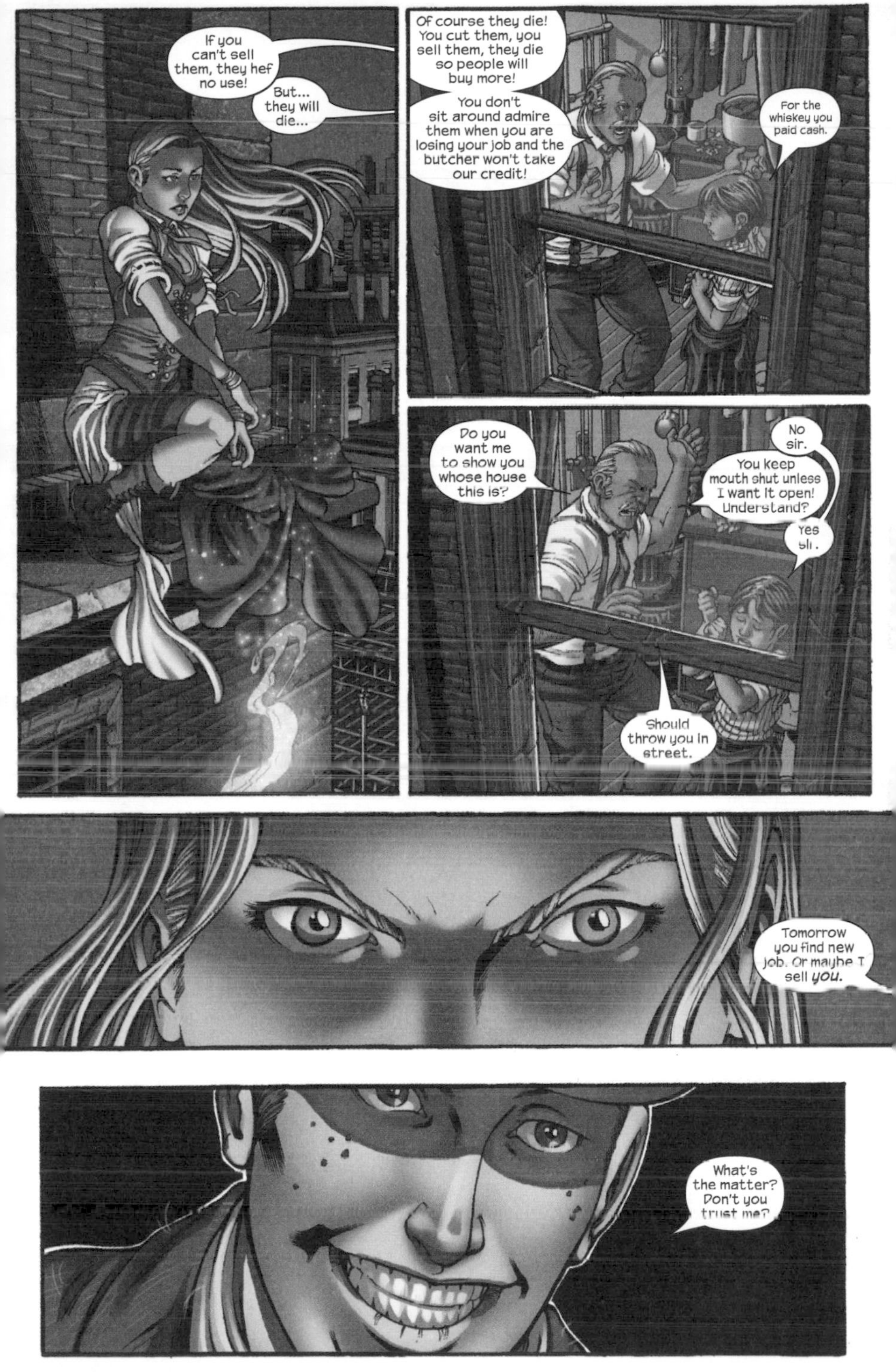

If you can't sell them, they hef no use!
But... they will die...
Of course they die! You cut them, you sell them, they die so people will buy more!
You don't sit around admire them when you are losing your job and the butcher won't take our credit!
For the whiskey you paid cash.
Do you want me to show you whose house this is?
No sir.
You keep mouth shut unless I want it open! Understand?
Should throw you in street.
Tomorrow you find new job. Or maybe I sell *you.*
What's the matter? Don't you trust me?

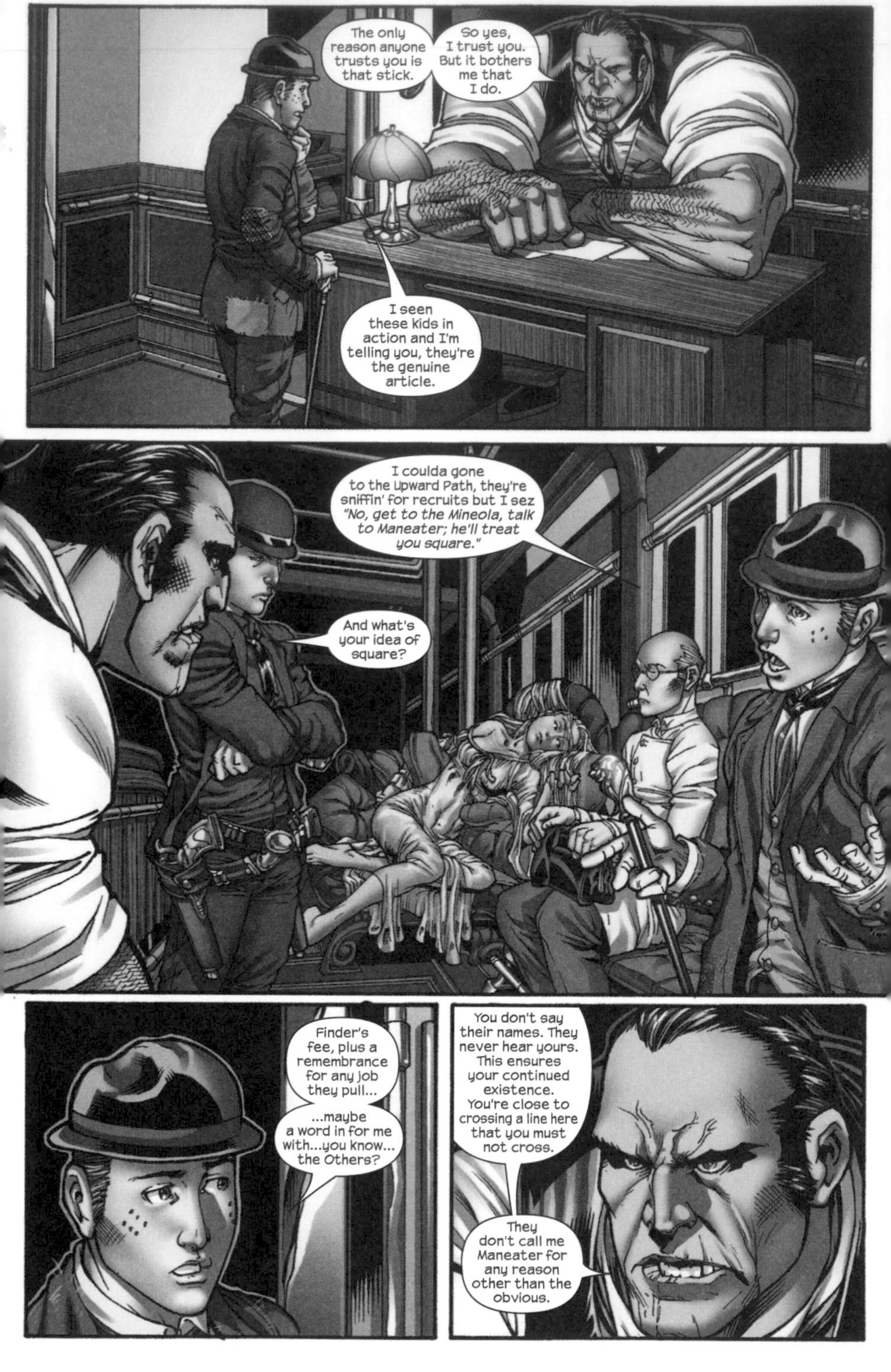
The only reason anyone trusts you is that stick.
So yes, I trust you. But it bothers me that I do.
I seen these kids in action and I'm telling you, they're the genuine article.
I coulda gone to the Upward Path, they're sniffin' for recruits but I sez *"No, get to the Mineola, talk to Maneater; he'll treat you square."*
And what's your idea of square?
Finder's fee, plus a remembrance for any job they pull...
...maybe a word in for me with...you know... the Others?
You don't say their names. They never hear yours. This ensures your continued existence. You're close to crossing a line here that you must not cross.
They don't call me Maneater for any reason other than the obvious.

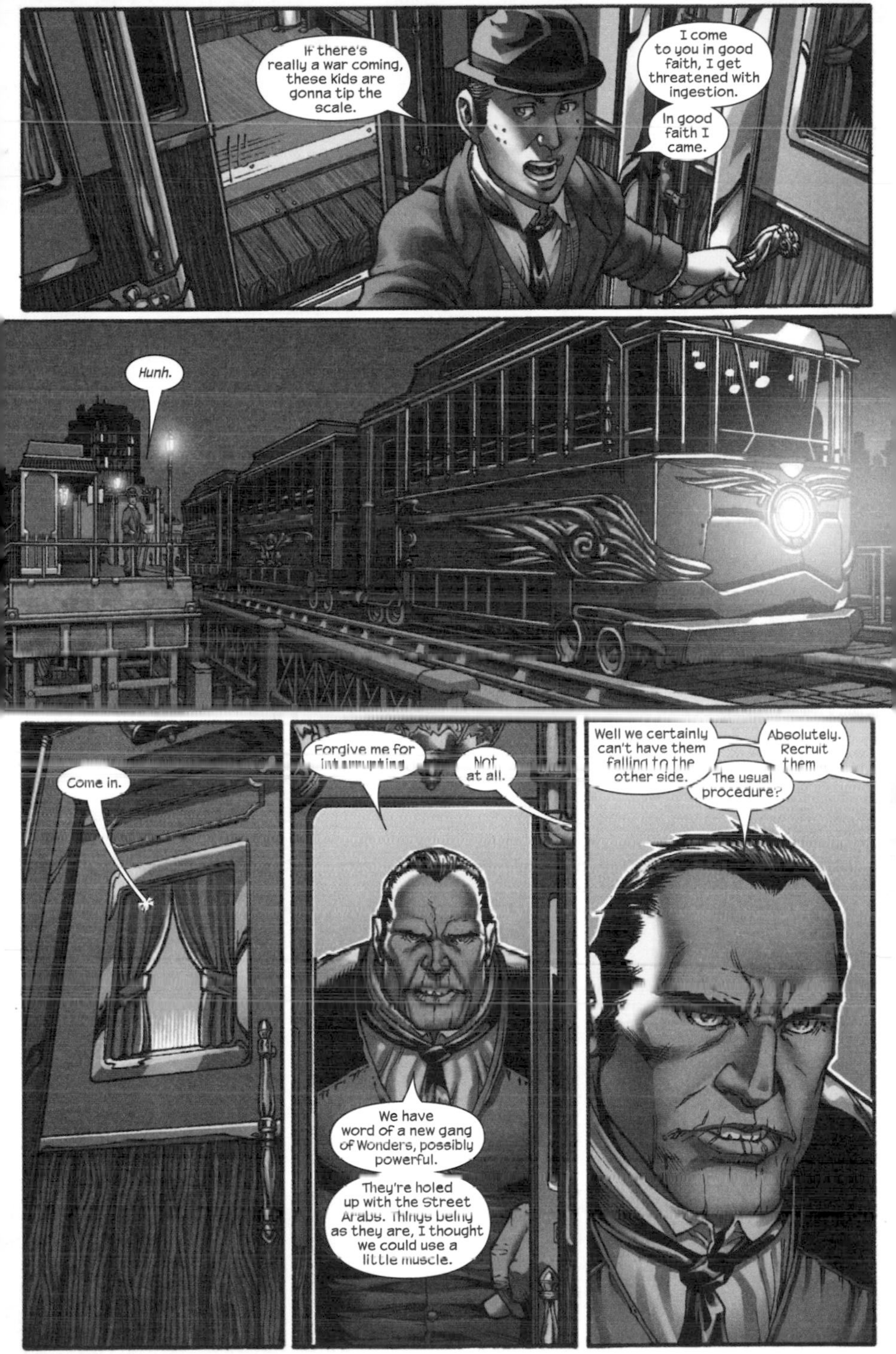
If there's really a war coming, these kids are gonna tip the scale.
I come to you in good faith, I get threatened with ingestion.
In good faith I came.
Hunh.
Come in.
Forgive me for interrupting
Not at all.
We have word of a new gang of Wonders, possibly powerful.
They're holed up with the Street Arabs. Things being as they are, I thought we could use a little muscle.
Well we certainly can't have them falling to the other side.
The usual procedure?
Absolutely. Recruit them

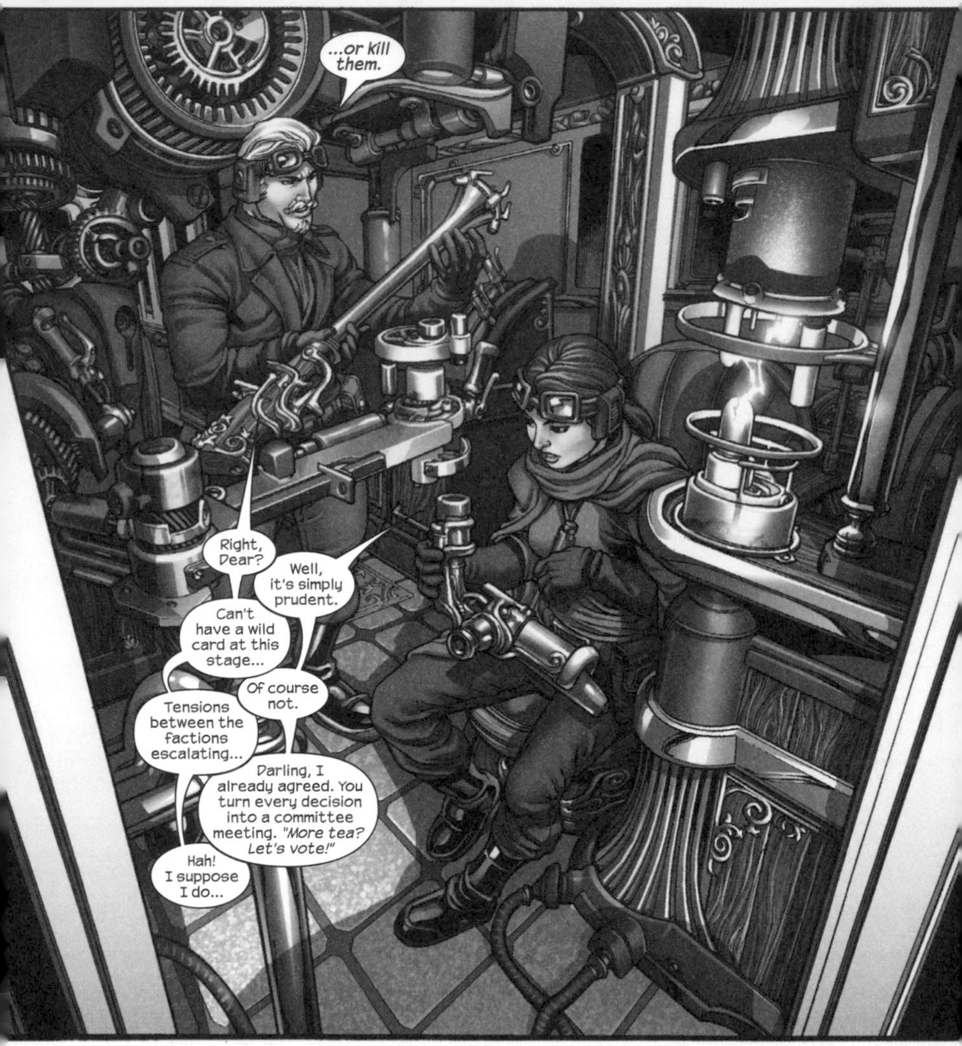
...or kill them.
Right, Dear?
Well, it's simply prudent.
Can't have a wild card at this stage...
Of course not.
Tensions between the factions escalating...
Darling, I already agreed. You turn every decision into a committee meeting. *"More tea? Let's vote!"*
Hah! I suppose I do...

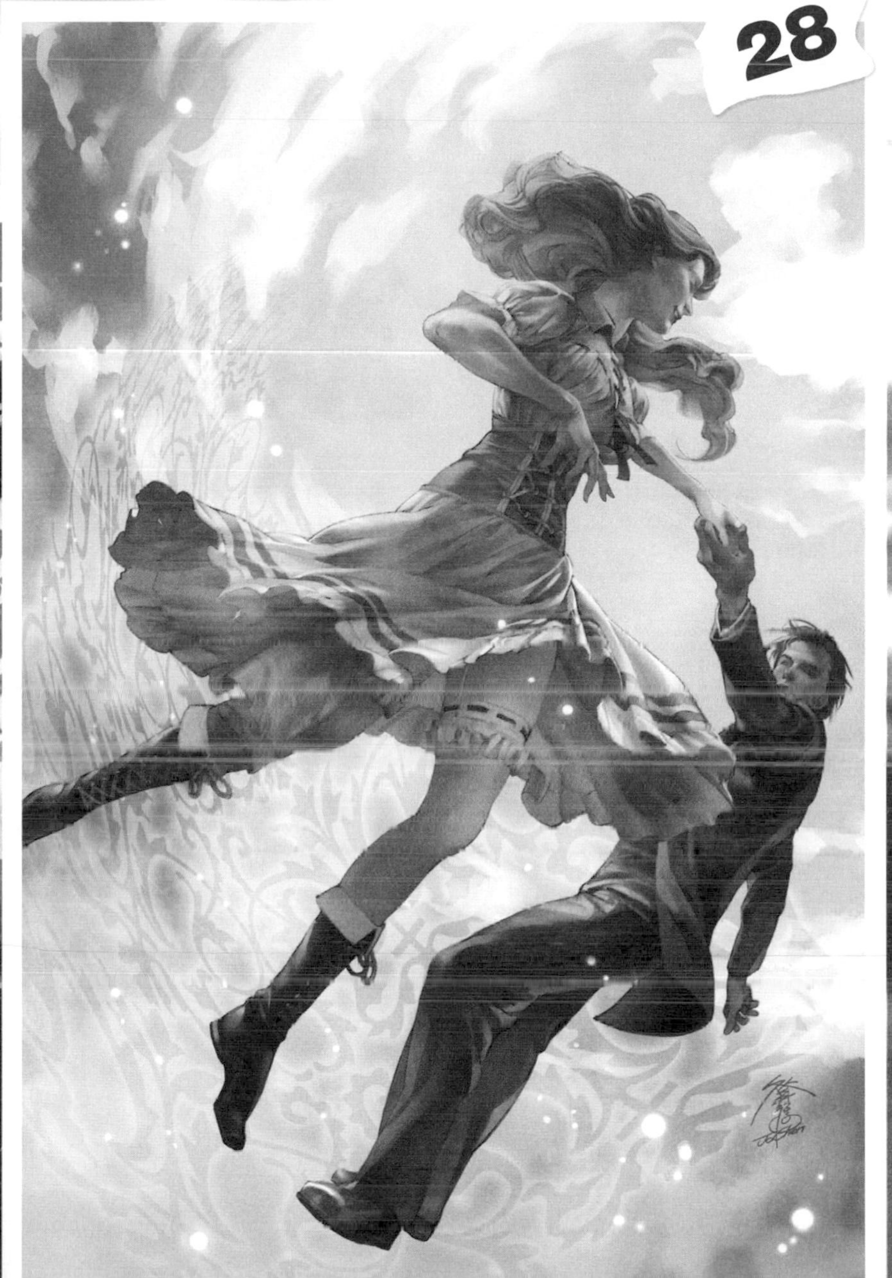
28

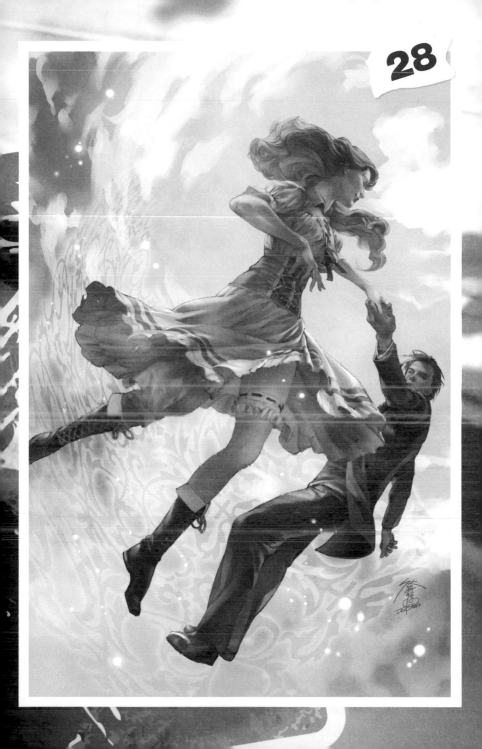

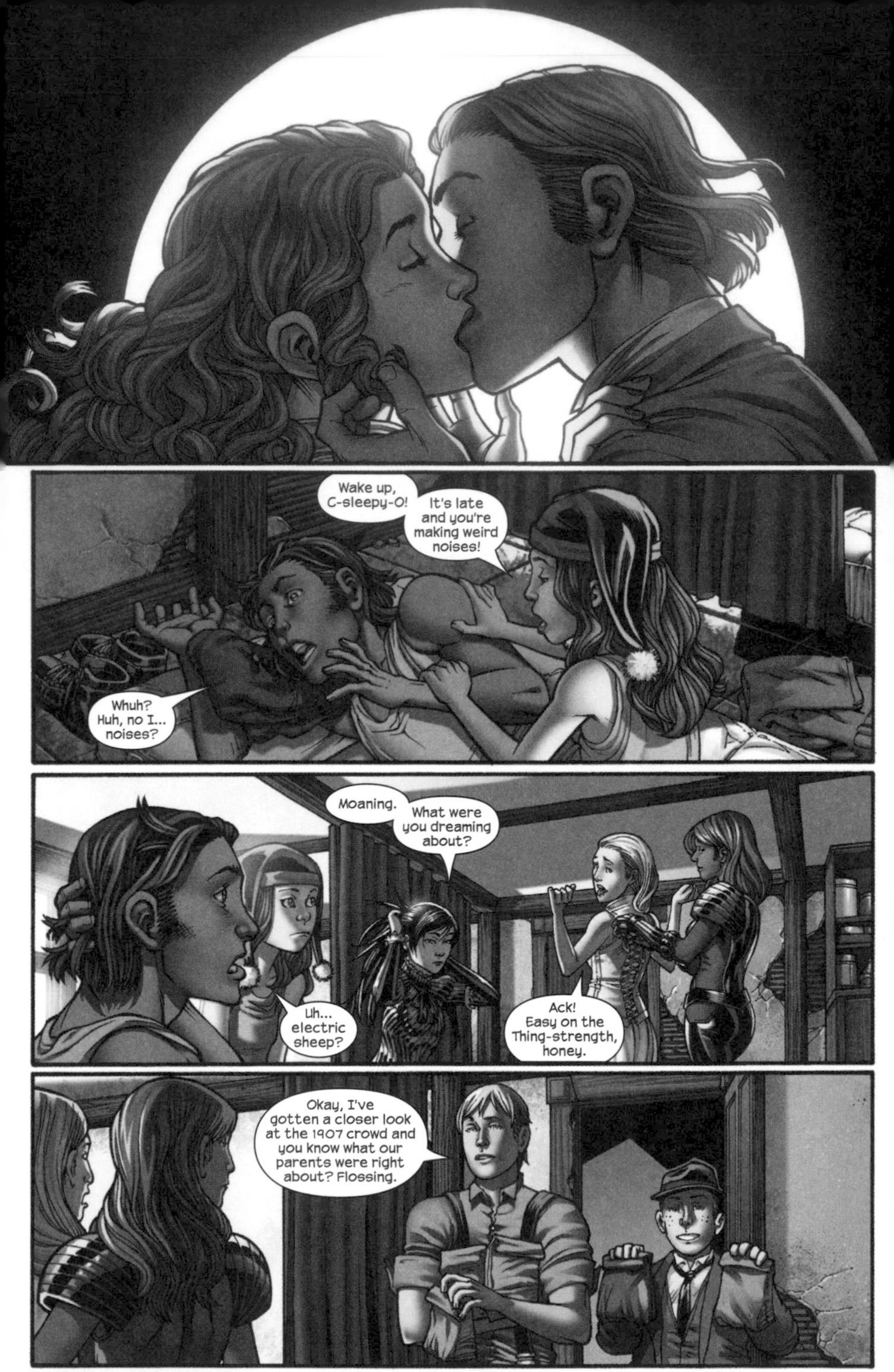

Wake up, C-sleepy-O!
It's late and you're making weird noises!
Whuh? Huh, no I... noises?
Moaning.
What were you dreaming about?
Uh... electric sheep?
Ack! Easy on the Thing-strength, honey.
Okay, I've gotten a closer look at the 1907 crowd and you know what our parents were right about? Flossing.

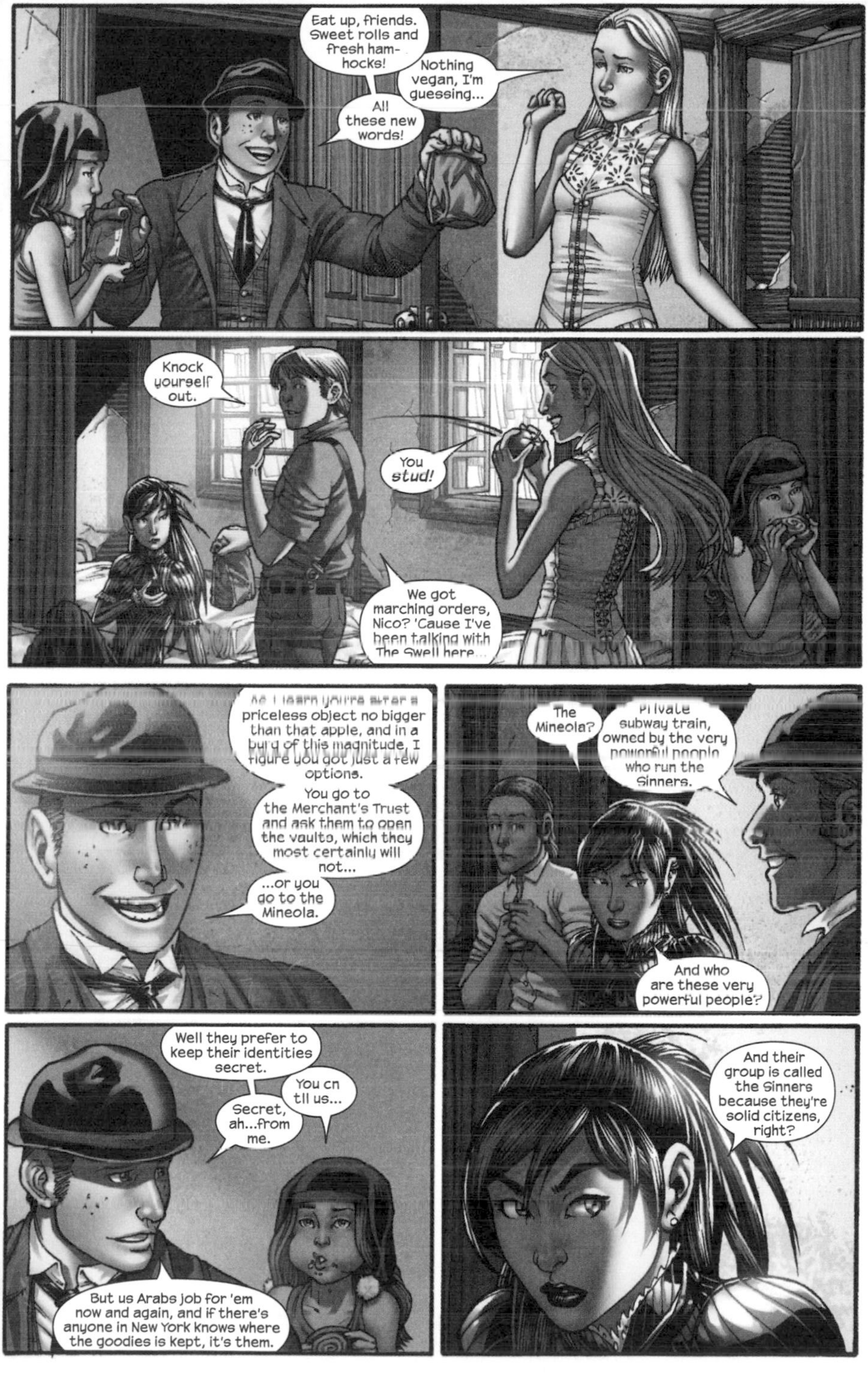
Eat up, friends. Sweet rolls and fresh ham-hocks!
Nothing vegan, I'm guessing...
All these new words!
Knock yourself out.
You *stud!*
We got marching orders, Nico? 'Cause I've been talking with The Swell here...
priceless object no bigger than that apple, and in a burg of this magnitude, I figure you got just a few options.
You go to the Merchant's Trust and ask them to open the vaults, which they most certainly will not...
...or you go to the Mineola.
The Mineola?
Private subway train, owned by the very powerful people who run the Sinners.
And who are these very powerful people?
Well they prefer to keep their identities secret.
You cn tll us...
Secret, ah...from me.
But us Arabs job for 'em now and again, and if there's anyone in New York knows where the goodies is kept, it's them.
And their group is called the Sinners because they're solid citizens, right?

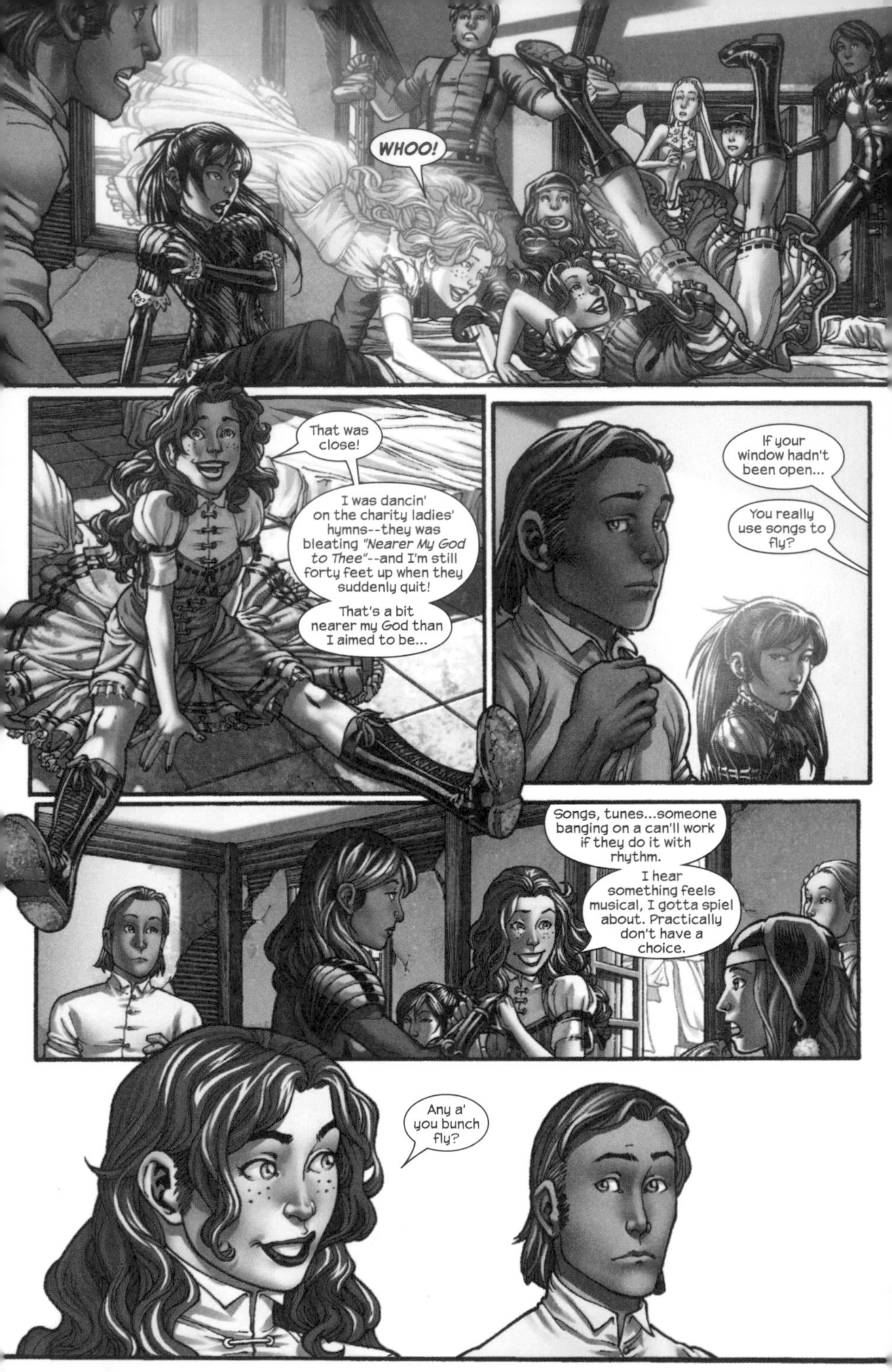
WHOO!
That was close!
I was dancin' on the charity ladies' hymns--they was bleating "Nearer My God to Thee"--and I'm still forty feet up when they suddenly quit!
That's a bit nearer my God than I aimed to be...
If your window hadn't been open...
You really use songs to fly?
Songs, tunes...someone banging on a can'll work if they do it with rhythm.
I hear something feels musical, I gotta spiel about. Practically don't have a choice.
Any a' you bunch fly?

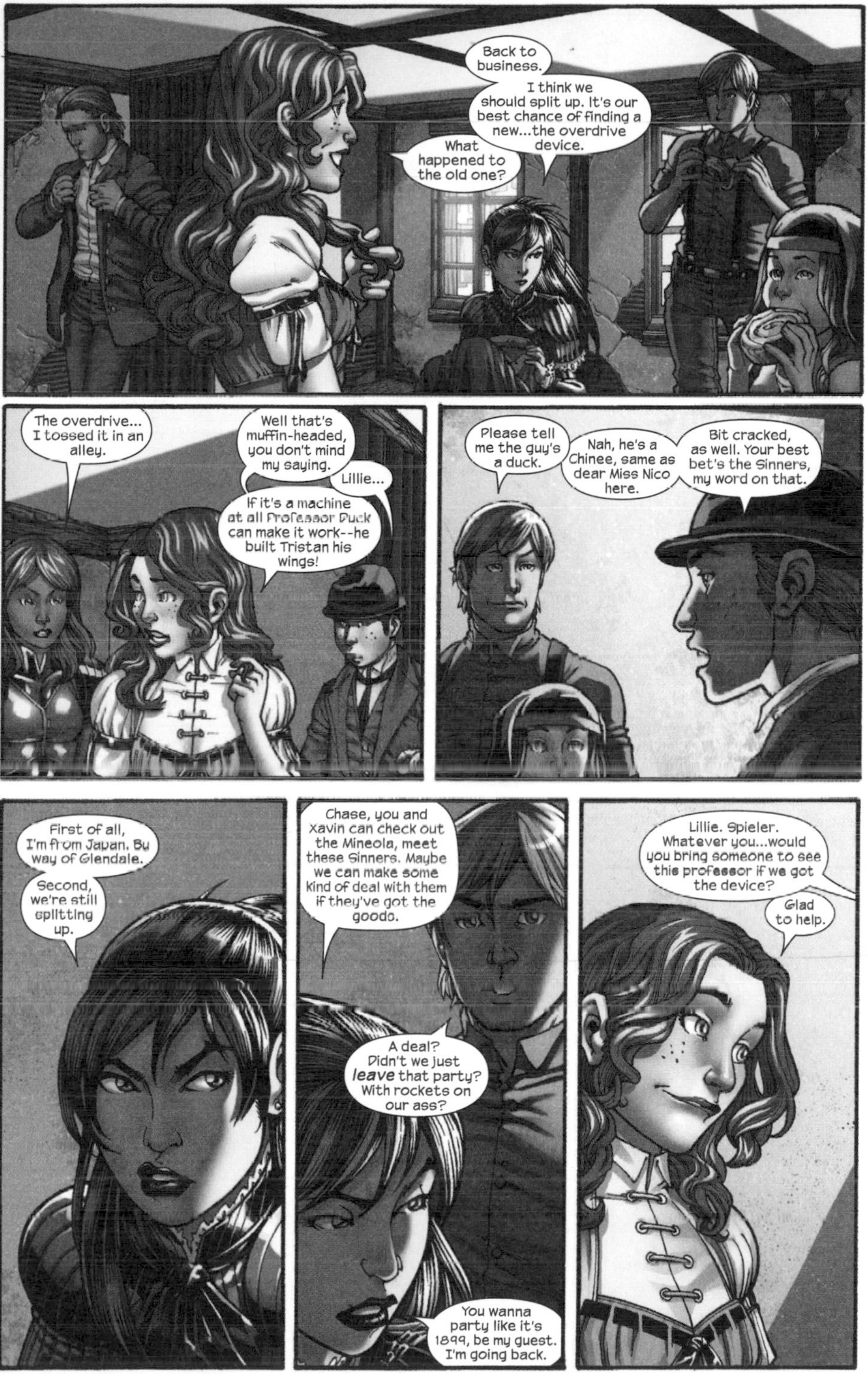
Back to business.
I think we should split up. It's our best chance of finding a new...the overdrive device.
What happened to the old one?
The overdrive... I tossed it in an alley.
Well that's muffin-headed, you don't mind my saying.
Lillie...
If it's a machine at all Professor Duck can make it work--he built Tristan his wings!
Please tell me the guy's a duck.
Nah, he's a Chinee, same as dear Miss Nico here.
Bit cracked, as well. Your best bet's the Sinners, my word on that.
First of all, I'm from Japan. By way of Glendale.
Second, we're still splitting up.
Chase, you and Xavin can check out the Mineola, meet these Sinners. Maybe we can make some kind of deal with them if they've got the goods.
A deal? Didn't we just *leave* that party? With rockets on our ass?
You wanna party like it's 1899, be my guest. I'm going back.
Lillie. Spieler. Whatever you...would you bring someone to see this professor if we got the device?
Glad to help.

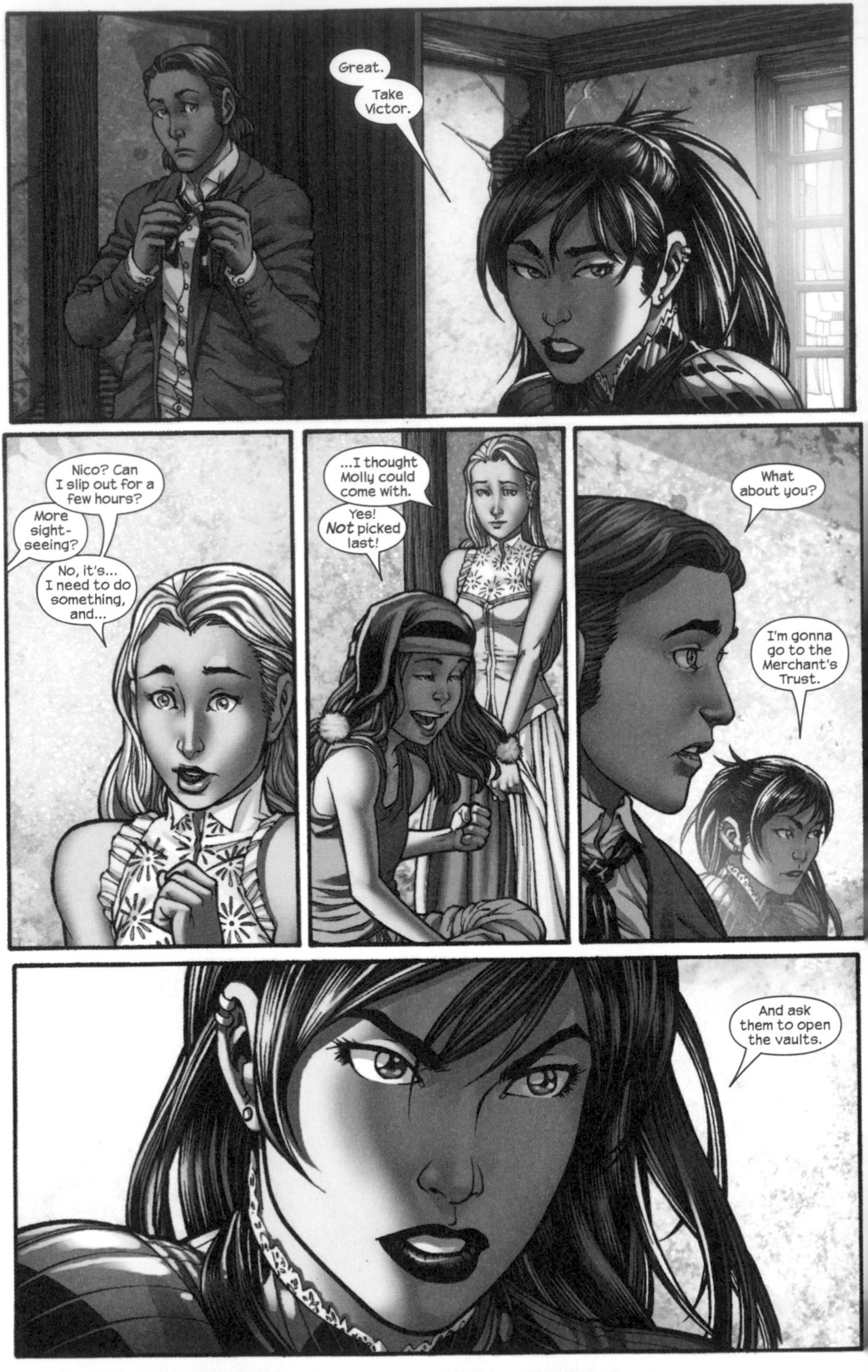
Great.
Take Victor.
Nico? Can I slip out for a few hours?
More sight-seeing?
No, it's... I need to do something, and...
...I thought Molly could come with.
Yes! *Not* picked last!
What about you?
I'm gonna go to the Merchant's Trust.
And ask them to open the vaults.

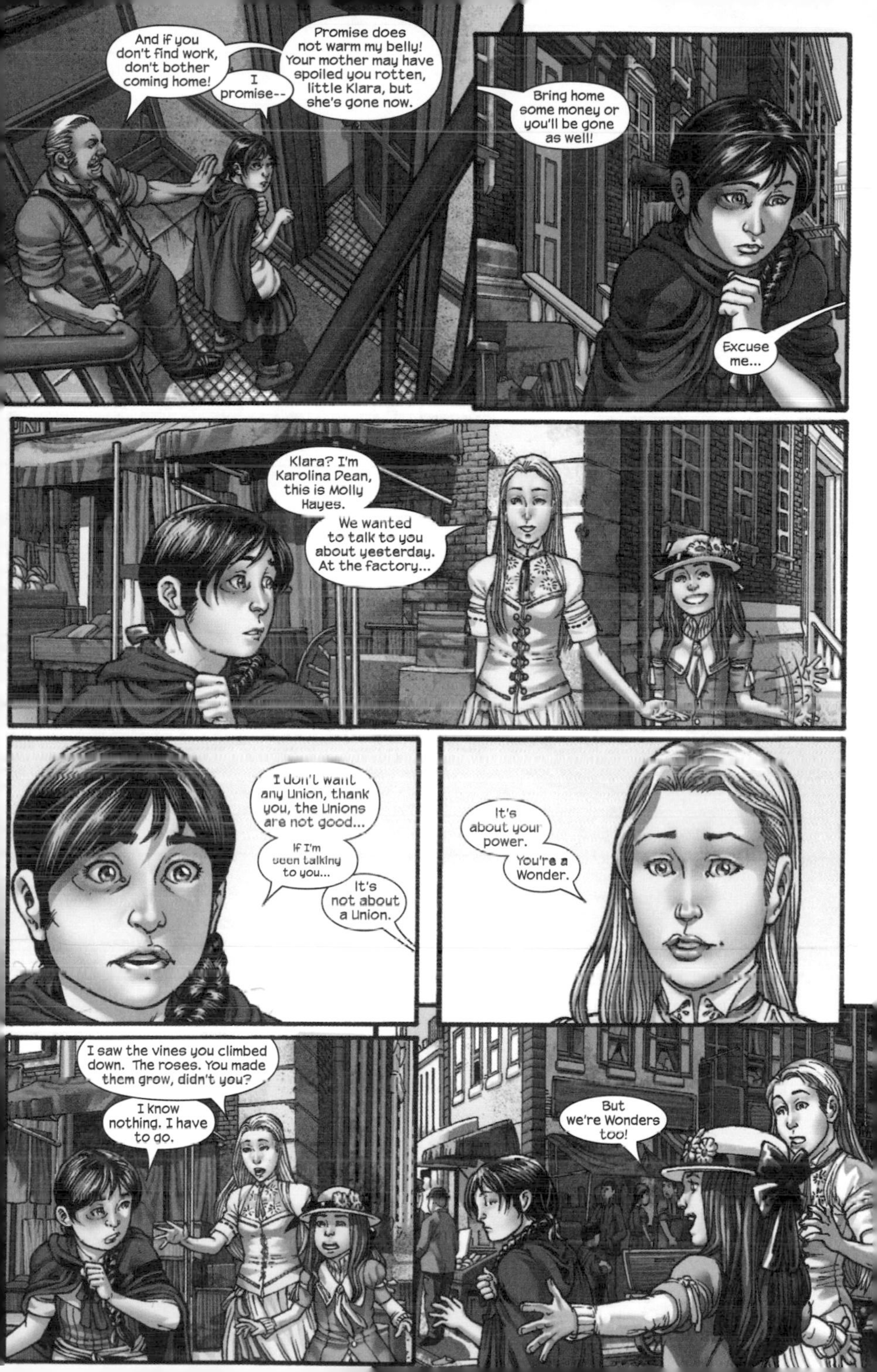
And if you don't find work, don't bother coming home!
I promise--
Promise does not warm my belly! Your mother may have spoiled you rotten, little Klara, but she's gone now.
Bring home some money or you'll be gone as well!
Excuse me...
Klara? I'm Karolina Dean, this is Molly Hayes.
We wanted to talk to you about yesterday. At the factory...
I don't want any Union, thank you, the Unions are not good...
If I'm seen talking to you...
It's not about a Union.
It's about your power.
You're a Wonder.
I saw the vines you climbed down. The roses. You made them grow, didn't you?
I know nothing. I have to go.
But we're Wonders too!

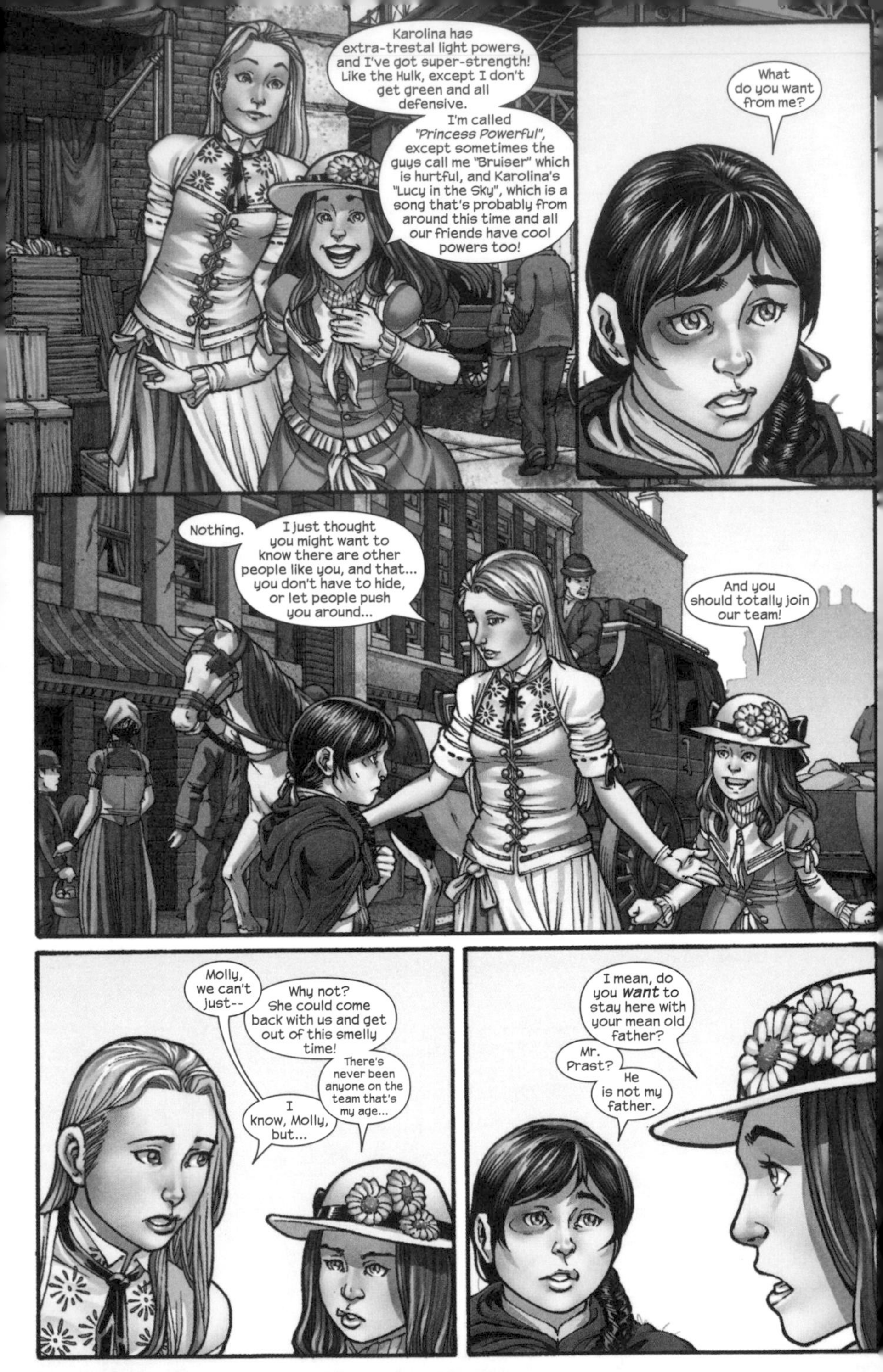
Karolina has extra-trestal light powers, and I've got super-strength! Like the Hulk, except I don't get green and all defensive.
I'm called "Princess Powerful", except sometimes the guys call me "Bruiser" which is hurtful, and Karolina's "Lucy in the Sky", which is a song that's probably from around this time and all our friends have cool powers too!
What do you want from me?
Nothing.
I just thought you might want to know there are other people like you, and that... you don't have to hide, or let people push you around...
And you should totally join our team!
Molly, we can't just--
Why not? She could come back with us and get out of this smelly time!
I know, Molly, but...
There's never been anyone on the team that's my age...
I mean, do you *want* to stay here with your mean old father?
Mr. Prast?
He is not my father.

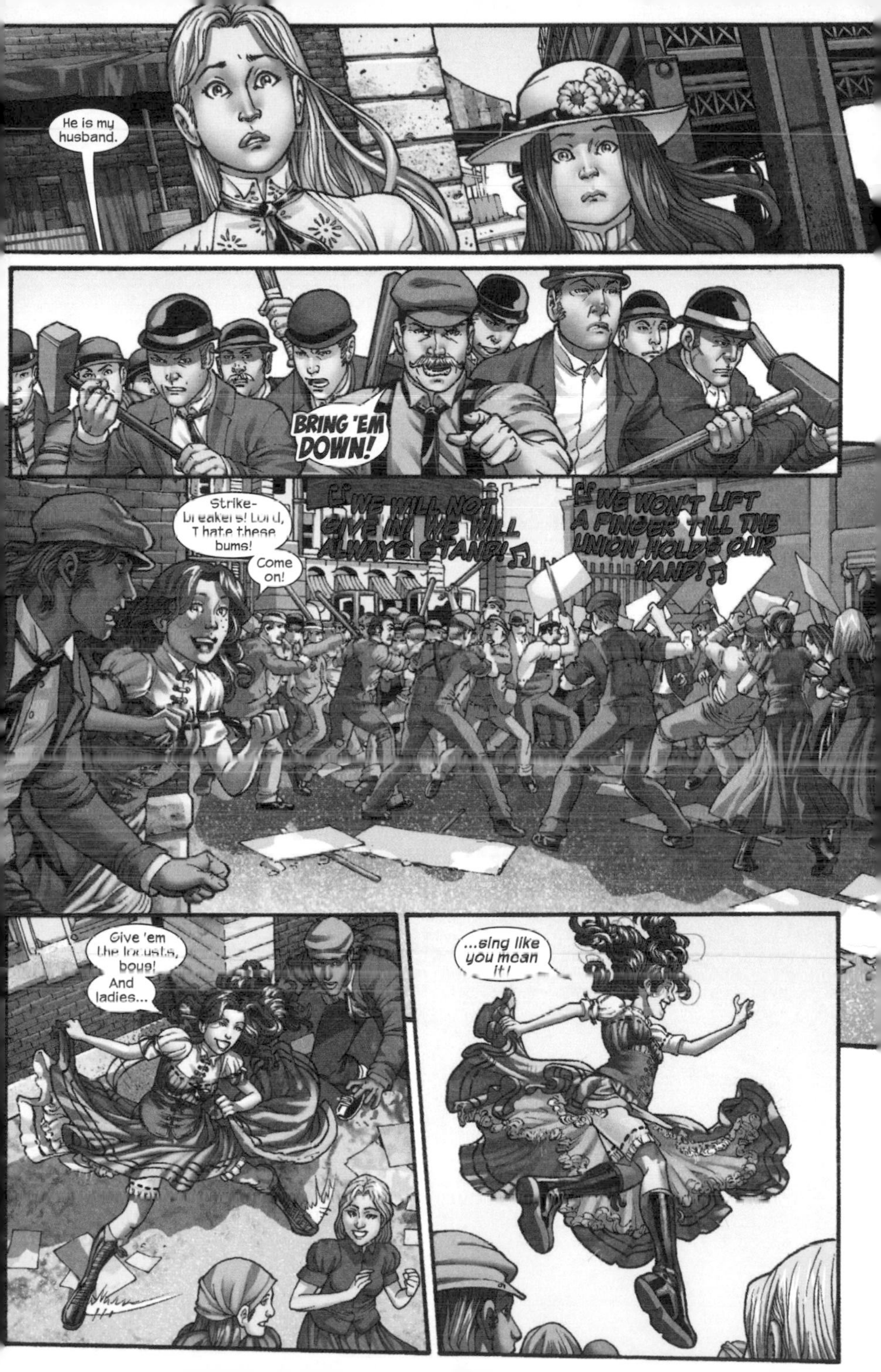
He is my husband.
BRING 'EM DOWN!
Strike-breakers! Lord, I hate these bums!
Come on!
WE WILL NOT GIVE IN! WE WILL ALWAYS STAND!
WE WON'T LIFT A FINGER TILL THE UNION HOLDS OUR HAND!
Give 'em the locusts, boys!
And ladies...
...sing like you mean it!

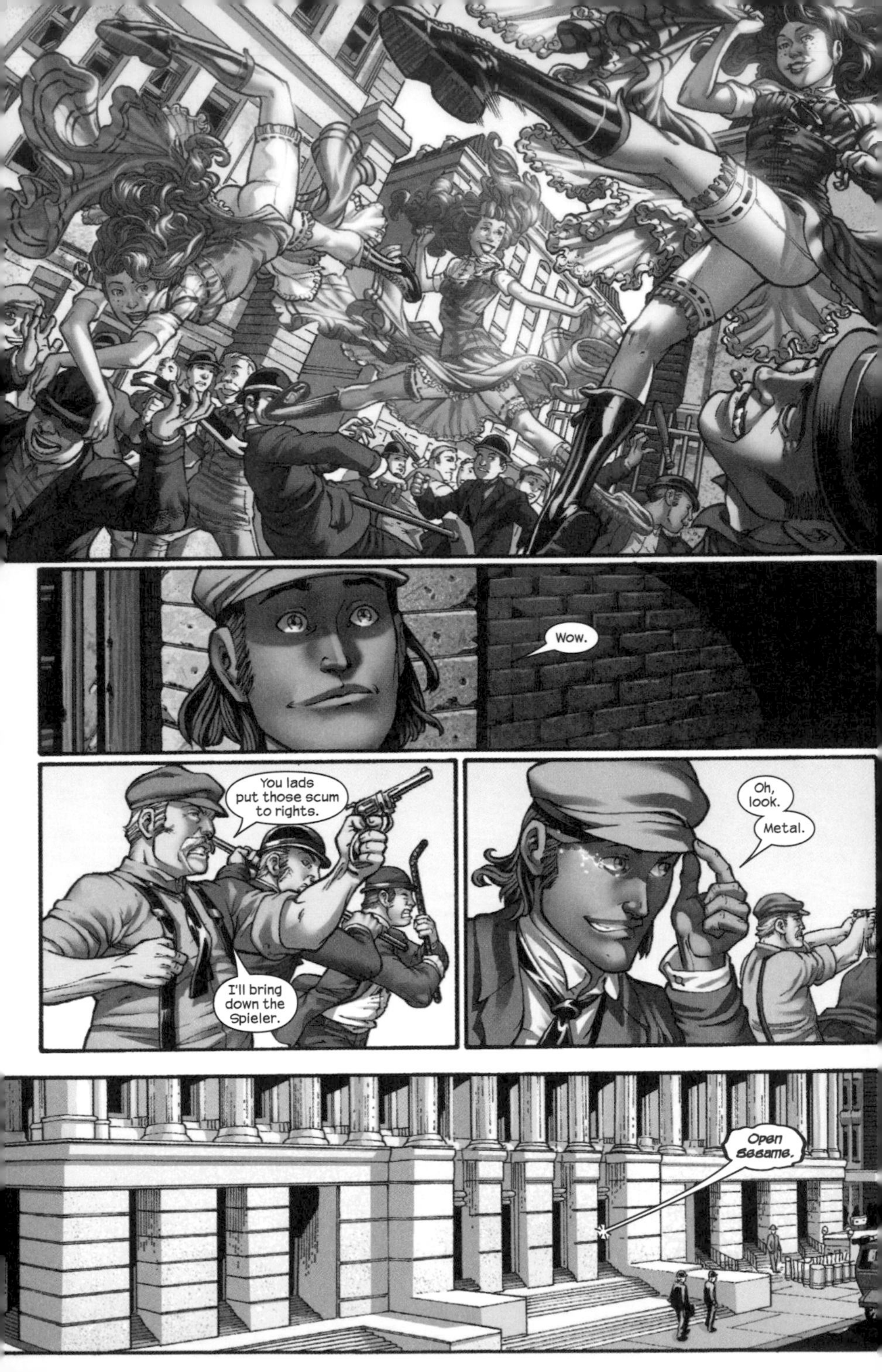

Wow.
You lads put those scum to rights.
I'll bring down the Spieler.
Oh, look.
Metal.
Open Sesame.

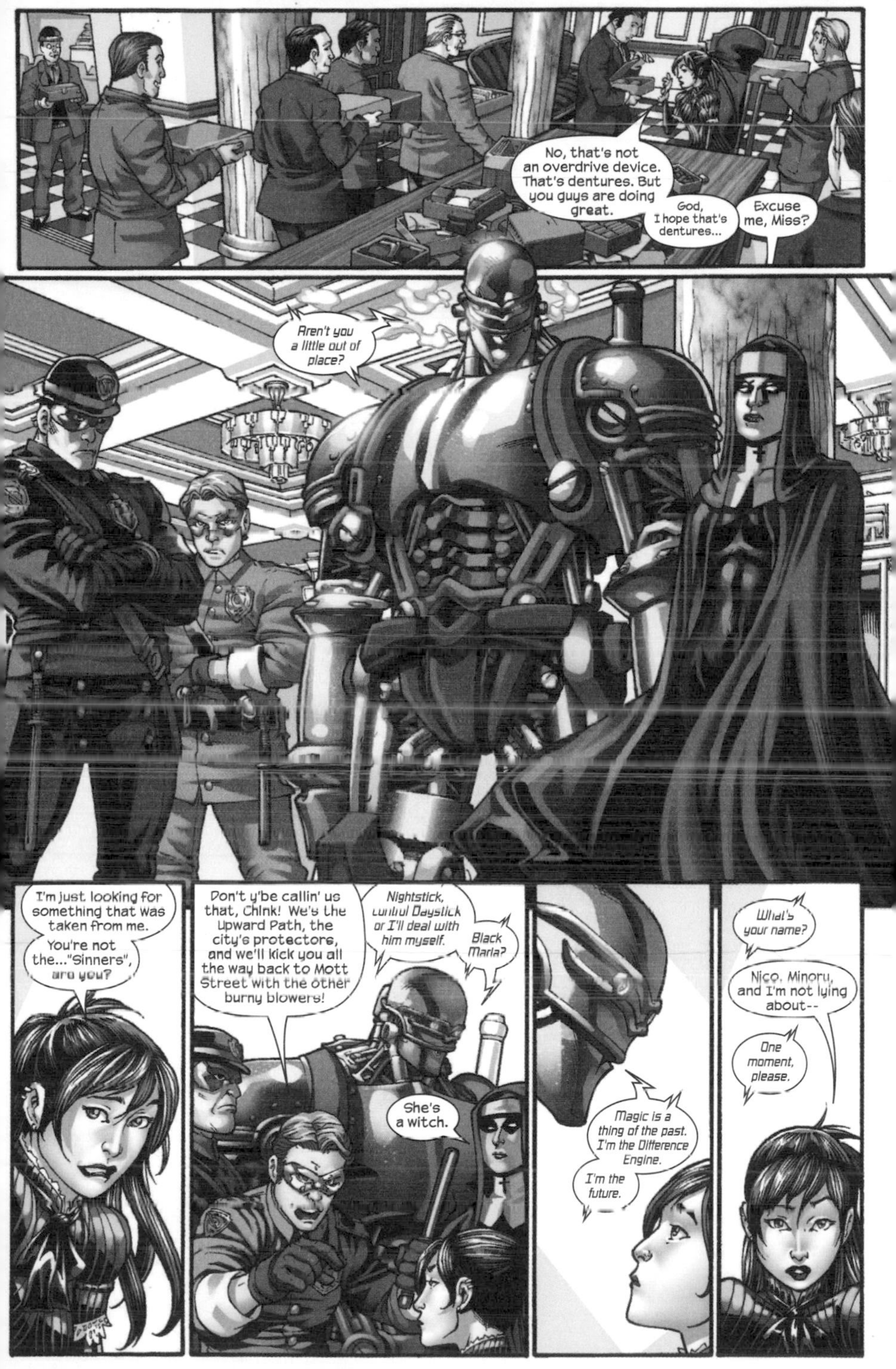
No, that's not an overdrive device. That's dentures. But you guys are doing great.
God, I hope that's dentures...
Excuse me, Miss?
Aren't you a little out of place?
I'm just looking for something that was taken from me.
You're not the..."Sinners", are you?
Don't y'be callin' us that, Chink! We's the Upward Path, the city's protectors, and we'll kick you all the way back to Mott Street with the other burny blowers!
Nightstick, control Daystick or I'll deal with him myself.
Black Maria?
She's a witch.
Magic is a thing of the past. I'm the Difference Engine.
I'm the future.
What's your name?
Nico. Minoru, and I'm not lying about--
One moment, please.

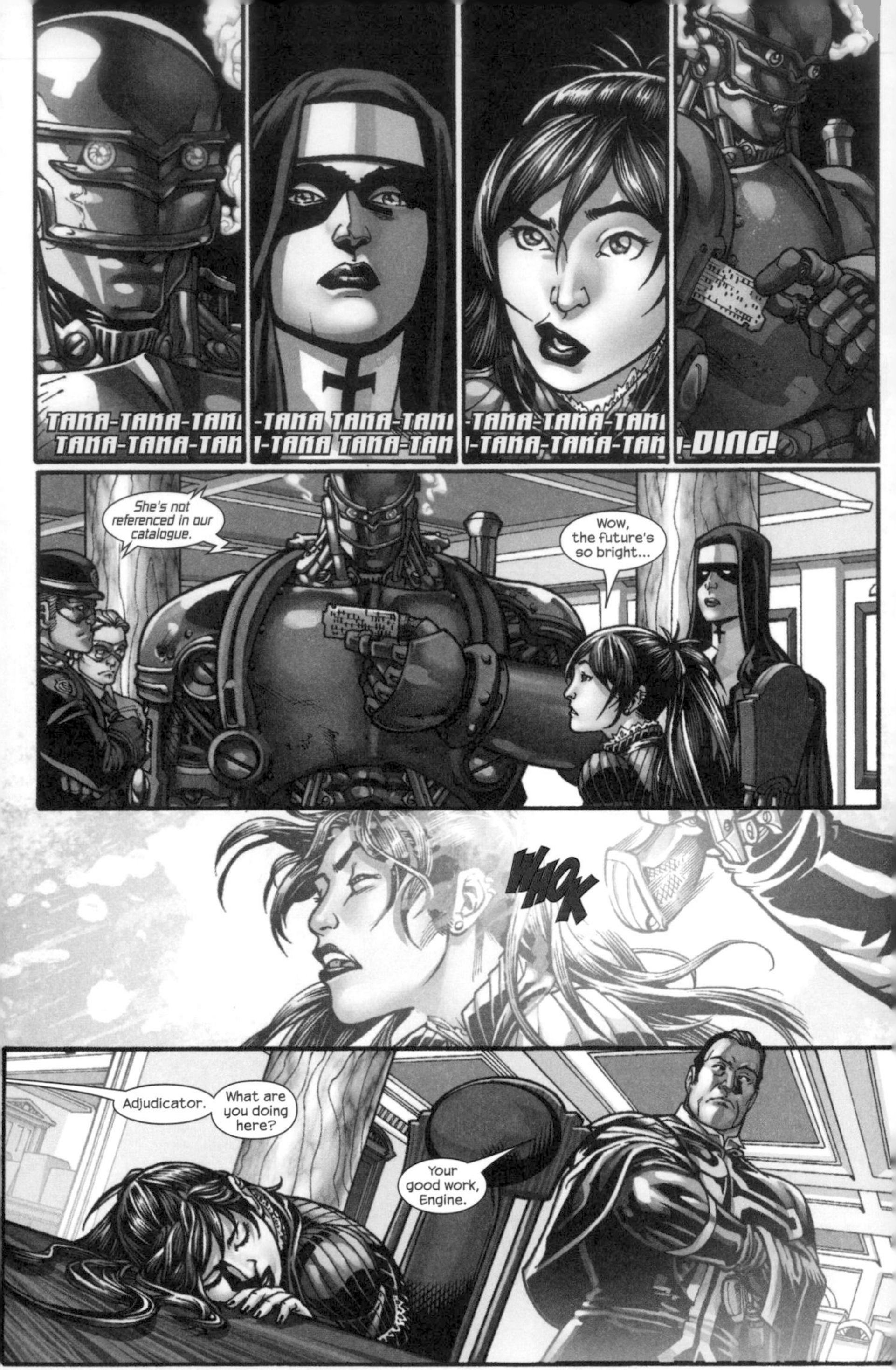
TAKA-TAKA-TAKA-TAKA TAKA-TAKA-TAKA-TAKA-TAKA-TAKA
TAKA-TAKA-TAKA-TAKA TAKA-TAKA-TAKA-TAKA-TAKA-TAKA-DING!
She's not referenced in our catalogue.
Wow, the future's so bright...
WHOK
Adjudicator.
What are you doing here?
Your good work, Engine.

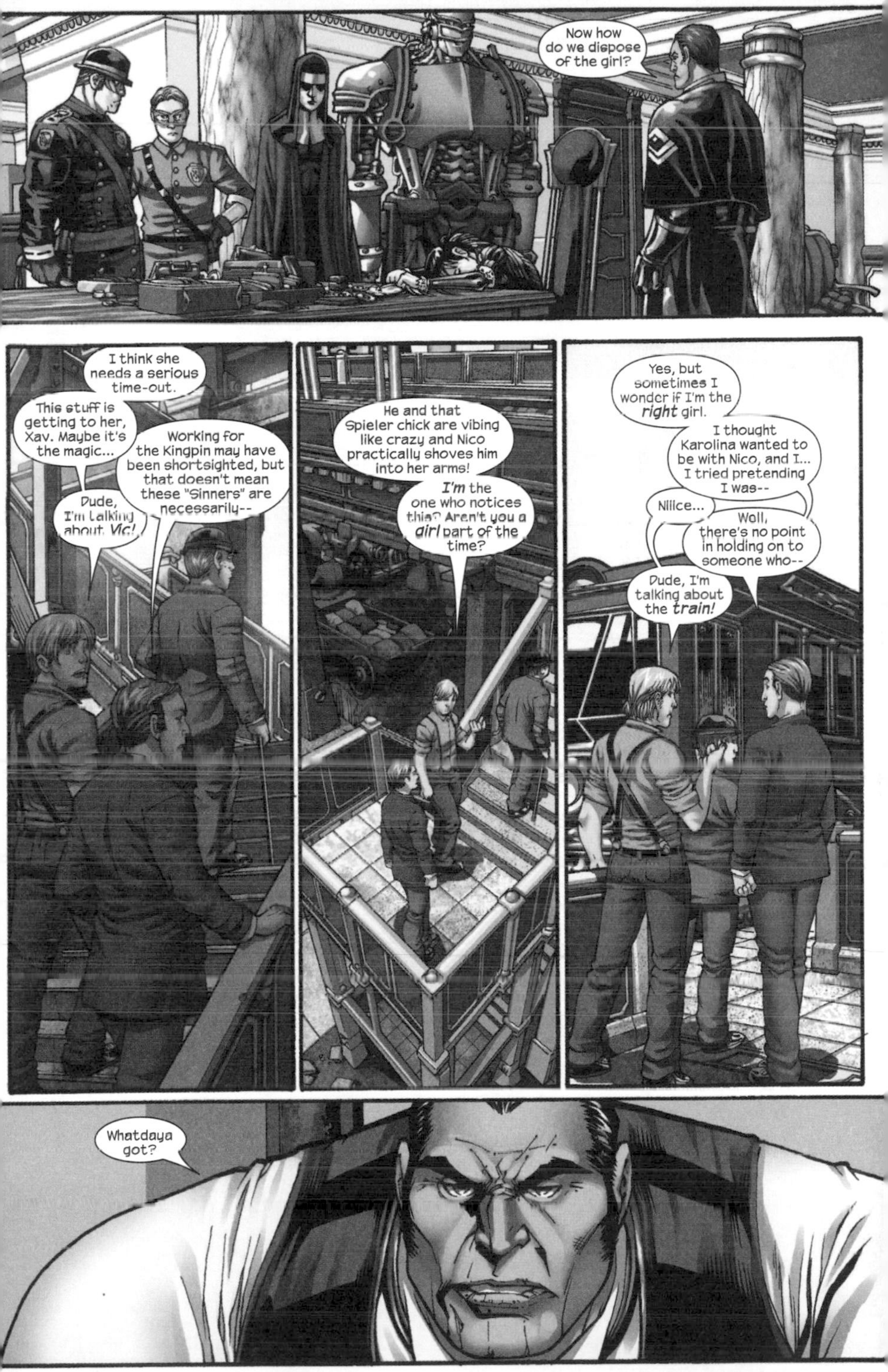
Now how do we dispose of the girl?
I think she needs a serious time-out.
This stuff is getting to her, Xav. Maybe it's the magic...
Working for the Kingpin may have been shortsighted, but that doesn't mean these "Sinners" are necessarily--
Dude, I'm talking about Vic!
He and that Spieler chick are vibing like crazy and Nico practically shoves him into her arms!
I'm the one who notices this? Aren't you a girl part of the time?
Yes, but sometimes I wonder if I'm the right girl.
I thought Karolina wanted to be with Nico, and I... I tried pretending I was--
Niiice...
Well, there's no point in holding on to someone who--
Dude, I'm talking about the train!
Whatdaya got?

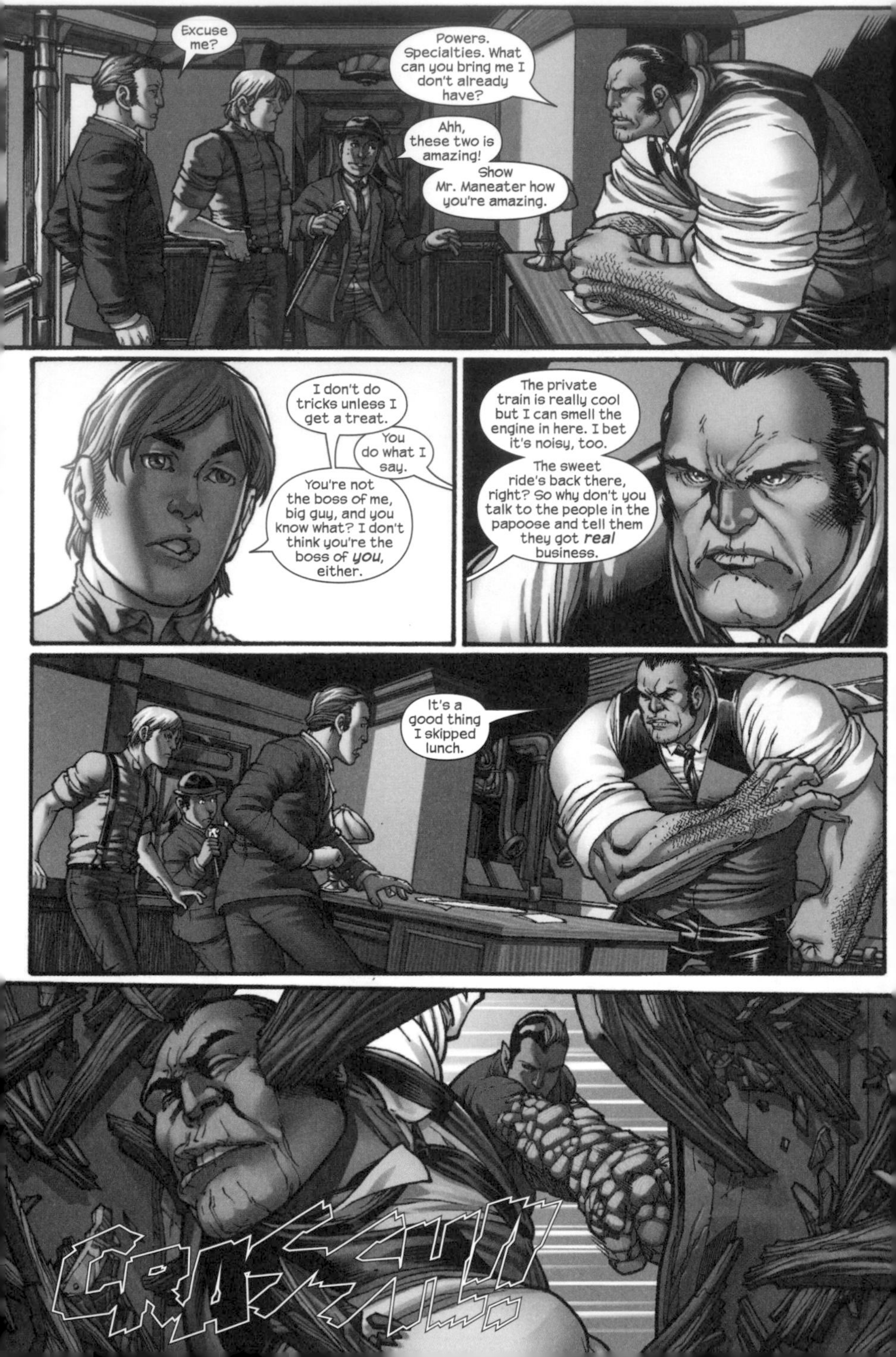
Excuse me?
Powers. Specialties. What can you bring me I don't already have?
Ahh, these two is amazing!
Show Mr. Maneater how you're amazing.
I don't do tricks unless I get a treat.
You do what I say.
You're not the boss of me, big guy, and you know what? I don't think you're the boss of *you*, either.
The private train is really cool but I can smell the engine in here. I bet it's noisy, too.
The sweet ride's back there, right? So why don't you talk to the people in the papoose and tell them they got *real* business.
It's a good thing I skipped lunch.
CRASSHH!

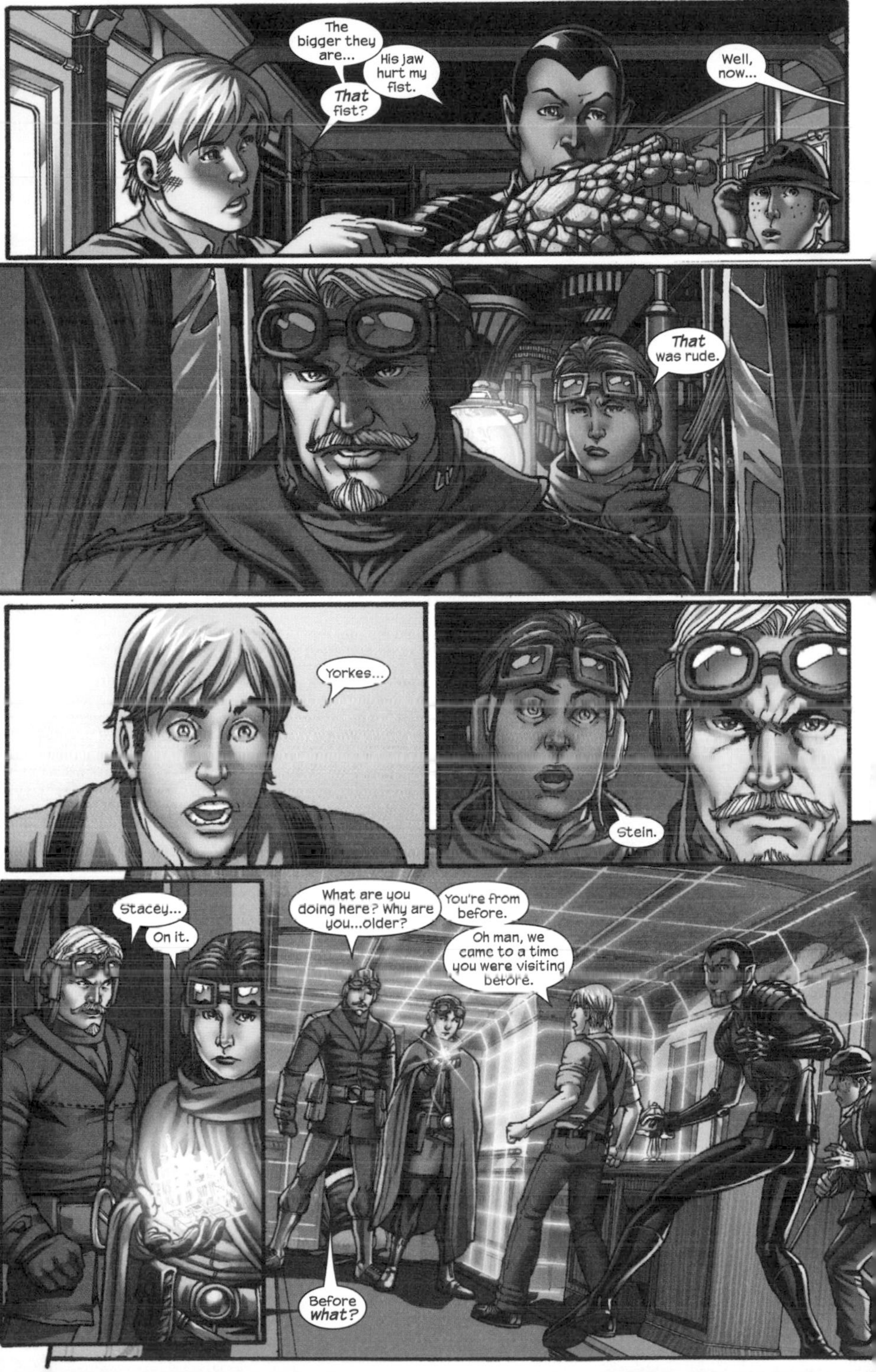
The bigger they are...
His jaw hurt my fist.
That fist?
Well, now...
That was rude.
Yorkes...
Stein.
Stacey...
On it.
What are you doing here? Why are you...older?
You're from before.
Oh man, we came to a time you were visiting before.
Before *what?*

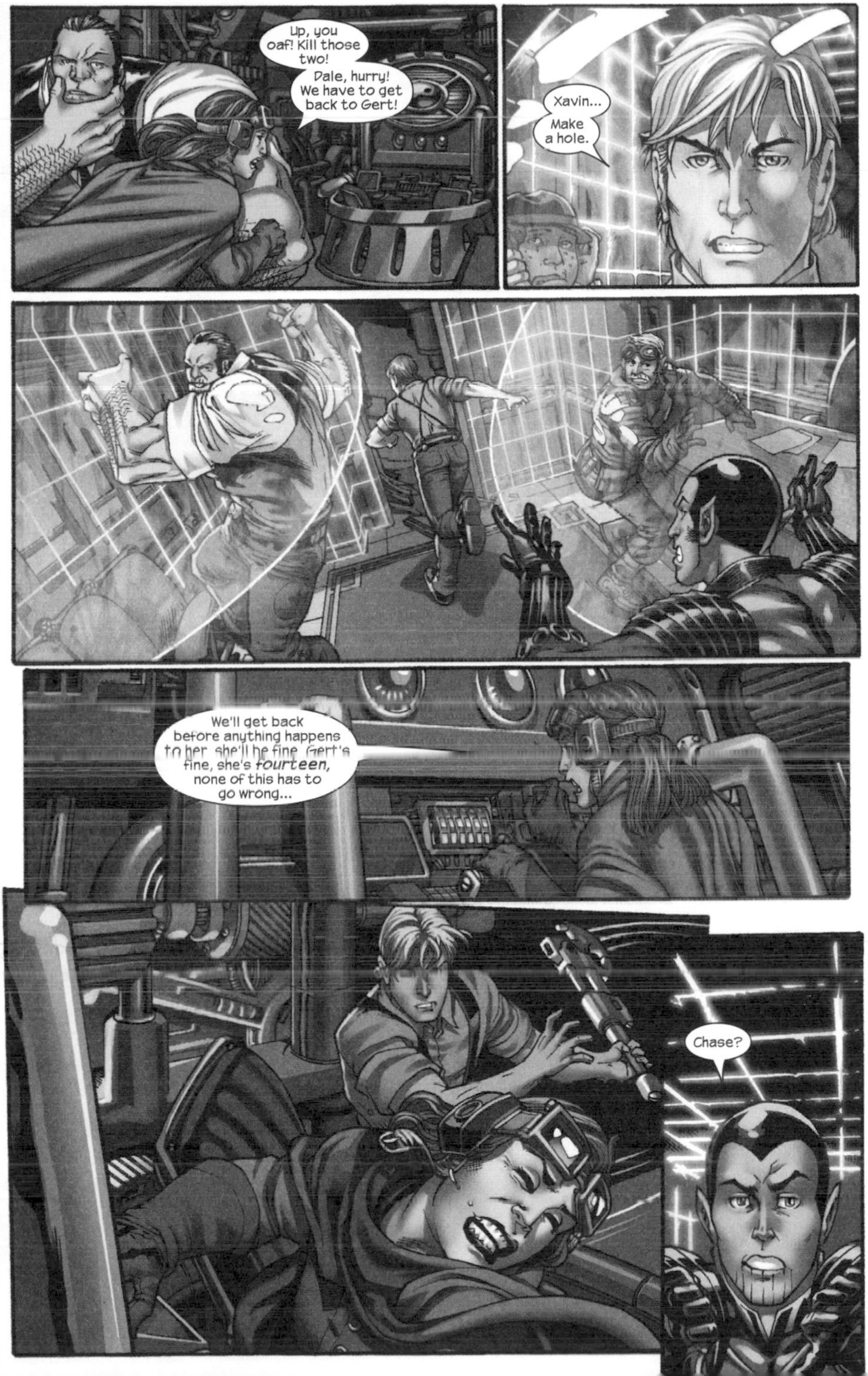
Up, you oaf! Kill those two!
Dale, hurry! We have to get back to Gert!
Xavin... Make a hole.
We'll get back before anything happens to her, she'll be fine. Gert's fine, she's *fourteen,* none of this has to go wrong...
Chase?

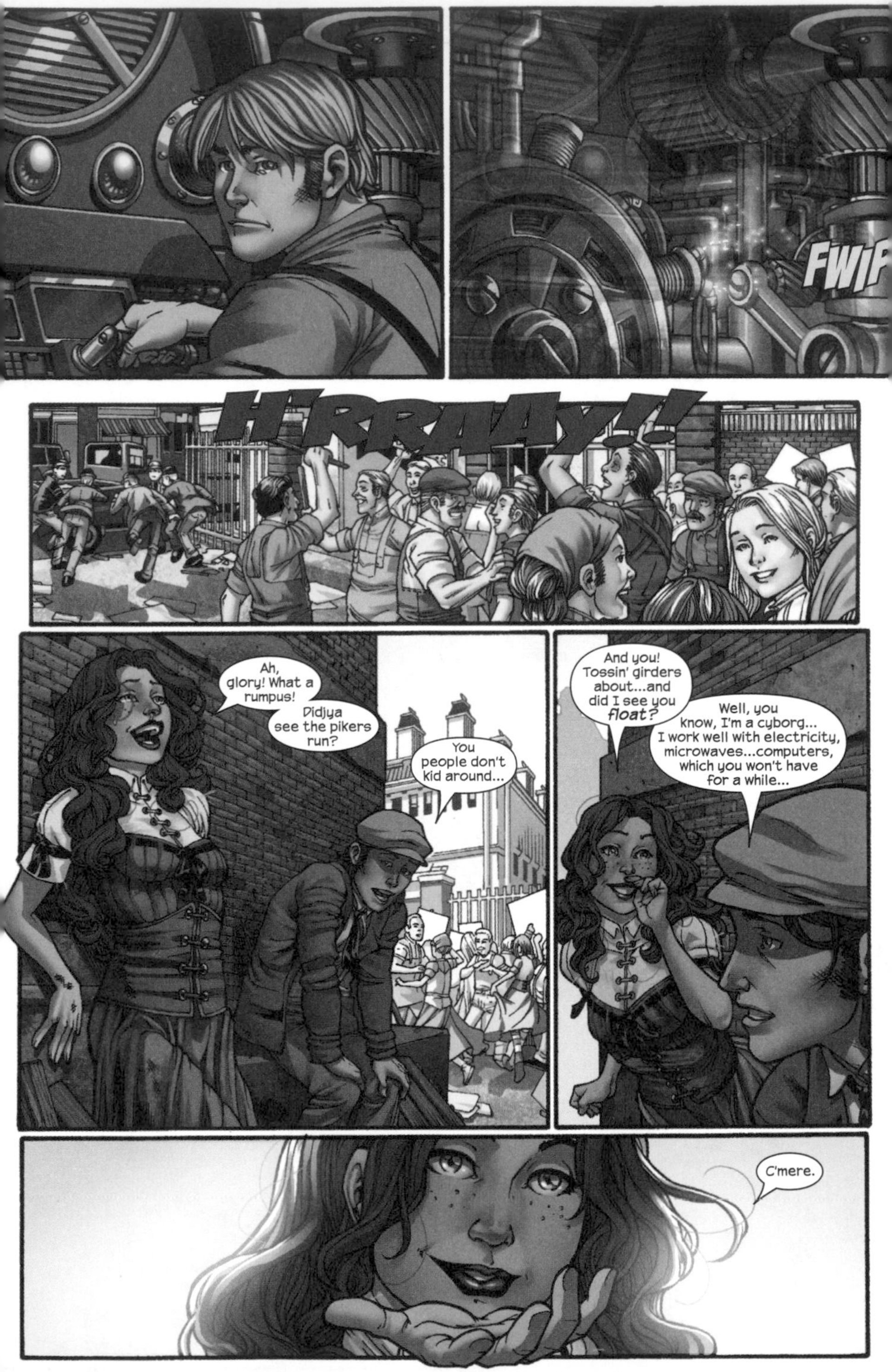
FWIP
H'RRAAY!!
Ah, glory! What a rumpus!
Didjya see the pikers run?
You people don't kid around...
And you! Tossin' girders about...and did I see you float?
Well, you know, I'm a cyborg... I work well with electricity, microwaves...computers, which you won't have for a while...
C'mere.

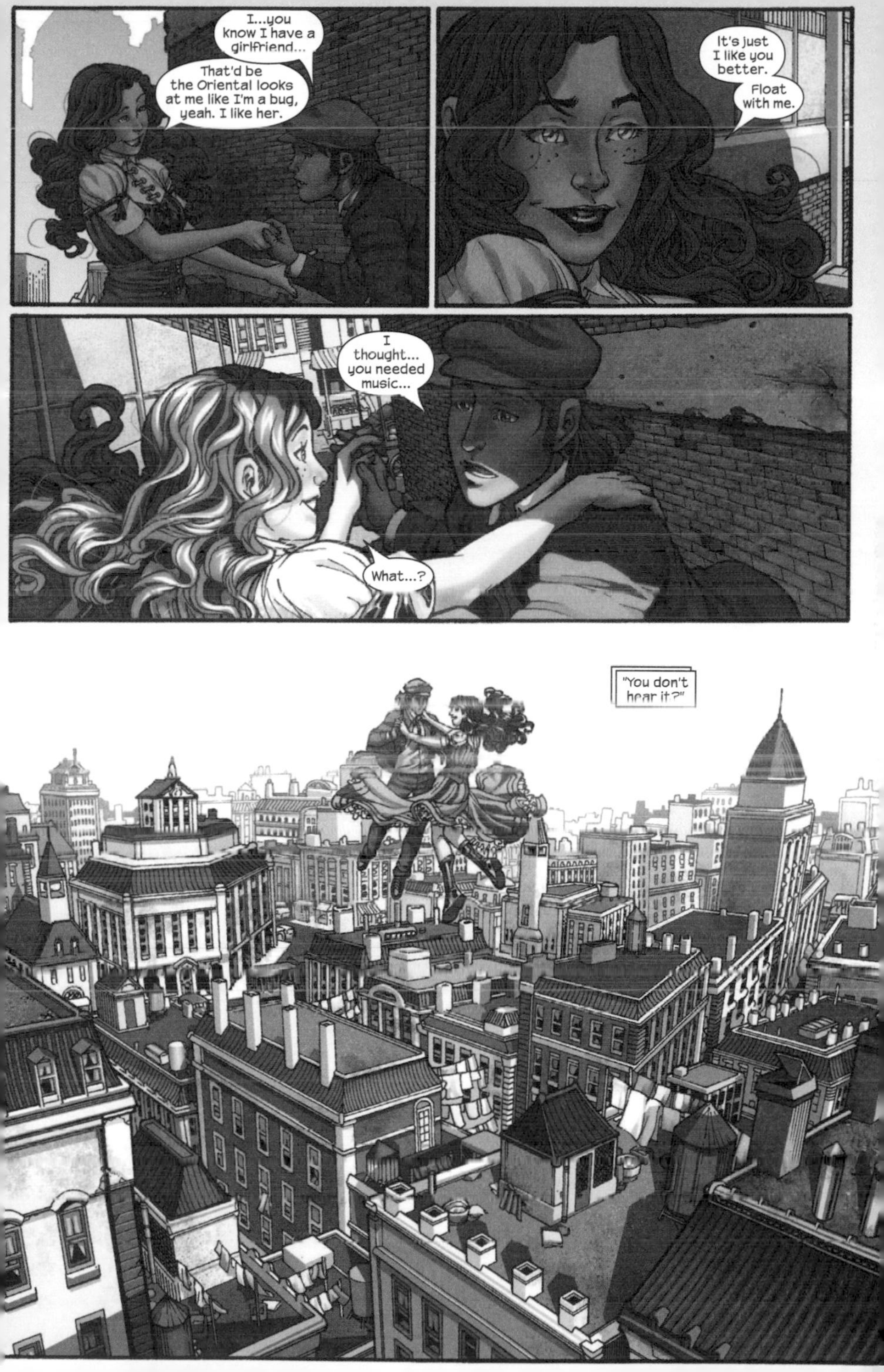
I...you know I have a girlfriend...
That'd be the Oriental looks at me like I'm a bug, yeah. I like her.
It's just I like you better.
Float with me.
I thought... you needed music...
What...?
"You don't hear it?"

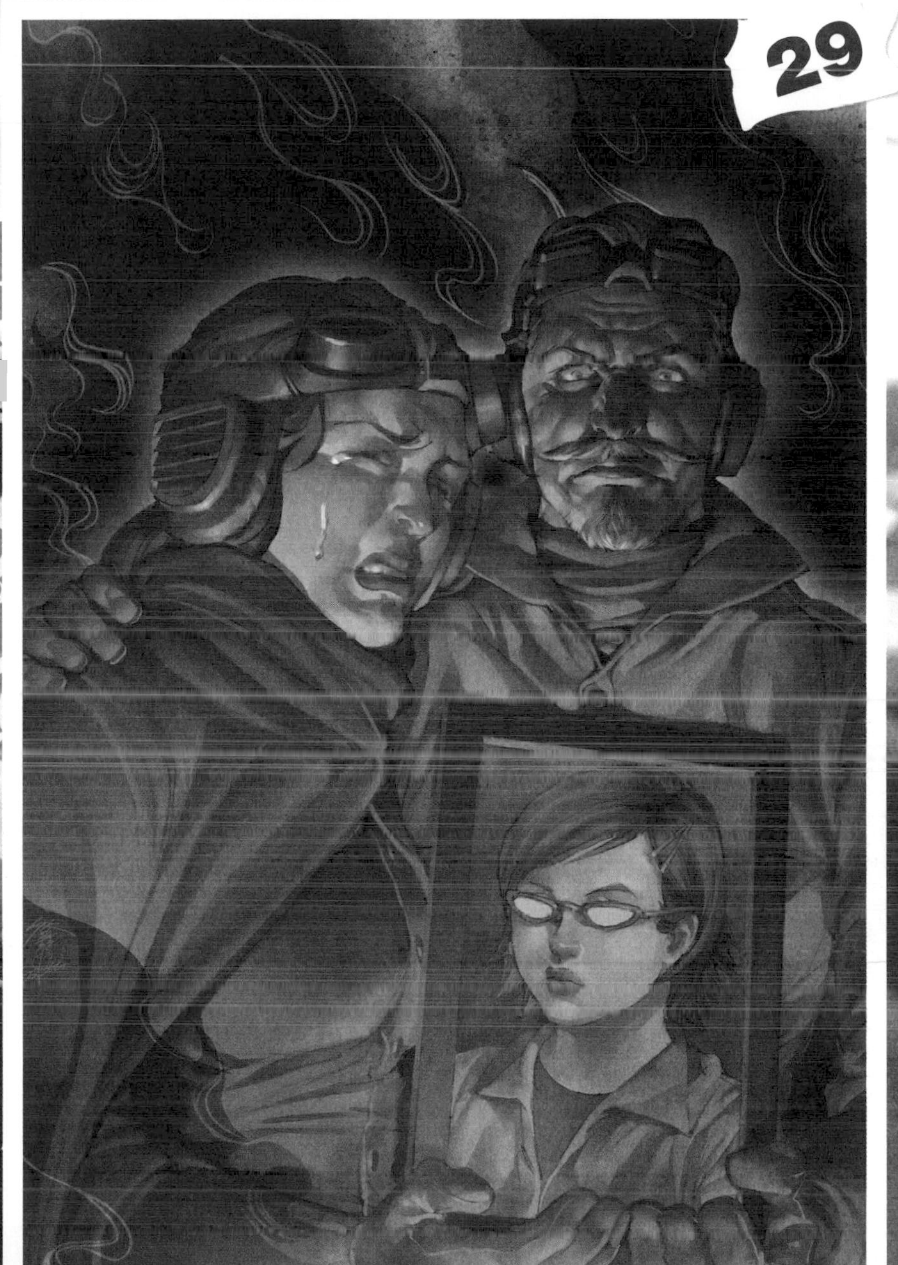
29

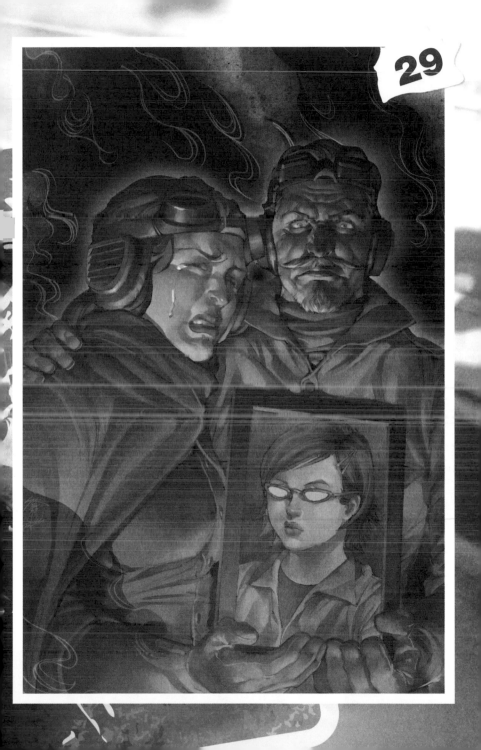

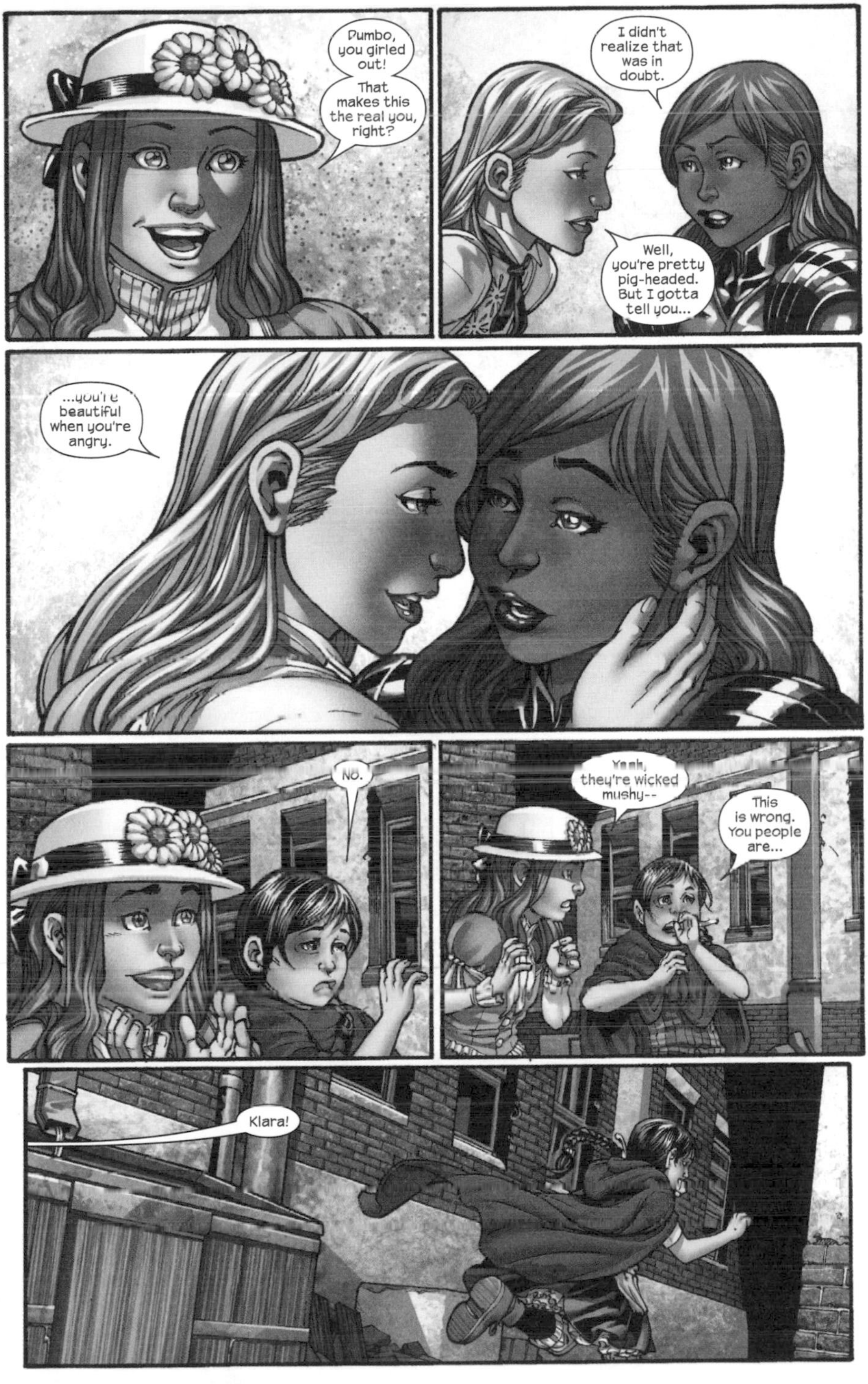

Dumbo, you girled out!
That makes this the real you, right?
I didn't realize that was in doubt.
Well, you're pretty pig-headed. But I gotta tell you...
...you're beautiful when you're angry.
No.
Yeah, they're wicked mushy--
This is wrong. You people are...
Klara!

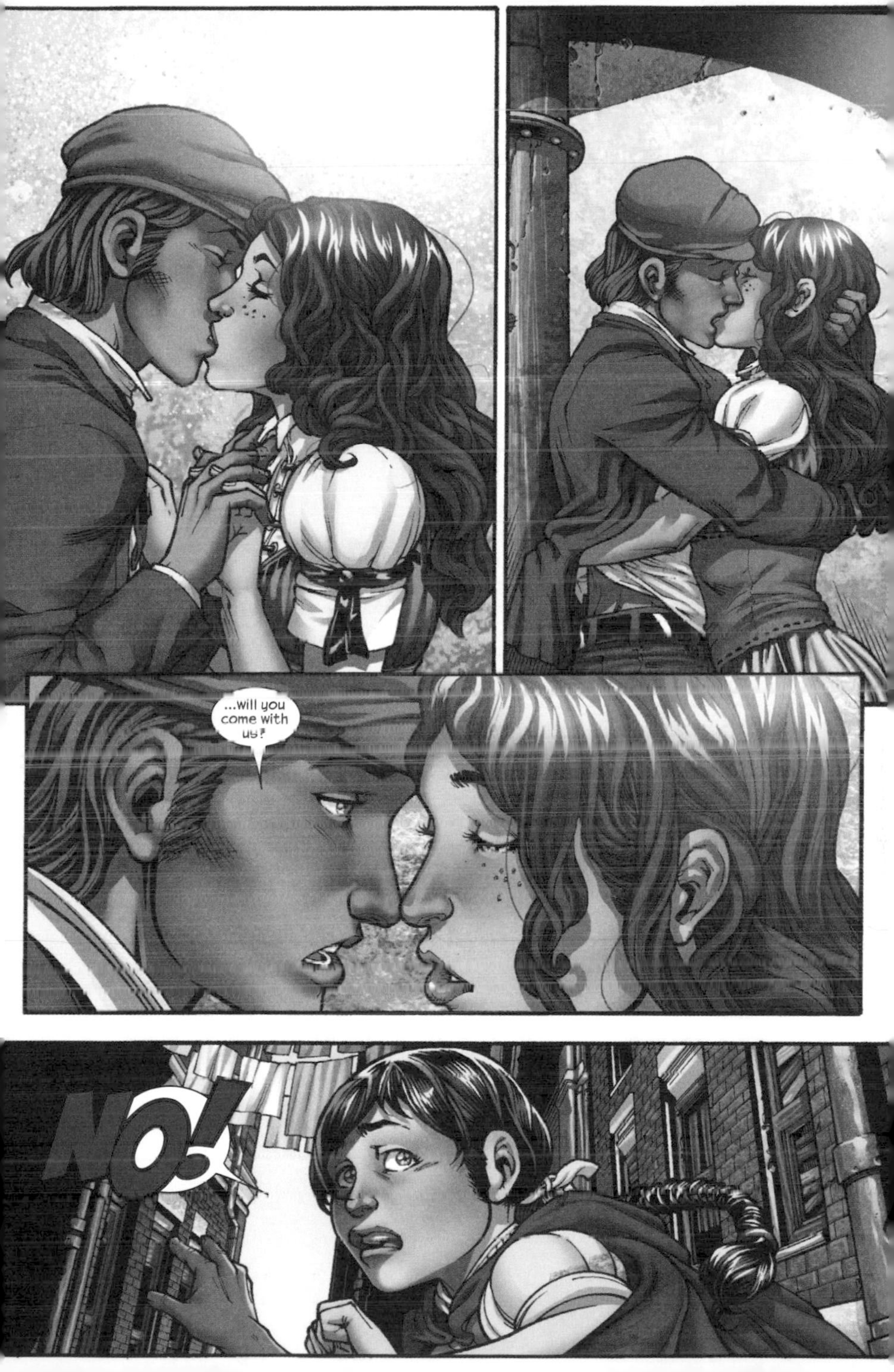
...will you come with us?
NO!

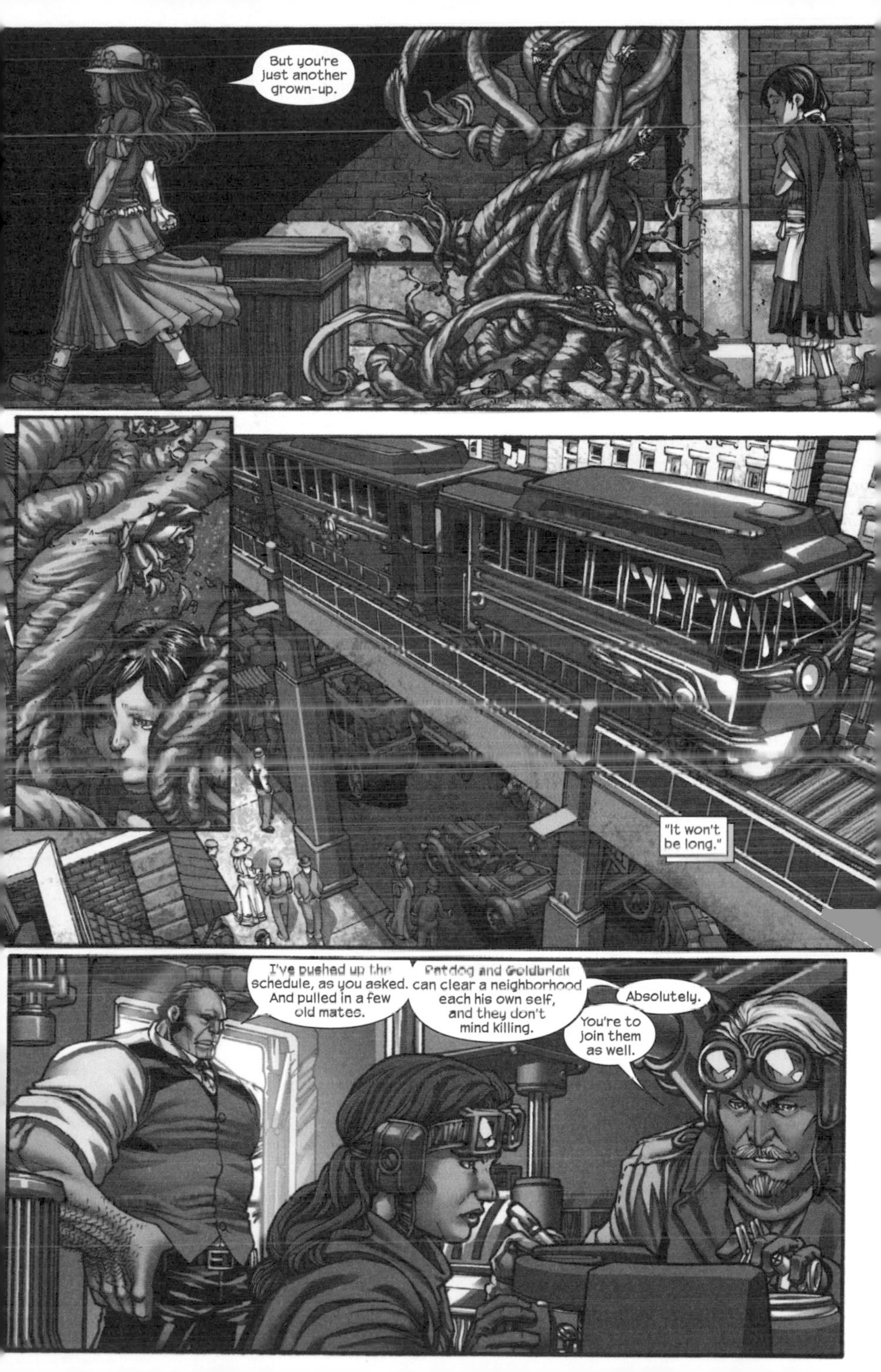
But you're just another grown-up.
"It won't be long."
I've pushed up the schedule, as you asked. And pulled in a few old mates.
Ratdog and Goldbrick can clear a neighborhood each his own self, and they don't mind killing.
Absolutely.
You're to join them as well.

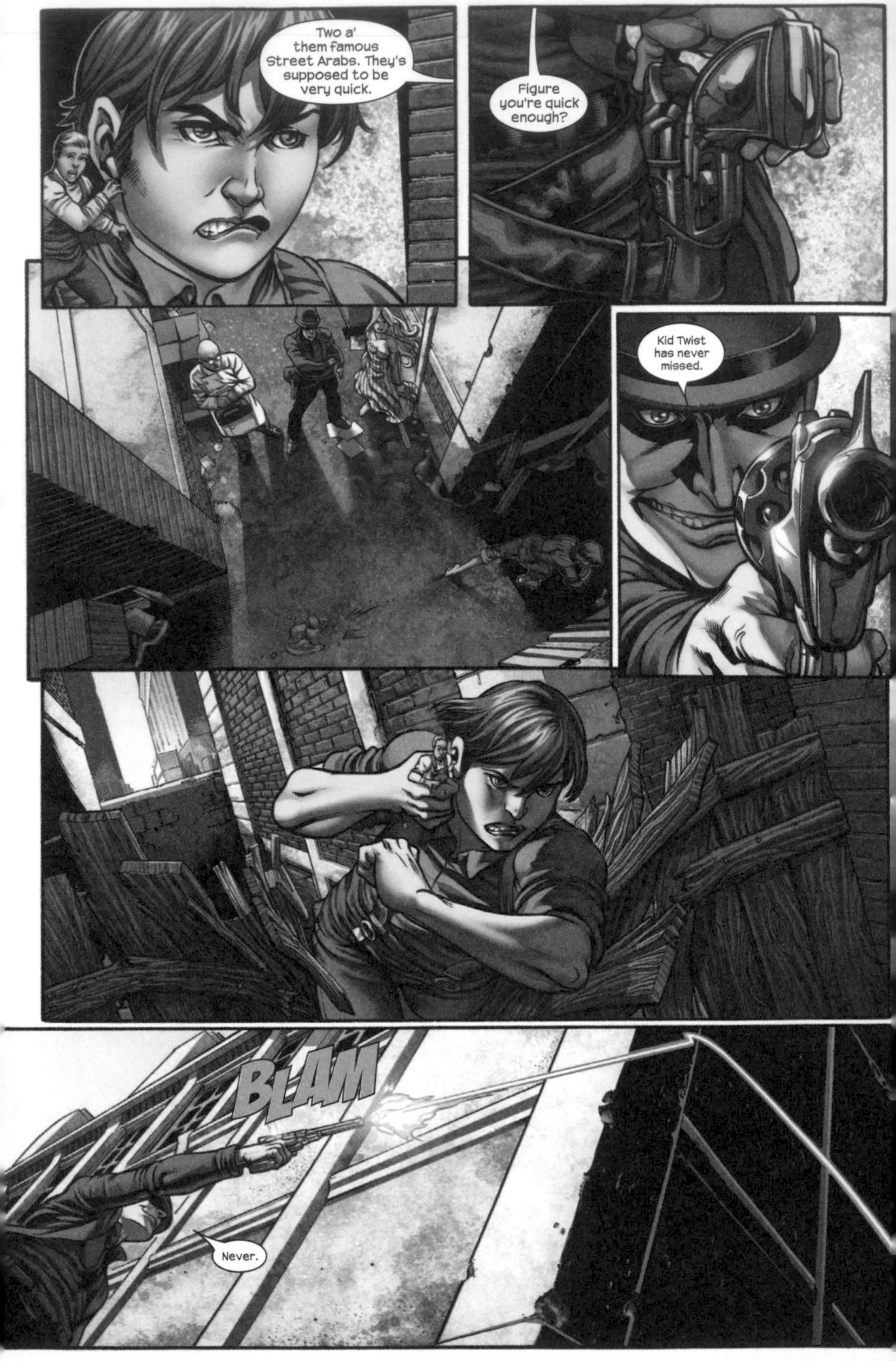

Two a' them famous Street Arabs. They's supposed to be very quick.
Figure you're quick enough?
Kid Twist has never missed.
BLAM
Never.

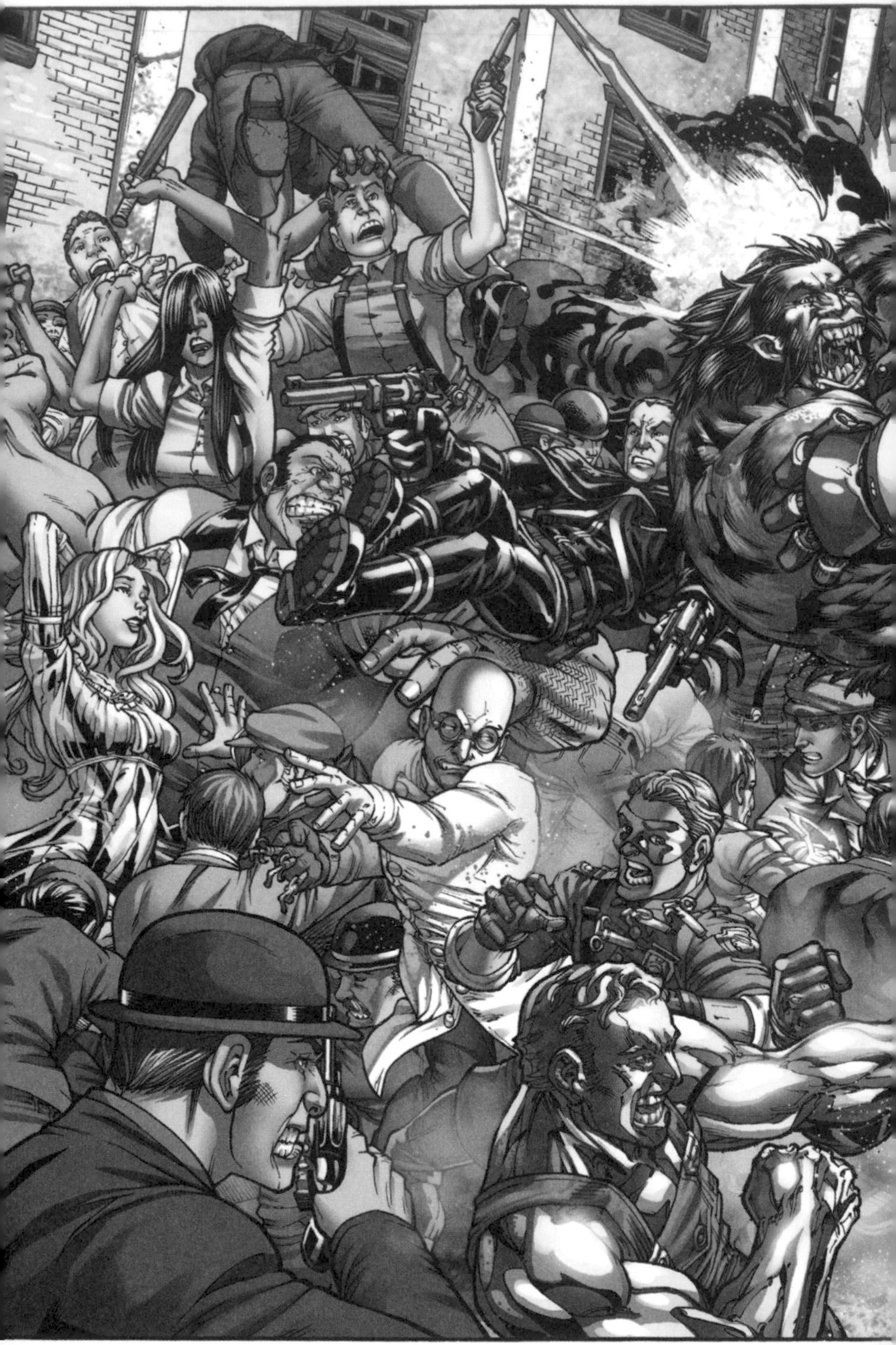

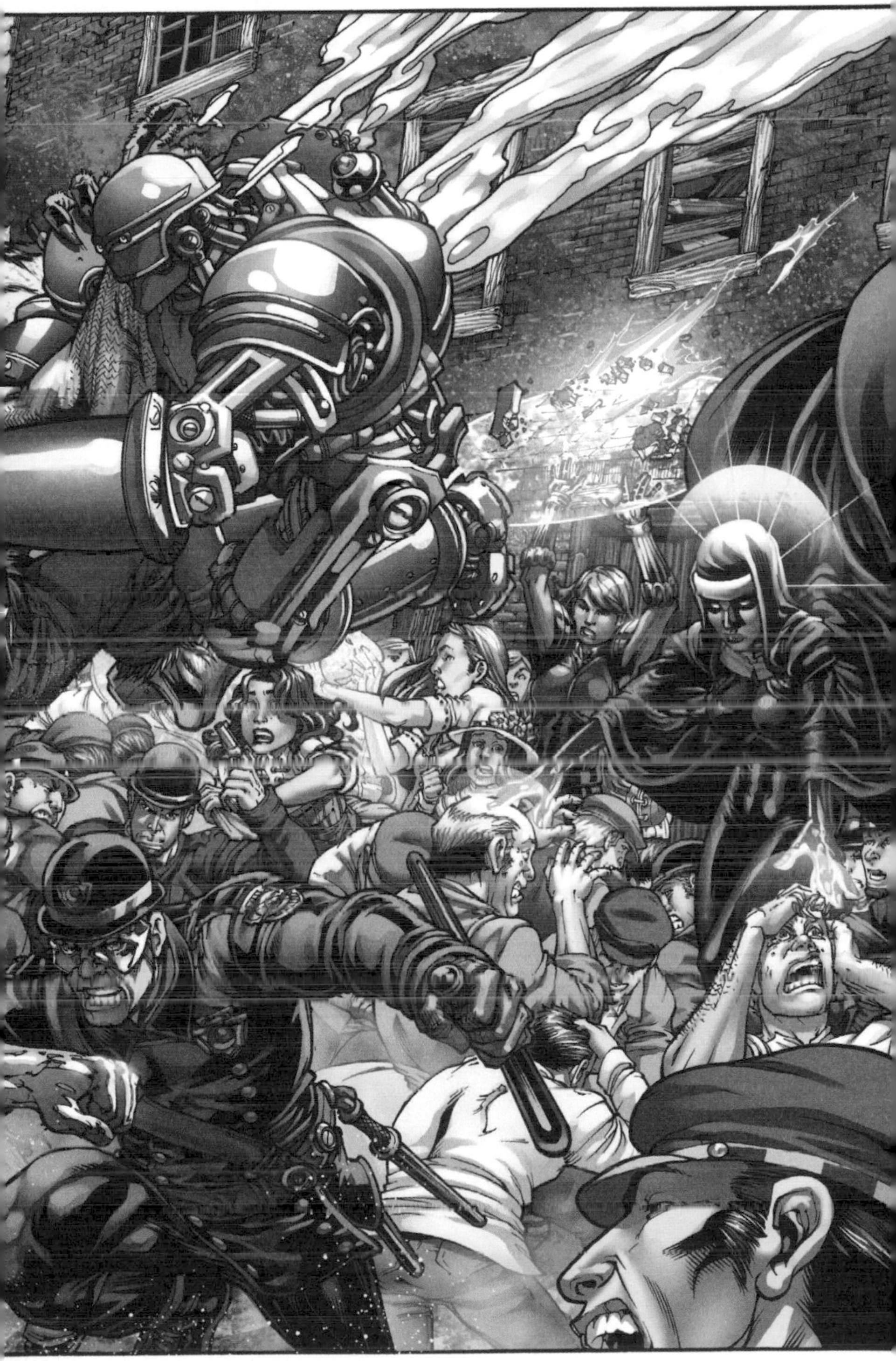

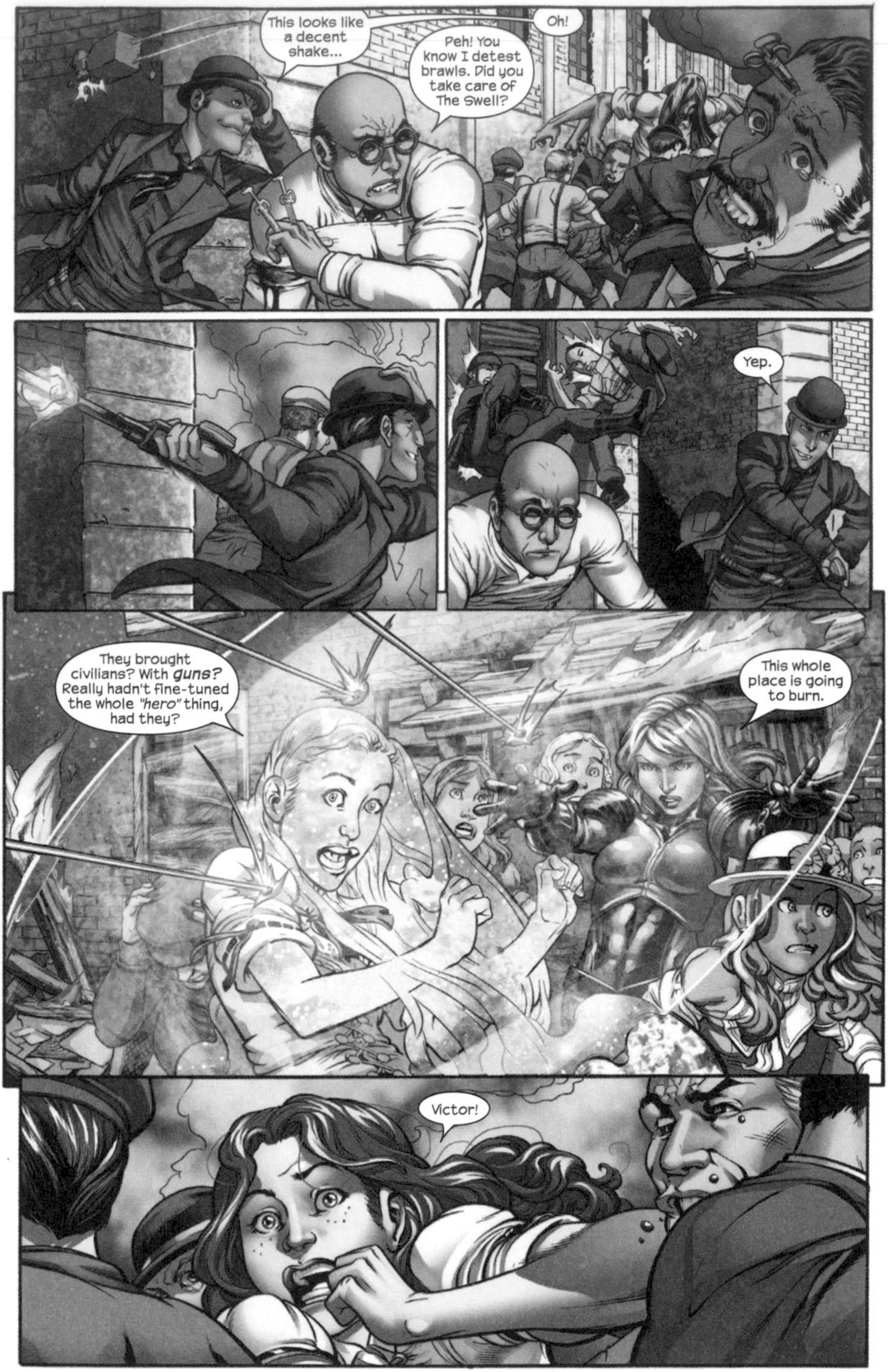
This looks like a decent shake...
Oh!
Peh! You know I detest brawls. Did you take care of The Swell?
Yep.
They brought civilians? With *guns?* Really hadn't fine-tuned the whole *"hero"* thing, had they?
This whole place is going to burn.
Victor!

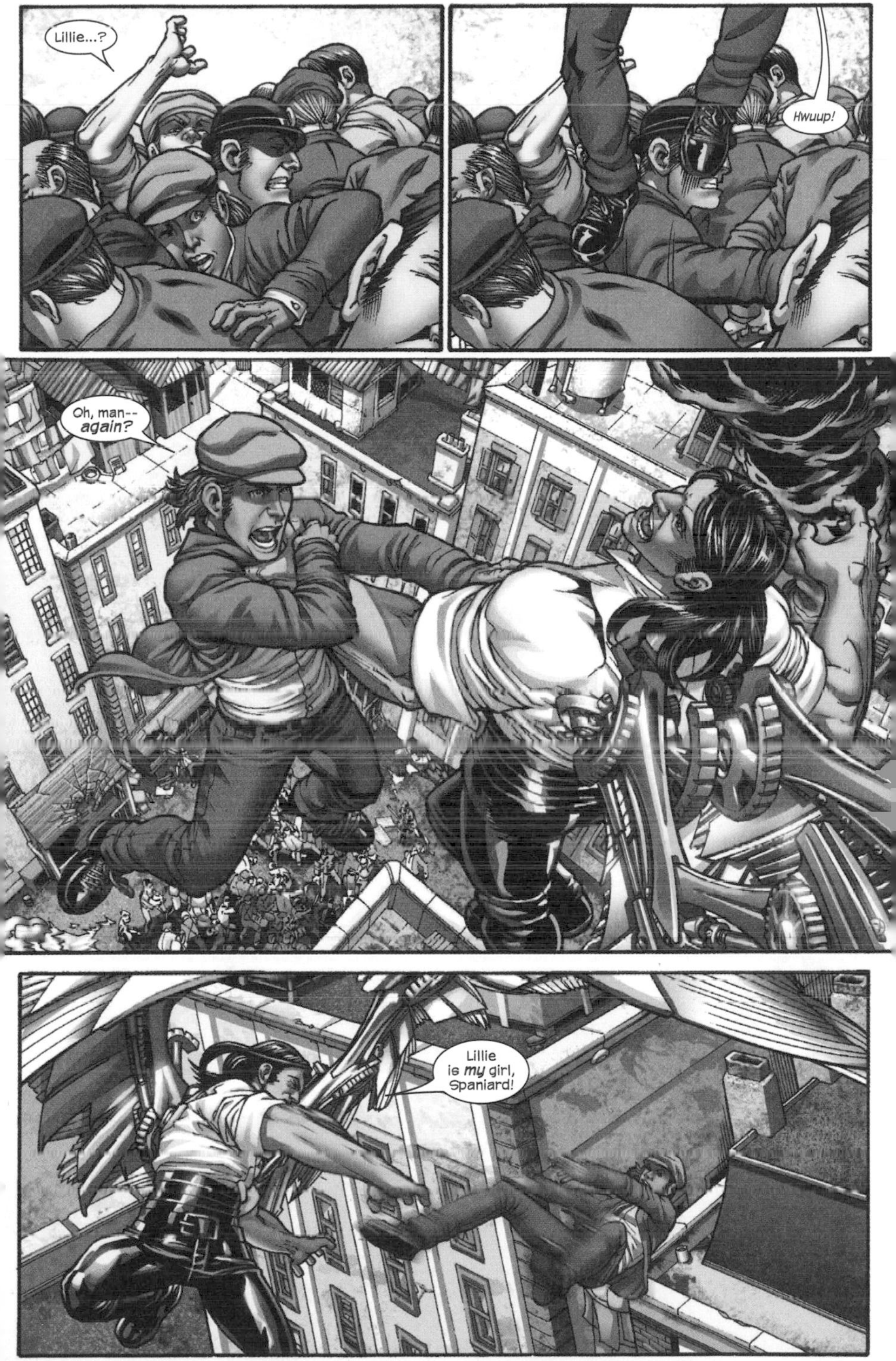
Lillie...?
Hwuup!
Oh, man--
again?
Lillie
is my girl,
Spaniard!

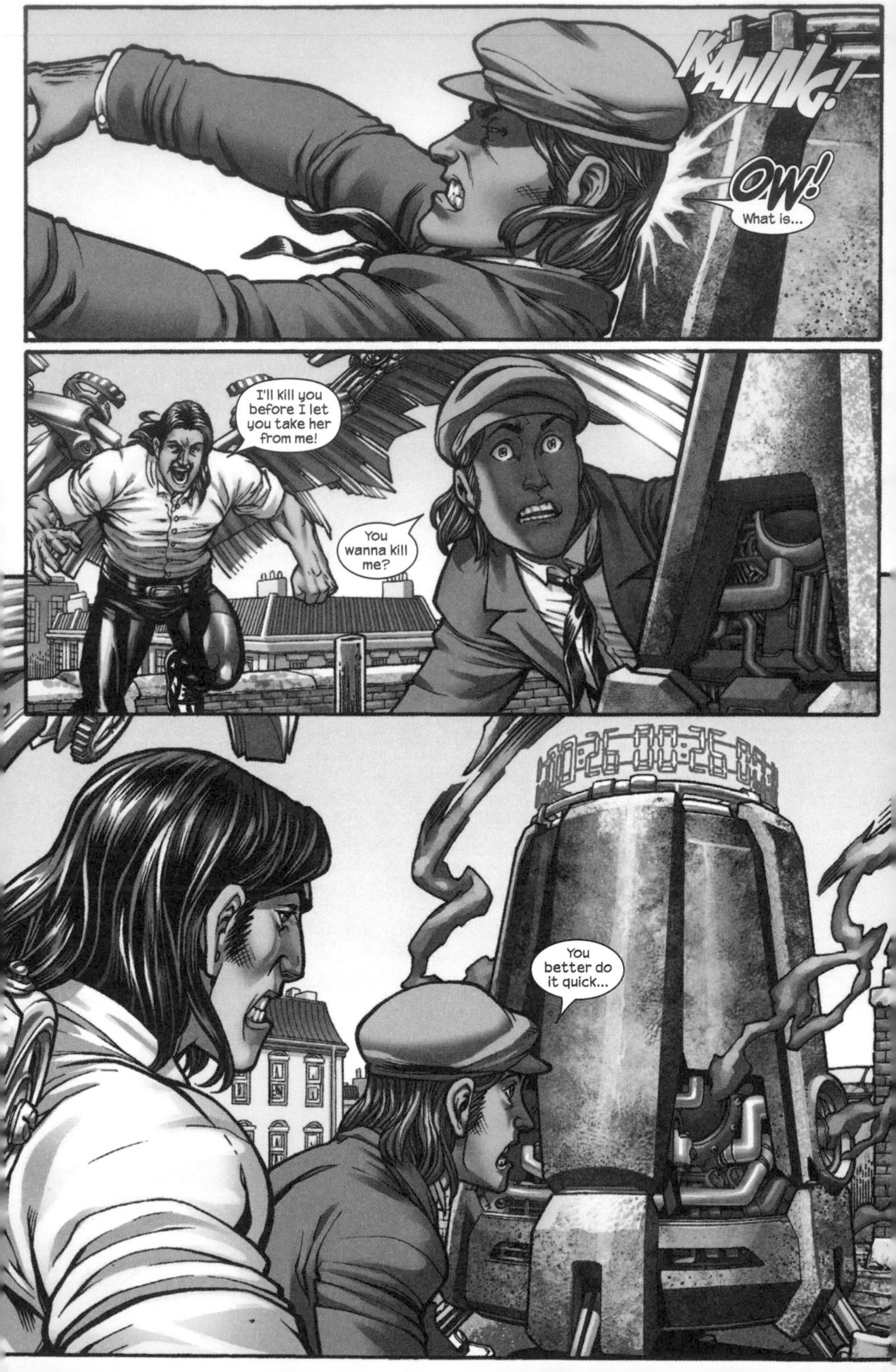
KANNG!
OW!
What is...
I'll kill you before I let you take her from me!
You wanna kill me?
You better do it quick...

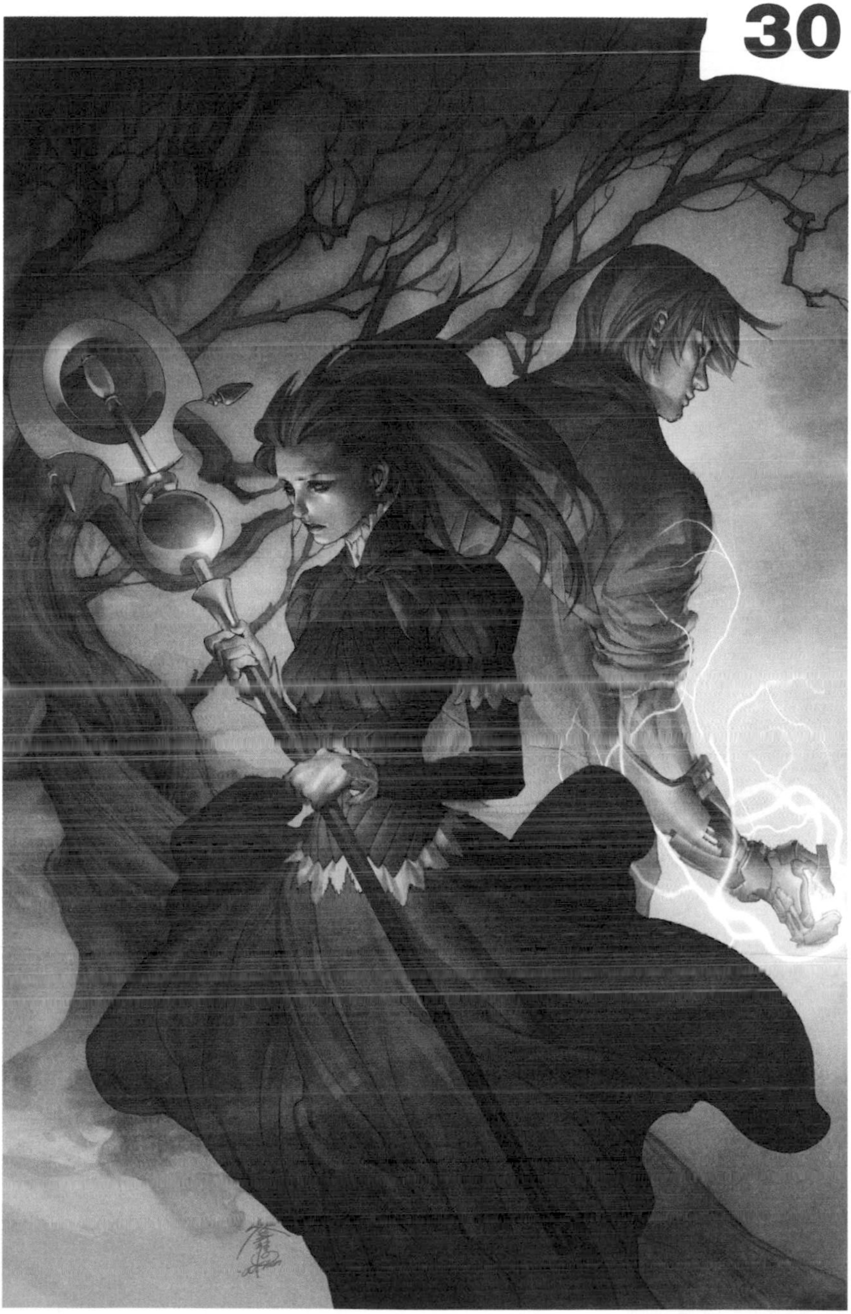

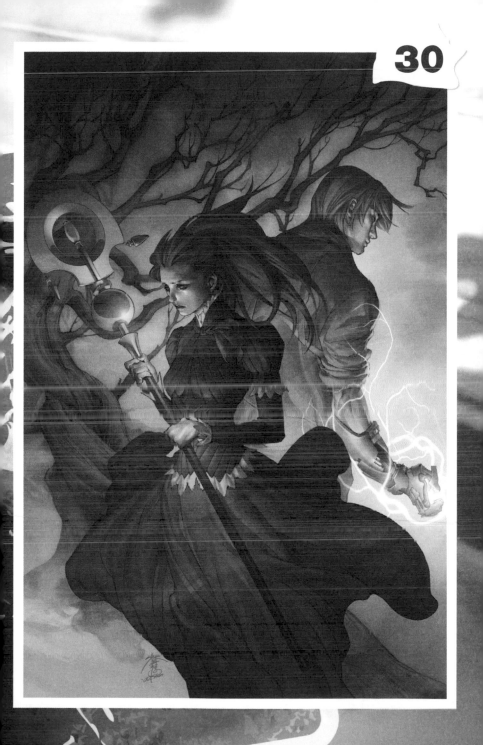

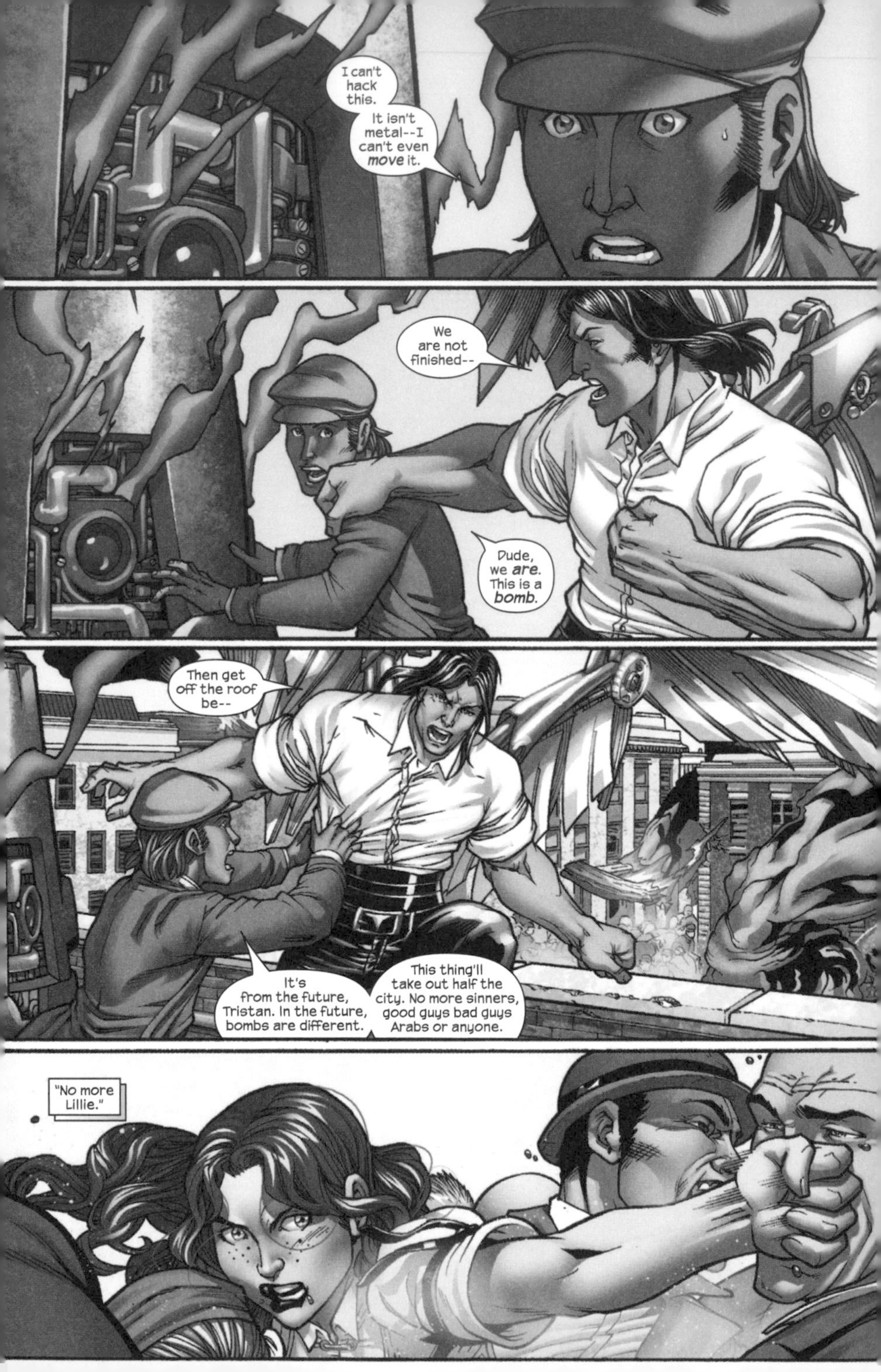

I can't hack this.
It isn't metal--I can't even *move* it.
We are not finished--
Dude, we *are*. This is a *bomb*.
Then get off the roof be--
It's from the future, Tristan. In the future, bombs are different.
This thing'll take out half the city. No more sinners, good guys bad guys Arabs or anyone.
"No more Lillie."

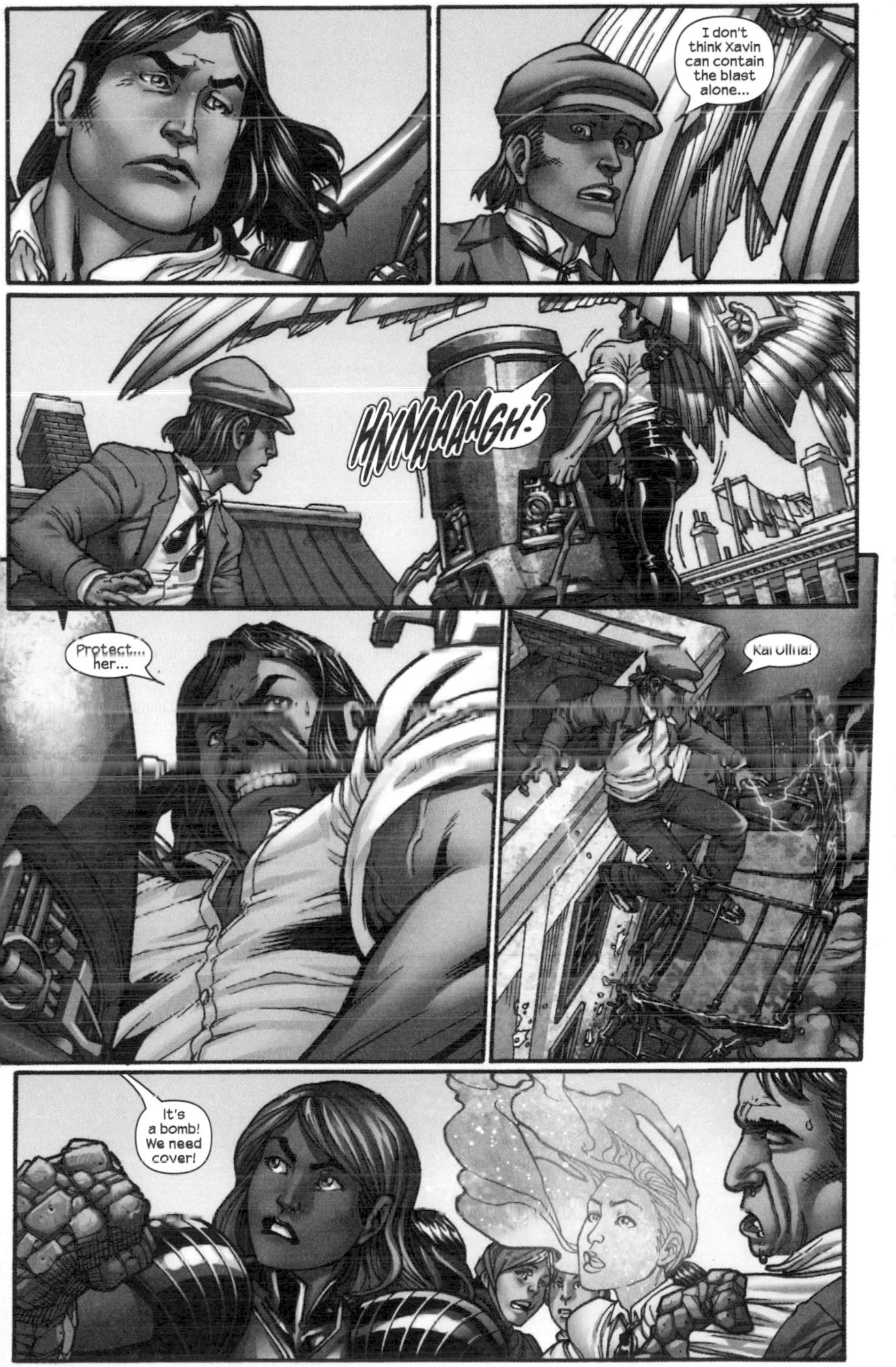
I don't think Xavin can contain the blast alone...
HNNAAAAAGH!
Protect... her...
Karolina!
It's a bomb! We need cover!

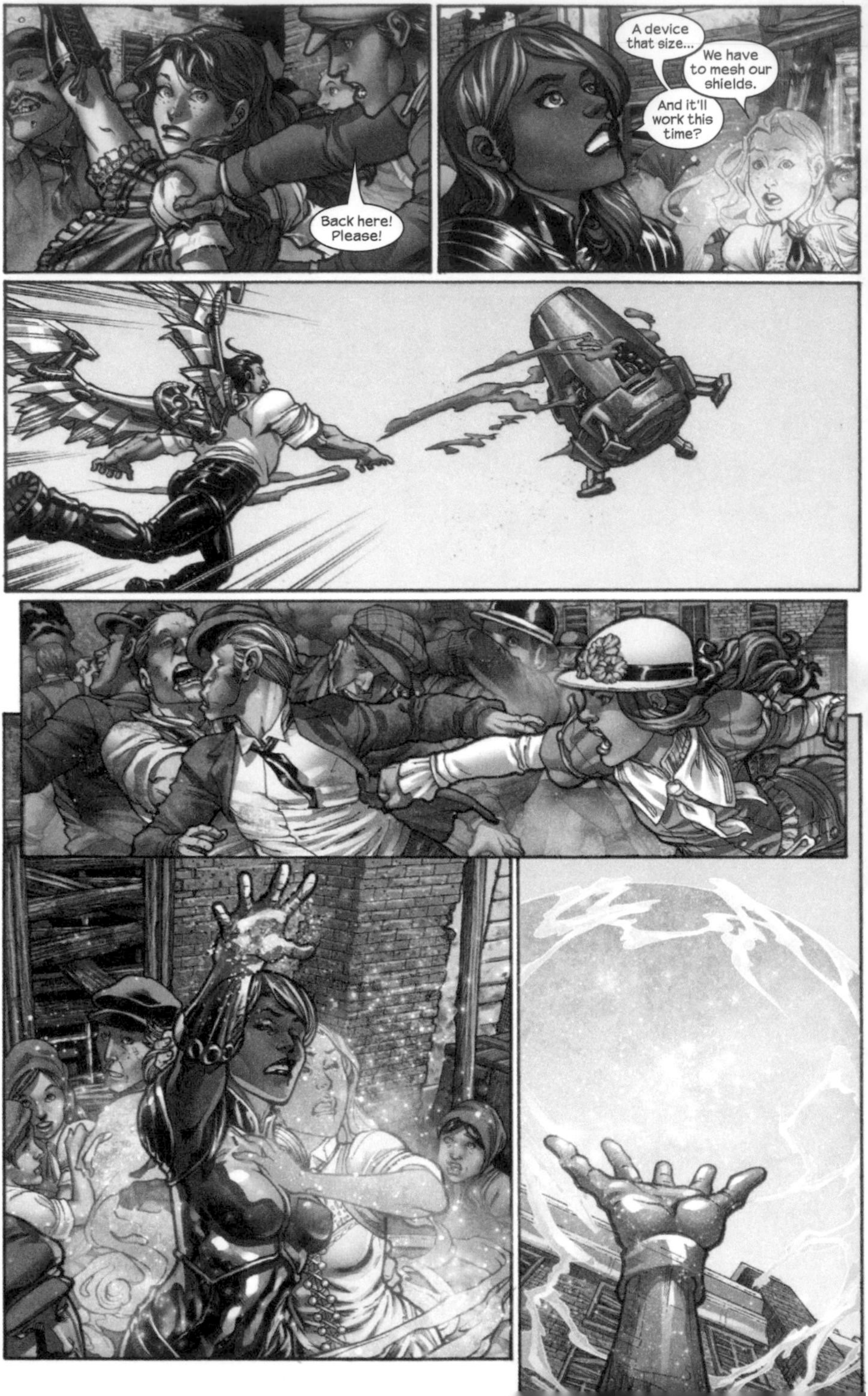
Back here! Please!
A device that size...
We have to mesh our shields.
And it'll work this time?

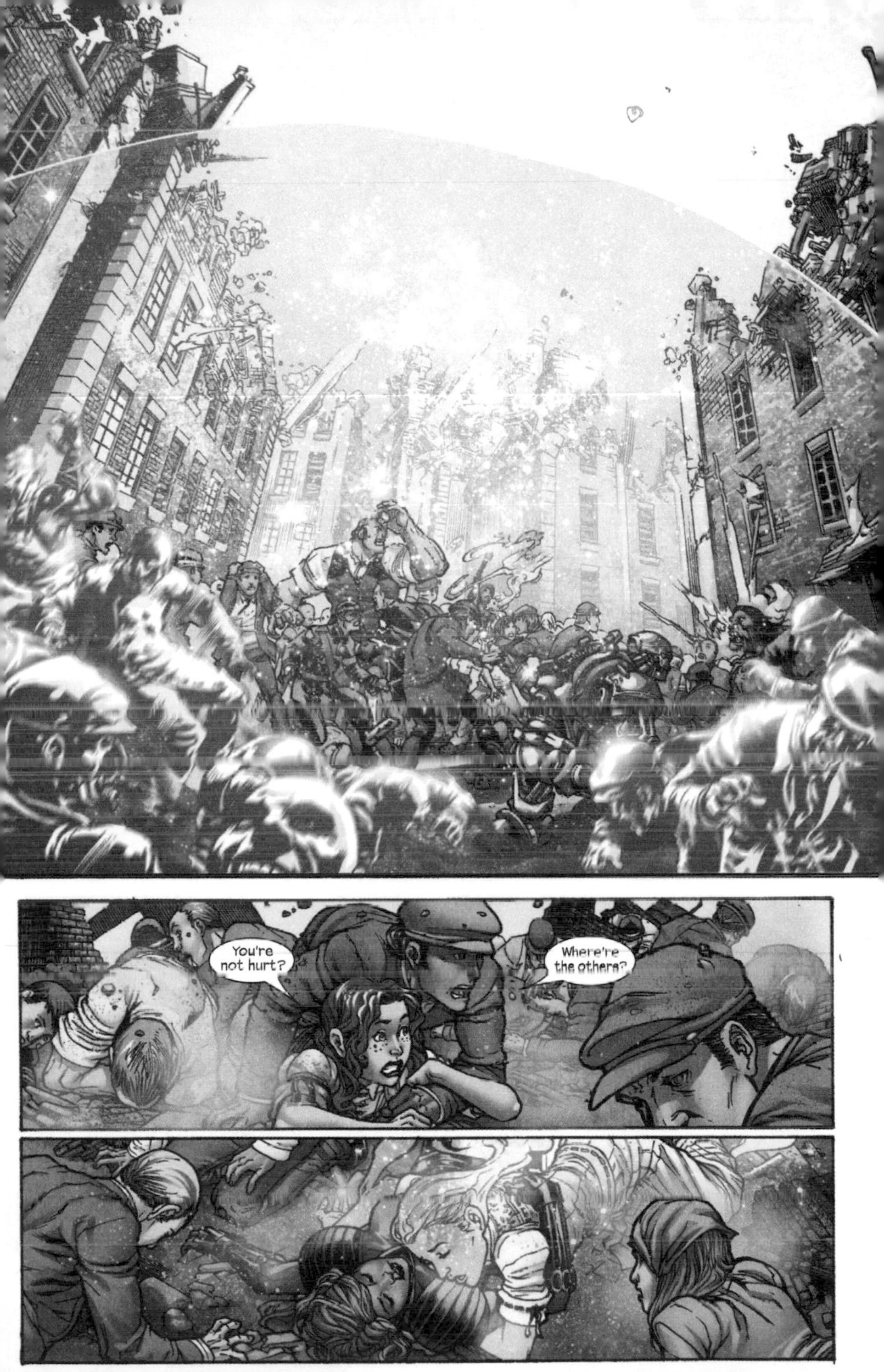
You're not hurt?
Where're the others?

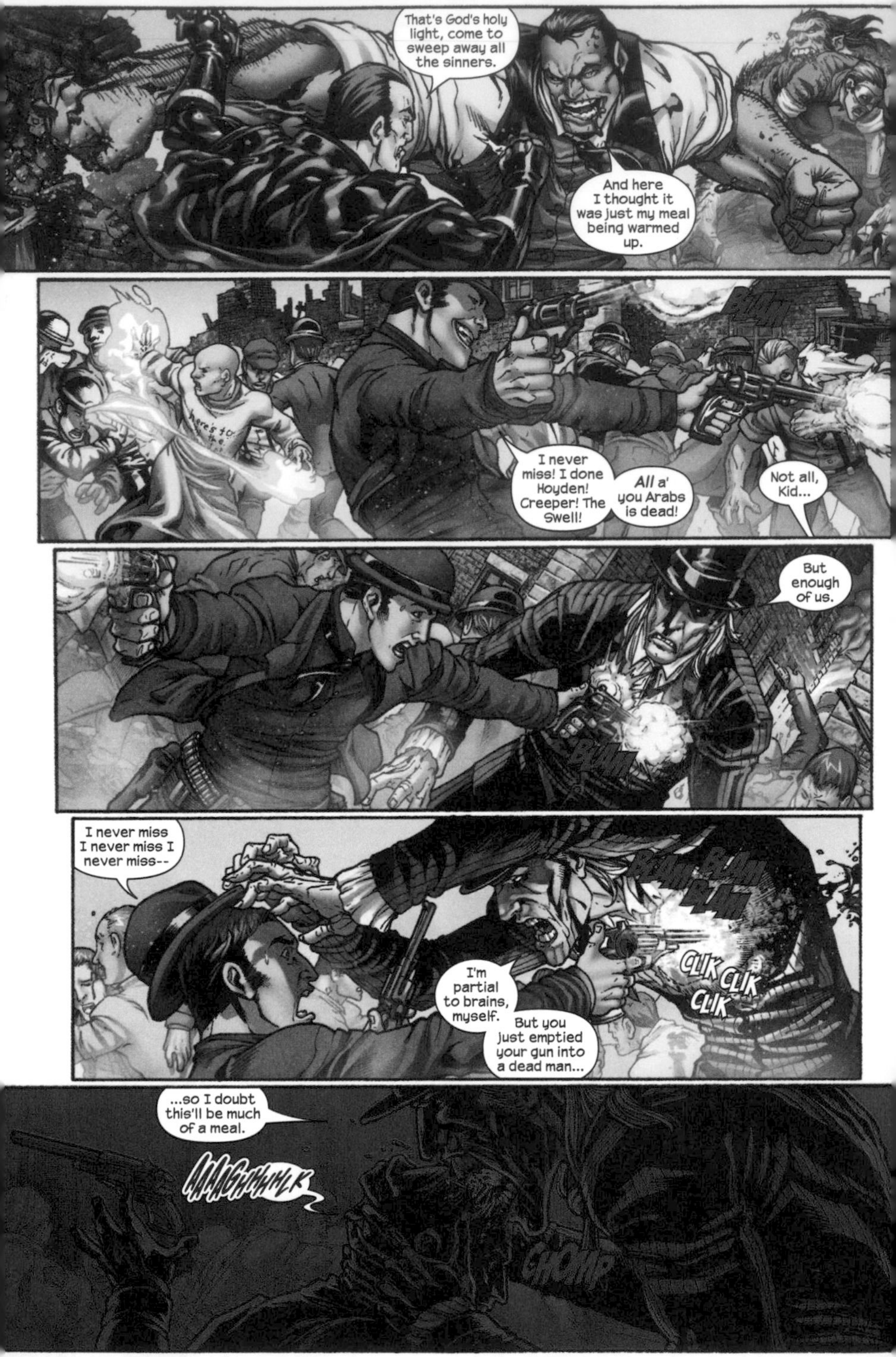

That's God's holy light, come to sweep away all the sinners.
And here I thought it was just my meal being warmed up.
BLAM
I never miss! I done Hoyden! Creeper! The Swell!
All a' you Arabs is dead!
Not all, Kid...
But enough of us.
BLAM
I never miss I never miss I never miss--
BLAM BLAM BLAM BLAM
CLIK CLIK CLIK
I'm partial to brains, myself.
But you just emptied your gun into a dead man...
...so I doubt this'll be much of a meal.
AAAAGHHHHLK
CHOMP

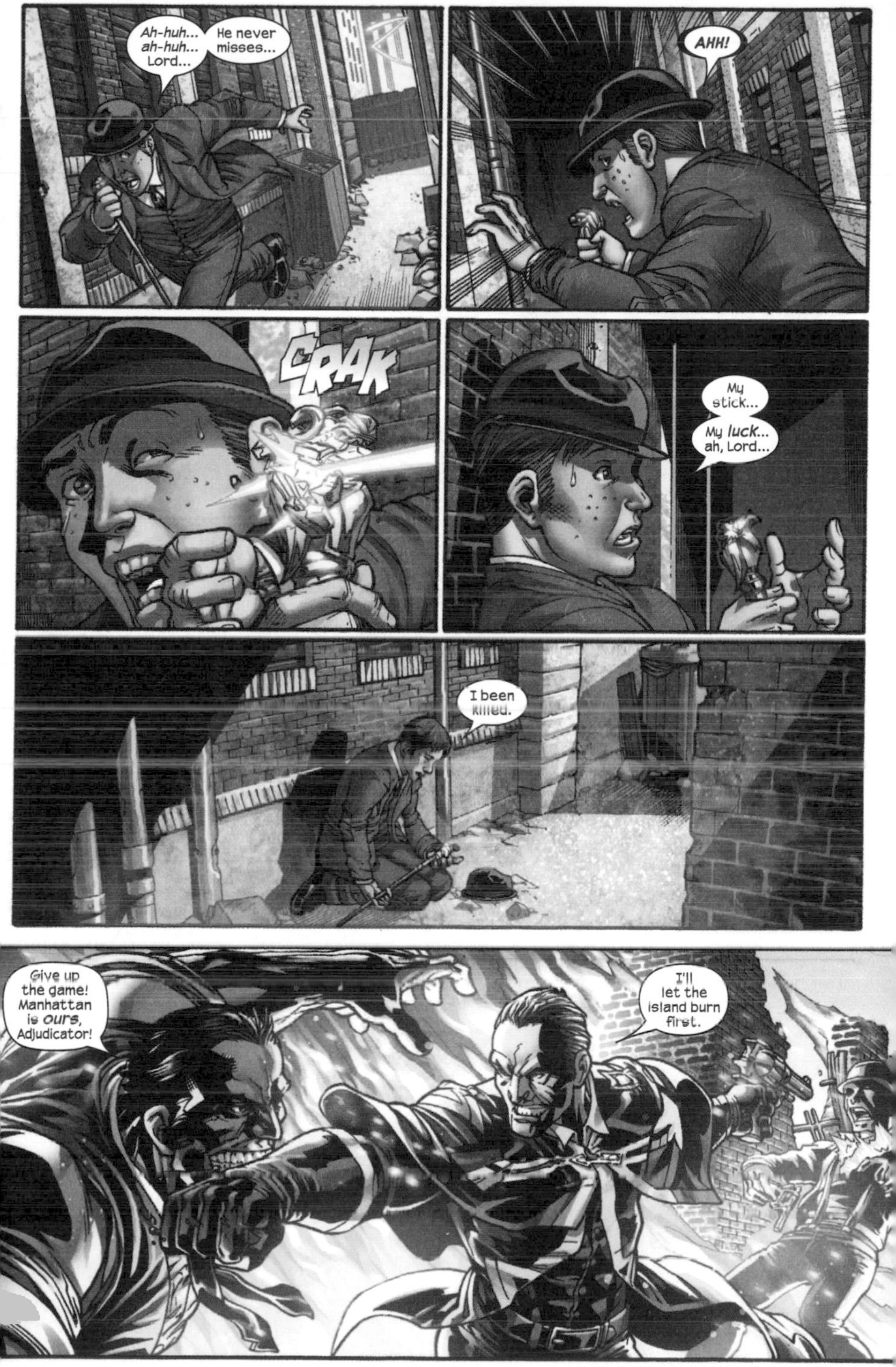
Ah-huh... ah-huh... Lord...
He never misses...
AHH!
CRAK
My stick...
My luck... ah, Lord...
I been killed.
Give up the game! Manhattan is ours, Adjudicator!
I'll let the island burn first.

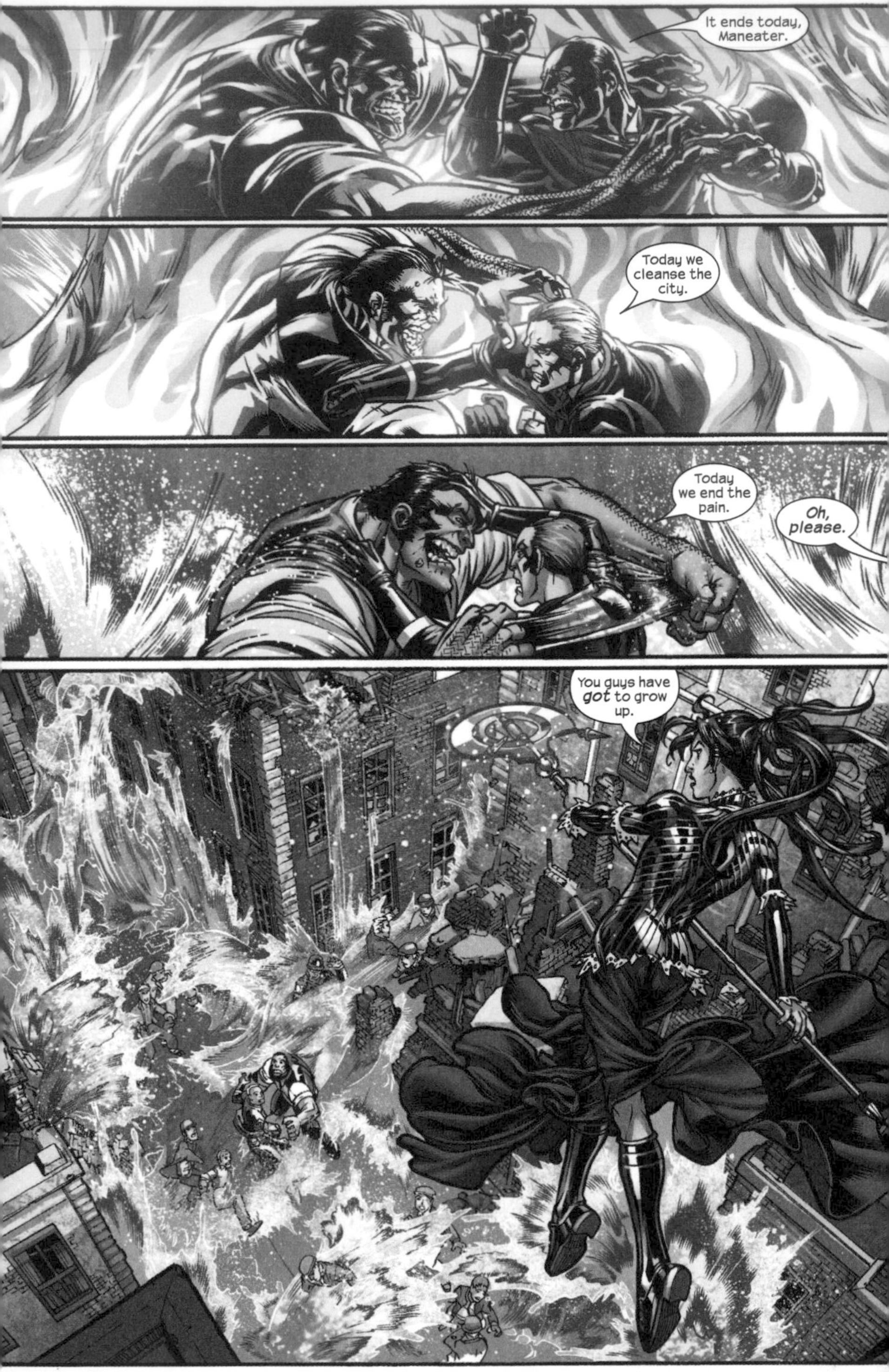
It ends today, Maneater.
Today we cleanse the city.
Today we end the pain.
Oh, please.
You guys have got to grow up.

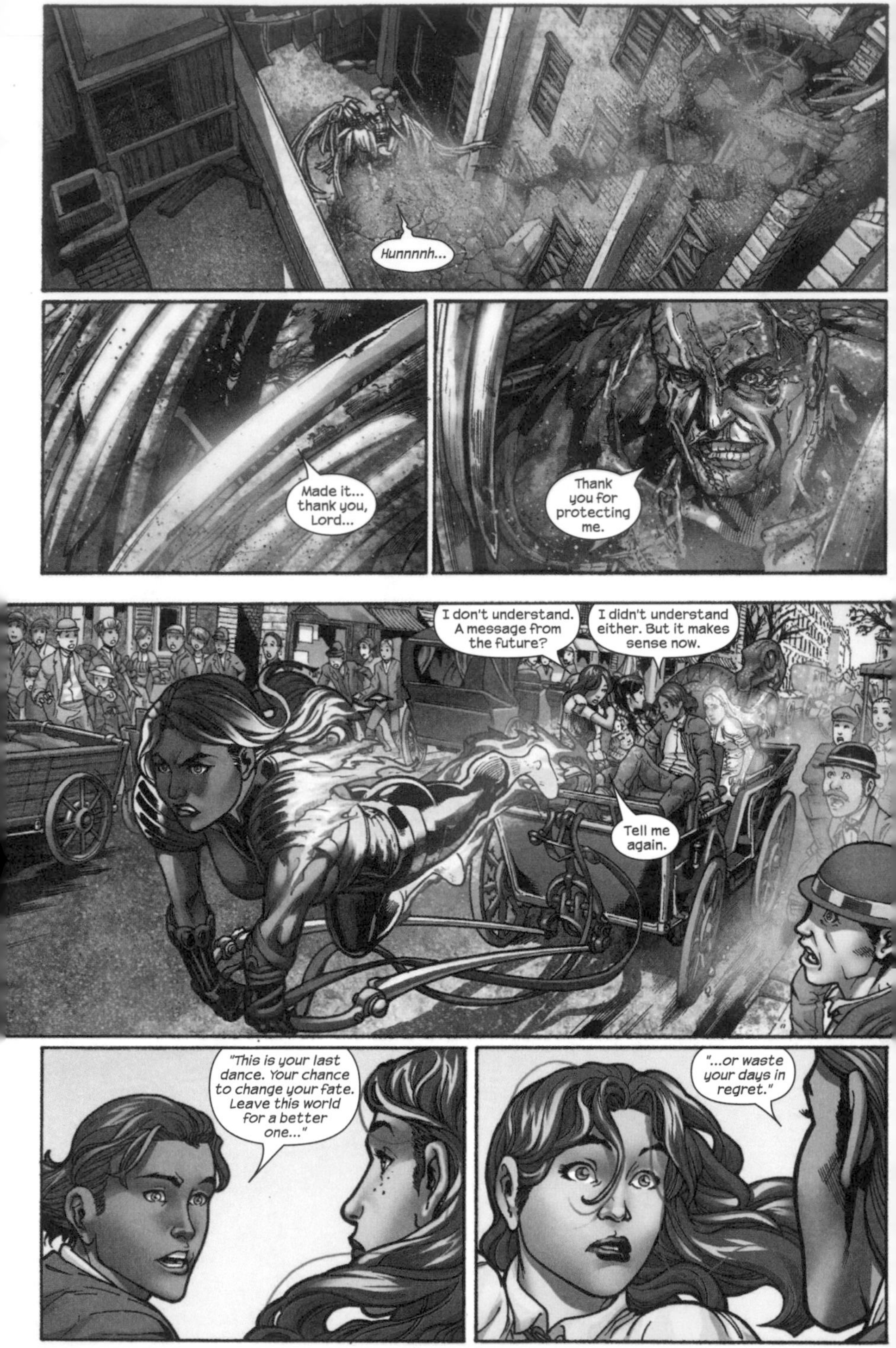
Hunnnnh...
Made it... thank you, Lord...
Thank you for protecting me.
I don't understand. A message from the future?
I didn't understand either. But it makes sense now.
Tell me again.
"This is your last dance. Your chance to change your fate. Leave this world for a better one..."
"...or waste your days in regret."

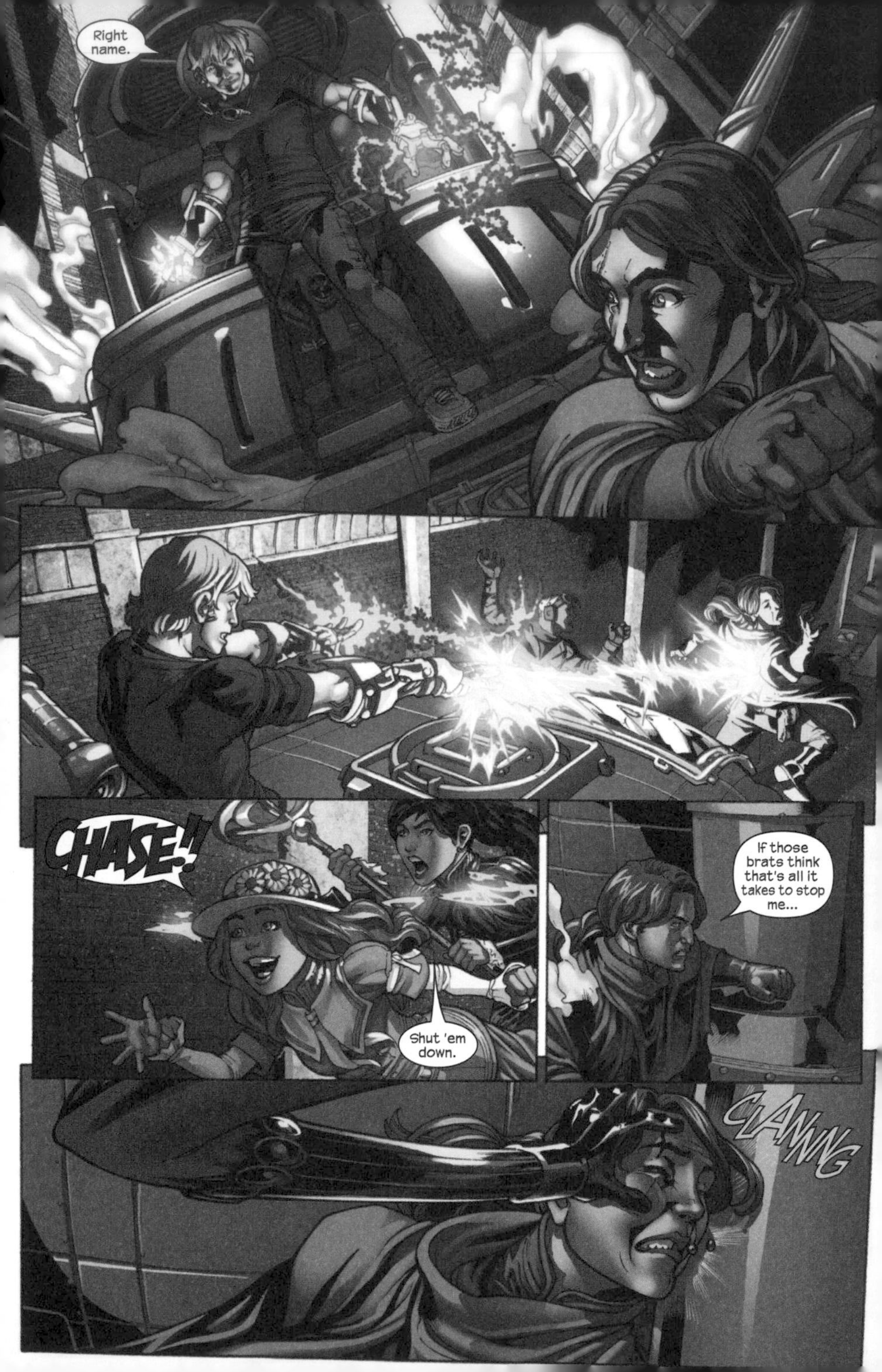
Right name.
CHASE!!
Shut 'em down.
If those brats think that's all it takes to stop me...
CLANNNG

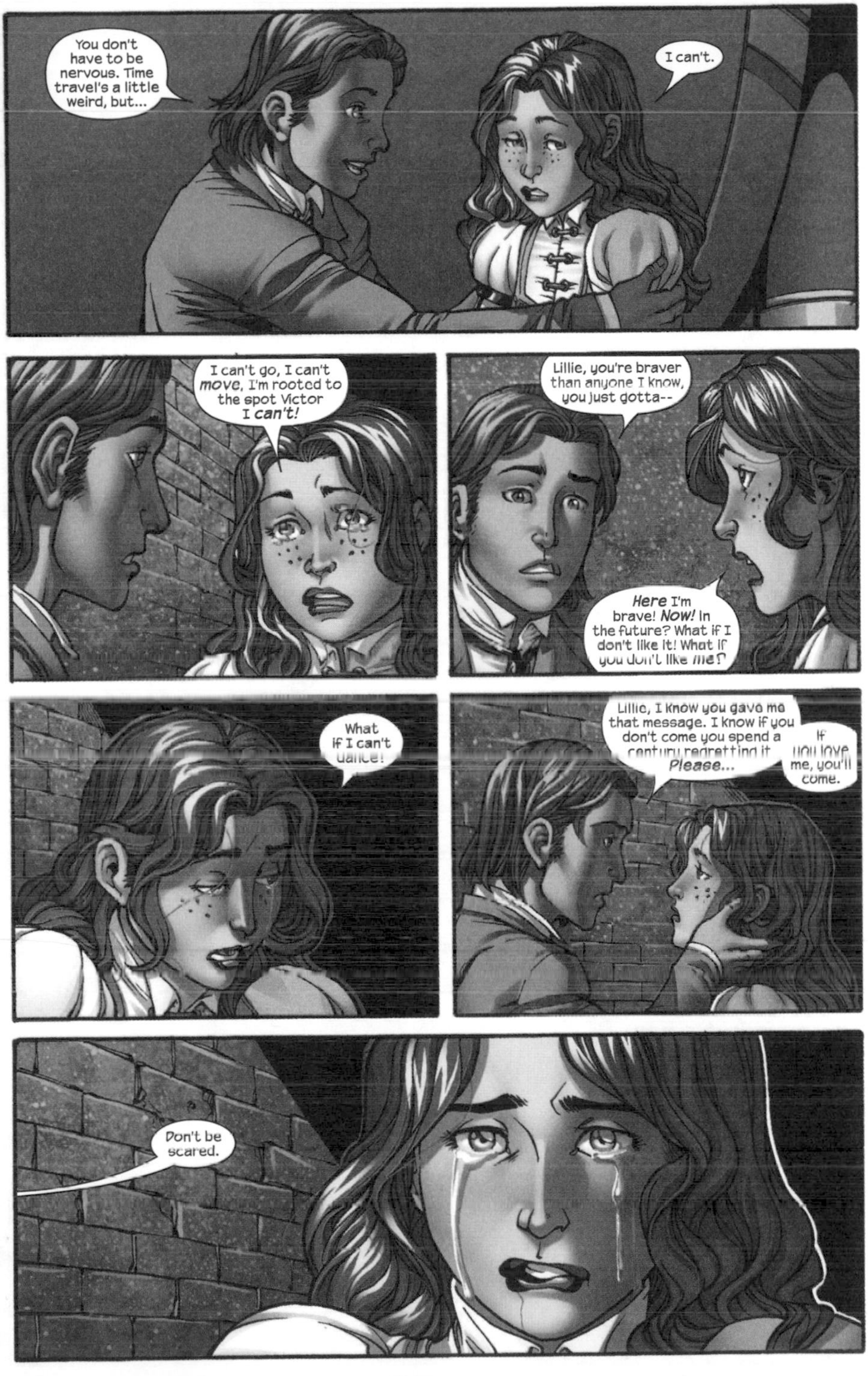
You don't have to be nervous. Time travel's a little weird, but...
I can't.
I can't go, I can't *move*, I'm rooted to the spot Victor I *can't!*
Lillie, you're braver than anyone I know, you just gotta--
Here I'm brave! *Now!* In the future? What if I don't like it! What if you don't like *me*?
What if I can't dance!
Lillie, I know you gave me that message. I know if you don't come you spend a century regretting it. *Please...*
If you love me, you'll come.
Don't be scared.

30

NICO & KAROLINA

CHASE

NICO

CHARACTER
SKETCHES
BY MICHAEL RYAN

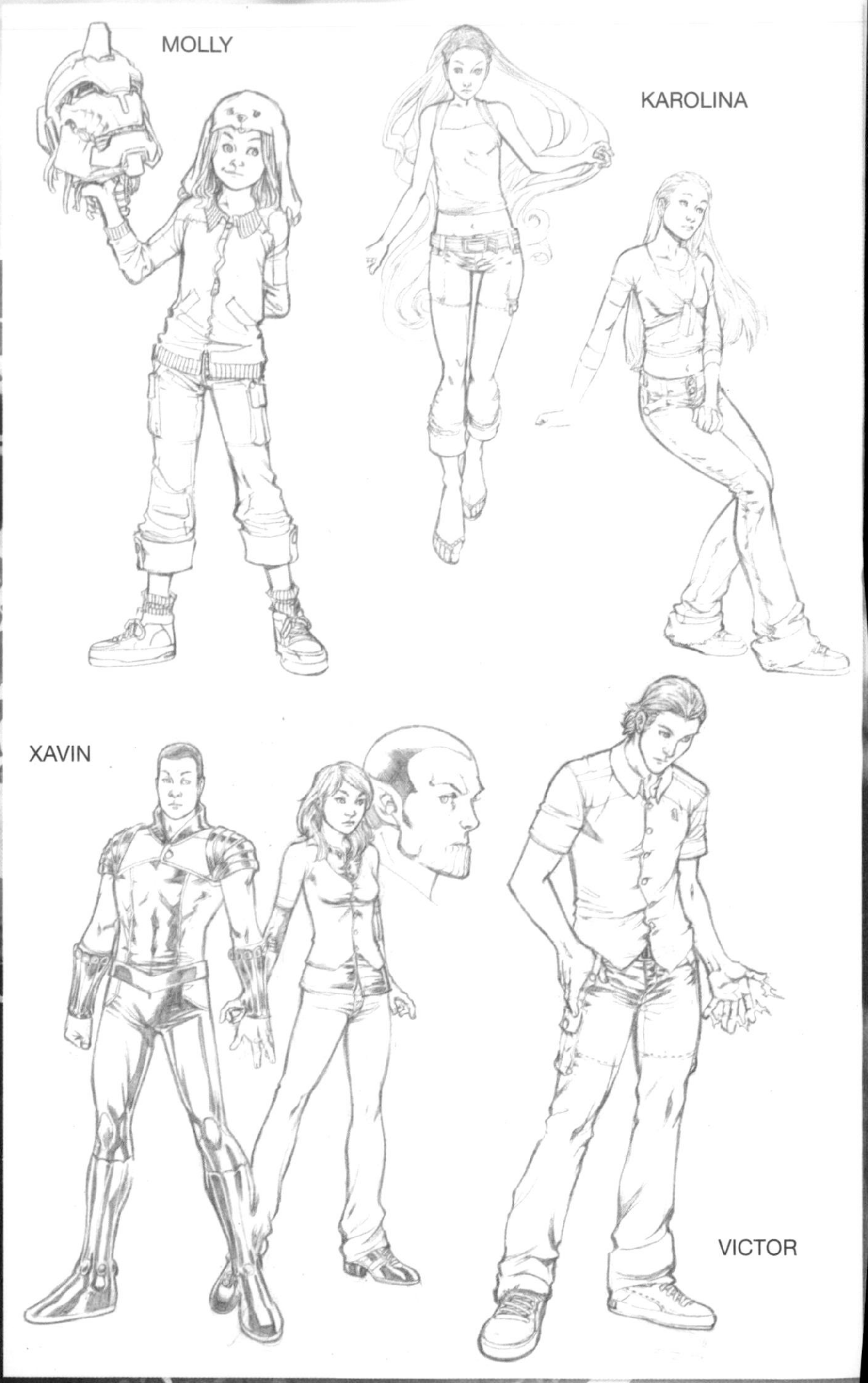
MOLLY
KAROLINA
XAVIN
VICTOR